Withdrawn

CIVIL LIBERTIES vs. NATIONAL SECURITY

Contemporary Issues

Series Editors: Robert M. Baird & Stuart E. Rosenbaum

Volumes edited by Robert M. Baird and Stuart E. Rosenbaum unless otherwise noted.

CIVIL LIBERTIES *vs.* NATIONAL SECURITY

IN A POST-9/11 WORLD

Edited by M. Katherine B. Darmer,
Robert M. Baird, and Stuart E. Rosenbaum

Prometheus Books

59 John Glenn Drive
Amherst, New York 14228-2197

Published 2004 by Prometheus Books

Inquiries should be addressed to
Prometheus Books
59 John Glenn Drive
Amherst, New York 14228–2197
VOICE: 716–691–0133, ext. 207
FAX: 716–564–2711
WWW.PROMETHEUSBOOKS.COM

08 07 06 05 04   5 4 3 2 1

Library of Congress Cataloging-in-Publication Data

Civil liberties vs. national security in a post-9/11 world / edited by M. Katherine B. Darmer, Stuart E. Rosenbaum & Robert M. Baird.
    p. cm. — (Contemporary issues)
  Includes bibliographical references.
  ISBN 1-59102-234-7 (pbk. : alk. paper)
  1. War and emergency powers—United States. 2. Civil rights—United States. 3. War on Terrorism, 2001—Law and legislation—United States. 4. Iraq War, 2003—Law and legislation—United States. I. Title: Civil liberties versus national security in a post-9/11 world. II. Darmer, M. Katherine B. III. Rosenbaum, Stuart E. IV. Baird, Robert M., 1937– V. Contemporary issues (Amherst, NY)

KF5060.C48 2005
342.7308'5—dc22
                                                                    2004013480

Every attempt has been made to trace accurate ownership of copyrighted material in this book. Errors and omissions will be corrected in subsequent editions, provided that notification is sent to the publisher.

Printed in the United States of America on acid-free paper

CONTENTS

PART TWO: DOMESTIC SURVEILLANCE

PART THREE: RACIAL PROFILING

PART FOUR: INTERROGATING SUSPECTS AND TORTURE

PART FIVE: HABEAS CORPUS AND "ENEMY COMBATANTS"

PART SIX: RECENT DEVELOPMENTS

ACKNOWLEDGMENTS

M. Katherine B. Darmer wishes to acknowledge the helpful research assistance of Sherry Powell, Homan Hosseinioun, and Rachel M. Pickens, JD candidates at the Chapman University School of Law, as well as the administrative support of Gloria L. Davis.

INTRODUCTION

M. Katherine B. Darmer

After September 11, 2001, questions that had preoccupied the country the prior year seemed trivial; the terrorist events rendered virtually irrelevant the question of whether the new millennium started in the year 2000 or the year 2001. After September 11, for our country at least, that line became the demarcation point: before and after. The world as we knew it changed, irrevocably, on that day in history.

Our national leaders inevitably responded, both militarily and otherwise. Congress passed the USA PATRIOT Act and the Justice Department acted aggressively in an effort to preempt any further attacks. The executive, legislative, and judicial branches of government continue to wrestle with the challenges to national security. Some believe that civil liberties have become a casualty in that process; others insist that the exigencies of national security demand restrictions on liberties. Questions related to trade-offs between security and liberty are the focus of this book.

This collection is not intended to provide a comprehensive analysis of the "War on Terror." In particular, the military dimensions of that war are addressed only peripherally. We hope, however, that the selections included here provide a starting point for those interested in security and liberty in a post-9/11 world.

While the events of September 11 were singular, the nation has faced national security challenges before, and several of this book's chapters involve historical matters that are directly relevant to today's concerns. The first selection in section one, for example, is a chapter from Chief Justice William Rehnquist's book *All the Laws but One: Civil Liberties in Wartime*. Written three years before the terrorist attacks of September 11, Rehnquist's book addresses such issues as President Lincoln's suspension of the writ of habeas corpus during the Civil War and the internment of Japanese Americans during World War II. In the chapter excerpted here, bearing the Latin phrase *Inter Arma Silent Leges* ("In time of war the laws are silent"), Rehnquist argues that, inevitably, the government is less deferential to civil liberties in times of war. Yet his message is ultimately one of optimism that the courts are equipped to balance government's claimed needs to protect security with competing claims for civil liberties.

The second piece, Aryeh Neier's introduction to a book critical of the current Justice Department's handling of security concerns after September 11, presents a less sanguine view. Neier argues that some of the "worst violations of civil liberties" have occurred during times of war and that those abuses did nothing to promote national security. In the current climate, he describes such measures as the USA PATRIOT Act, secret detention hearings, and the denial of lawyers to prisoners at Guantanamo Bay as "failures of the war against terrorism." While Neier, like Rehnquist, suggests that the judiciary has played an important historic role in safeguarding liberties, Neier implies that the current Court may not be as receptive to liberty claims as were earlier courts. Neier's pessimism notwithstanding, the Supreme Court on June 28, 2004, issued two opinions asserting a role for the courts in assessing the habeas claims of both Guantanamo Bay detainees and alleged citizen–enemy combatants. Those opinions, one of which appears in section six of the book, have been widely viewed as vindicating traditional liberty interests.

Excerpts from the United States Constitution and the text of the habeas corpus statute are included after Neier's piece, providing points of reference for the rest of the book. Habeas corpus is the traditional means by which a prisoner can challenge the legality of his confinement and was at issue in the Court's recent decisions about the president's authority to detain enemy combatants. Indeed, questions about liberty and national security raise issues that go to the core of the nation's values and to fundamental questions about the balance of powers among the executive, legislative, and judicial branches of government. Certain executive and legislative measures also directly implicate constitutional protections contained in the Bill of Rights. The Fourth Amendment, for example, protects citizens against unreasonable government searches and seizures, and the Fifth Amendment prohibits compelled self-incrimination and provides for due process of law. The words of the Constitution themselves are open to debate, of course. What is a "reasonable search"? What process is due an alleged terrorist?

Section two addresses the question of reasonable searches, as it deals with domestic surveillance with a particular emphasis on provisions of the USA PATRIOT Act. The first selection, by Jay Stanley and Barry Steinhardt from the American Civil Liberties Union's Technology and Liberty Program, is highly critical of what it describes as a growing "surveillance society." While the ACLU criticizes increasing corporate surveillance, its biggest worry is government surveillance, and it analyzes the PATRIOT Act from that perspective. It points out that the act makes access to records easier, loosens the requirements for obtaining intelligence wiretaps, and allows for searches without immediately notifying the targets. The ACLU calls into question the premise that increased surveillance can make the country safer and sees vast potential for abuse of the data being collected. It calls for comprehensive privacy laws and a revivification of the Fourth Amendment to act as an effective bulwark against increasing encroachment on privacy.

The ACLU does identify one recent "bright spot": the Supreme Court's 2001 opinion in *Kyllo v. United States*, which is also excerpted in this section. *Kyllo* held that the Fourth Amendment forbade the government's use of certain thermal imaging technology to discern heat levels in a home. Though *Kyllo* was decided three months before September 11, and involved a marijuana grower and not a suspected terrorist, it is relevant in illustrating the Supreme Court's recent thinking about the parameters of the Fourth Amendment's limits on the use of advanced technology in law enforcement.

In the next piece, "No Checks, No Balances," Professor Stephen J. Schulhofer argues that the current administration's reaction to September 11 is deeply flawed from the perspective of both liberty *and* security. In particular, he is critical of the broadened investigative powers brought about by changes to the Foreign Intelligence Surveillance Act, which now permits expanded surveillance for law enforcement, as opposed to just intelligence gathering, purposes.

A piece by Professor Viet Dinh, former assistant attorney general and a chief architect of the PATRIOT Act, follows. Professor Dinh defends the Act as both constitutional and necessary to national security. He starts from the premise that the age-old dichotomy between security and liberty is false and submits that liberty cannot exist without order. "Freedom," in his view, includes freedom from the type of fear perpetrated by terrorists. He concedes that the Department of Justice has responded aggressively to thwart terrorism, but asserts that this approach is necessary to combat terrorist enemies who act with stealth and who themselves are willing to die.

Finally, Christian Parenti provides another view critical of the government. He details the proliferation of everyday surveillance and invokes the historical examples of Mahatma Gandhi and Martin Luther King Jr. in arguing that political protest—even illegal forms of it—might be necessary to "wind back" the "soft cage" of surveillance.

Section three addresses the controversial practice of "racial profiling." If today's government uses race as a factor in deciding whom to investigate or detain, it does so in the shadow of the Japanese internment cases of World War II, including the most famous case of that era, *Korematsu v. United States*. Korematsu challenged the legality of laws excluding him from his home and forcing him to go to a Japanese relocation center during the height of anti-Japanese hysteria during World War II. Although the Supreme Court upheld the exclusion order, Korematsu was vindicated years later when a court granted him a writ of *coram nobis*, effectively expunging his conviction. Although the internment orders are now almost universally condemned, the Supreme Court's decision itself has never been overruled and remains a viable precedent. The majority decision of the deeply divided Court is excerpted here, along with the opinion of one of the four dissenters.

Frank H. Wu's piece, the second in this section, argues that the Japanese internment of World War II is the "obvious precedent" for the post-9/11 treatment of Arab and Muslim Americans. Wu points out that the Japanese internment was widely supported during World War II and that even the national ACLU refused to challenge it. He contends that volatile emotions, generated by the attack on Pearl Harbor, were displaced onto Japanese Americans. Wu argues further that the Supreme Court, while deciding a series of internment cases, evaded the ultimate question of the constitutionality of the incarceration of a racial group. While the internment has recently been widely condemned, Wu expresses concern that, post 9/11, "respected voices" have advocated racial profiling. He argues that we must articulate anew the reasons why internment was wrong in order to respond appropriately to the challenges of September 11.

Wu's piece is followed by the views of Stuart Taylor Jr. and David Harris, who differ with each other about whether it is "common sense" to use racial profiling in the wake of 9/11. While conceding that the chances that any Middle Eastern passenger on an airplane is a terrorist are "tiny," Taylor argues that the odds that future al Qaeda terrorists will be Middle Eastern, rather than native-born Americans, make ignoring apparent national origin in airline screening potentially disastrous. He warns that future terrorists may provide no behavioral clues of their intentions, suggesting that profiling may be the only tool that could work to prevent acts of terror by innocent-seeming perpetrators. Harris, on the other hand, argues that this reasoning is incorrect, suggesting that, historically, racial profiling has not led to effective law enforcement. He argues that observation of behavior, rather than appearance, is the "gold standard" of policing and that law enforcement resources will be overwhelmed if the suspect pool is enlarged by employing techniques of profiling.

Section three concludes with the Department of Justice's current guidelines regarding the use of race in law enforcement investigations. While asserting that "racial profiling" is both wrong and ineffective, the guidelines permit federal law enforcement officers to consider race or ethnicity, pursuant to "existing legal and constitutional standards," when members of identifiable ethnic groups pose threats to the nation's security.

Section four confronts issues of torture, issues that have become all too real in the wake of the recent Abu Ghraib prison abuse scandal. The world has now seen explicit photographs depicting abuse and humiliation of Iraqi detainees at the hands of United States forces. There has been virtually universal condemnation of the abuse perpetrated at Abu Ghraib, but not everyone agrees that the use of torture is always unjustified. In fact, this section leads off with Alan M. Dershowitz's provocative proposal regarding torture. He argues that we must face the real possibility that, in some instances, torture might be the only way to avert a catastrophic terrorist event. Arguing that torture will occur "under the table" whether or not it is officially condoned or recognized, Dershowitz argues that a democratic society is obligated to confront the issue head-on, rather than taking a "Don't Ask, Don't Tell" approach. His suggestion is that judicial "torture warrants" be authorized in extreme circumstances.

Both Philip B. Heymann and Eyal Press take strong issue with Dershowitz in the second and third selections in this section. Heymann argues that such warrants would increase the incidence of torture and that any system for authorizing torture would necessarily involve errors. In his view, the long-term cost of any such system would "far outweigh" any short-term benefits. Press points out the difficulty in drawing the line at when torture might properly be used and argues that there is a parallel between terrorism and torture in that both dehumanize their victims.

In the final piece in this section, Profs. John T. Parry and Welsh S. White take a middle ground. While arguing that torture is and should be illegal, they also argue that any law enforcement agent who uses torture should be able to defend the "necessity" of his actions in a particular case. Thus, in a "ticking time bomb" scenario, a law enforcement agent would not be authorized to use torture, but he would have a potential defense if he did employ torture and later faced criminal prosecution.

Section four was initially completed before the situation at Abu Ghraib came to light. As a result, additional material on both torture and Abu Ghraib is included in a sixth section, covering recent developments. Following the revelation of mistreatment of prisoners at Abu Ghraib, the administration condemned the abuse. Some commentators, however, have suggested that the administration has not taken an unequivocal stand against torture. On August 1, 2002, Department of Justice lawyers drafted a memorandum regarding "Standards of Conduct for Interrogation." A brief excerpt of the memo, substantial portions of which were leaked to the press in June of 2004, is included in this final section. The memorandum suggests that only the harshest of interrogation methods are banned by statutes and treaties proscribing torture, argues that the president may not be bound even by limits on torture, and argues that defenses of necessity and of self-defense may be available to officials accused of torture. While the administration has strongly disavowed the views expressed in the memorandum, the memorandum's arguments—and indeed its very existence—have been widely criticized. Richard Cohen's *Washington Post* column, "A Plunge from the Moral Heights," provides one such critical perspective. Professor John Yoo, on the other hand, defends the memo.

Section five deals with the question of the executive branch's authority to detain "enemy combatants." Following September 11, the government has relied heavily on the World War II precedent of *In re Quirin*, a case involving German saboteurs, in justifying the use of the designation "enemy combatant." An "enemy combatant," unlike a civilian wrongdoer, can be detained without charge and tried before a military tribunal without the rights and protections of an ordinary criminal defendant. In *Quirin*, the saboteurs—including one who claimed United States citizenship—were convicted by a military tribunal and sentenced to death. The Supreme Court upheld the convictions, and the case is excerpted here. In the course of its opinion, the Court explained that the Constitution vests the president with the duty to execute laws and makes him commander in chief of the armed forces. The Court also drew upon historical practice in finding a distinction between lawful and unlawful combatants, the latter group being subject to trial and punishment by military tribunals.

The Second Circuit Court of Appeals opinion in *Padilla v. Rumsfeld* follows. Jose Padilla, a United States citizen suspected of seeking to detonate a so-called dirty bomb, was detained in Chicago at O'Hare International Airport. Ultimately, the president designated him an "enemy combatant" with ties to al Qaeda and detained him, without charge, at a naval brig in Charleston. Padilla then petitioned for a writ of habeas corpus.

The district court ruled that the government's detention of Padilla was proper, but that Padilla must be permitted to meet with his counsel. On appeal, the Second Circuit reversed the district court, holding that the executive branch, through Secretary of Defense Rumsfeld, was acting beyond the scope of its authority in detaining Padilla. In particular, it found that a Non-Detention Act passed by Congress in the wake of the Japanese internment cases forbids the type of detention at issue in Padilla's case and that authorization for such a detention was not contained in Congress's Joint Resolution of September 18, 2001, which authorized the president to use "all necessary and appropriate force" to prevent future terrorism. The three-judge panel was divided 2–1 on this issue, and both the majority and dissenting opinions are excerpted here. The *Padilla* decision is followed by Nat Hentoff's opinion piece supportive of the judgment of the Second Circuit Court and a *Chicago Tribune Herald* editorial that is critical.

The Supreme Court reviewed the Second Circuit decision but did not decide the merits, instead ruling that the New York courts lacked jurisdiction over the case and that Padilla must refile his petition in South Carolina. A brief excerpt of that decision is included in section six. Also included in that section is *Hamdi v. Rumsfeld*, a closely related case in which the Supreme Court held that the president was within his authority in detaining without charge Yaser Hamdi, an alleged enemy combatant captured in Afghanistan, but that Hamdi must be given a meaningful process for challenging that detention. The Supreme Court justices issued four separate opinions in *Hamdi*, arguing passionately about the scope of presidential powers and the civil liberties of an alleged enemy combatant. While they disagreed about the scope of presidential authority in initially detaining Hamdi, eight of the nine justices agreed that Hamdi was entitled at least to further due process. Several of the justices would have gone further and would have released the petitioner unless he was formally charged.

In an opinion particularly relevant to the issues addressed in this book, Justice Antonin Scalia says the following: "The Founders well understood the difficult tradeoff between safety and freedom." Quoting Hamilton in *The Federalist*, No. 8, Scalia notes that "even the ardent lover of liberty," when challenged by external danger, risks being willing to give up freedoms.

"The Founders warned us about the risk," Scalia continues, "and equipped us with a Constitution to deal with it." Responding specifically to the notion that *inter arma silent leges*, Scalia emphasizes that, "whatever the general merits" of such a notion, "that view has no place in the interpretation and application of a Constitution designed precisely to confront war, and in a manner that accords with democratic principles, to accommodate it."

Scalia's opinion in *Hamdi* garnered only one other vote, but it is perhaps appropriate that this book's selections are book-ended by differing perspectives on the notion that in time of war, the laws are silent. From the time of our country's founding and continuing through today and beyond, perhaps no question is as important for a society to consider as the proper balance between security and liberty. In the words of Justice David Souter in another of the *Hamdi* opinions, "The defining character of American constitutional government is its constant tension between security and liberty, serving both by partial helpings of each."

Editor's Note: Many of the selections included in this book were edited in the interest of space. In several instances, including in court opinions, footnotes and citations were omitted without indication. Otherwise, editors' omissions are generally reflected with ellipses and alterations with brackets. The publisher has made minor additional alterations to some selections.

MKBD

PART 1.

CIVIL LIBERTIES IN WARTIME

AN OVERVIEW

1.

INTER ARMA
SILENT LEGES

William Rehnquist

The United States has been engaged in several armed conflicts since the end of World War II, but in none of them has Congress declared war on another nation. Recent presidents have been eager to establish their authority to engage United States troops in foreign military operations without such a declaration, and Congress has never declared war without having been requested to do so by the president. When North Korea invaded South Korea in 1950, President Truman relied on a United Nations resolution to commit US troops to fight in Korea. When the war in Vietnam escalated during the mid-1960s, President Lyndon Johnson similarly relied on the Gulf of Tonkin Resolution, enacted by Congress in 1964, for similar authority. Before the Gulf War in 1991, President Bush received approval to use armed force against Iraq from both houses of Congress. In each case, Congress has appropriated the necessary funds for the military effort, but in none was there a declaration of war.

Reprinted from *All the Laws but One* by William H. Rehnquist. Copyright © 1998 by William H. Rehnquist. Used by permission of Alfred A. Knopf, a division of Random House, Inc.

Without question the government's authority to engage in conduct that infringes civil liberty is greatest in time of declared war. . . . In *The Prize Cases*,[1] decided in 1863, the Supreme Court held that an insurrection could be treated by the government as the equivalent of a declared war.

There are marked differences between the government's conduct during the Civil War, during World War I, and during World War II. One of the main differences is that in the Civil War, the Lincoln administration relied on presidential authority or on the orders of military commanders to curtail civil liberties, while in the twentieth century wars, the executive branch resorted much more to laws passed by Congress. Neither Lincoln's original suspension of the writ of habeas corpus, nor Stanton's order for the trial of civilians by military commissions, was authorized by Congress. The same was true of Postmaster General Montgomery Blair's suspension of the mailing privileges of New York newspapers. Those privileges were suspended during World War I by Postmaster General Albert Burleson, but he acted under a provision of the Espionage Act passed by Congress. President Roosevelt authorized the internment of west coast Japanese during World War II, but Congress immediately ratified his action.

It may fairly be asked by those whose civil liberty is curtailed, whether they are any better off because Congress as well as the executive has approved the measure. As a practical matter, the answer may be no, but from the point of view of governmental authority under the Constitution, it is clear that the president may do many things in carrying out a congressional directive that he may not be able to do on his own. Justice Robert Jackson, in his now authoritative concurring opinion in the *Steel Seizure* cases decided during the Korean War, observed:

When the President acts pursuant to an expressed or implied authorization of Congress, his authority is at its maximum, for it includes all that he possesses in his own right plus all that Congress can delegate. In these circumstances, and in these only, may he be said (for what it may be worth), to personify the federal sovereignty. If his act is held unconstitutional under these circumstances, it usually means that the Federal Government as an undivided whole lacks power.[2]

It should be added that Congress may not always grant the president all of the authority for which he asks. It refused, for example, President Wilson's request for censorship authority during World War I.

The second notable difference in the treatment of civil liberty is the increasing resort to the courts since the Civil War. This is partly because of the very limited jurisdiction of the lower federal courts in the 1860s. They could issue writs of habeas corpus, and a defendant might raise a constitutional claim as a defense. But for someone who had neither been detained nor sued but wished to challenge an action taken by the government, the only practical remedy was to sue in the state courts. Not until 1875 did Congress grant lower federal courts authority to hear cases where the plaintiff based his lawsuit on a violation of the federal Constitution. Thus, the publishers who were denied mailing privileges by Blair would have found it difficult, if not impossible, to assert any constitutional claim in a federal court. By the time of World War II, [those subject to Japanese internment orders] were able to initiate claims of constitutional violation as plaintiffs in federal court.

There were no similar limitations on state courts, but many of these courts were neither experienced in, nor hospitable to, claims arising under the United States Constitution.

But an even more important reason for court involvement was increasing reliance by the government on prosecution in the federal courts for acts which had been made criminal by congressional legislation. In the Civil War, Clement Vallandigham was tried before a military commission, not for an offense against a law passed by Congress, but for violation of an order issued by the commanding general of a military department. During World War I, there were no such prosecutions; those who violated the Espionage Act were tried in civil courts by juries. In these prosecutions, the defendant was able to urge constitutional claims before judges who, if not particularly sympathetic, were far more neutral and detached than the members of a military commission. The result of these trials and appeals from them was the development by the Supreme Court of a body of case law interpreting the First Amendment.

A third great difference between the Civil War and the later conflicts was the extent to which the government sought to suppress public criticism of the administration's war effort. During the Civil War, the government used a heavy-handed, blunderbuss approach; local agents in the field would seize newspapers and confiscate the presses of those who opposed its policy. There was simply no federal challenge to these gross violations of the First Amendment. During World War I, Burleson successfully suppressed radical criticism of the administration, but at least his actions were subject to review by the courts. During World War II, there was no overt effort by the government to suppress public criticism of government war policy. Some of this change may have been due to the fact that the United States' entry into World War II was a defensive reaction to the Japanese bombing of Pearl Harbor and the German declaration of war. There was much less opposition to that war than to either the Civil War or World War I. But part of the change also resulted from the fact that the First Amendment had come into its own.

Despite this generally ameliorative trend, however, there remains a sense that there is some truth to the maxim *Inter arma silent leges*, at least in the purely descriptive sense. *Quirin*, decided during the darkest days of World War II, actually cut back on some of the extravagant dicta favorable to civil liberty in *Milligan*. Of the three Japanese internment cases, only *Endo*, decided near the end of World War II, represented even a minor victory for civil liberty. And as for *Duncan*, the good news for the people of Hawaii was that the Court held that martial law there during World War II had been unlawful; the bad news was that the decision came after the war was over, and a year and a half after martial law had been ended by presidential order. Again, part of the delay in such decisions is endemic to the legal process; given a hierarchical system of courts, a decision by the Supreme Court usually occurs months, if not years, after the lawsuit was begun. But there is also the reluctance of courts to decide a case against the government on an issue of national security during a war.

Is this reluctance a necessary evil—necessary because judges, like other citizens, do not wish to hinder a nation's "war effort"—or is it actually a desirable phenomenon? Judicial reluctance can manifest itself in more ways than one. A court may simply avoid deciding an important constitutional question in the midst of a war. . . . A court may also decide an issue in favor of the government during a war, when it would not have done so had the decision come after the war was over. Would, for example, *Duncan* have come out the same way in 1943 as it actually did in 1946?

Viewed as a matter of legal or constitutional principle, the law governing a particular set of facts—in *Duncan*, for example, whether a stockbroker could be tried for fraud by a military court in Hawaii in 1943—should not be different in 1946 than three years earlier. But one need not wholly accept Justice Holmes's aphorism that "the life of the law has not been logic, it has been experience" to recognize the human factor that inevitably enters into even the most careful judicial decision. If, in fact, courts are more prone to uphold wartime claims of civil liberties after the war is over, may it not actually be desirable to avoid decision on such claims during the war?

Lambdin Milligan, imprisoned after his trial before a military commission, surely would answer no to this question. While the body of case law might benefit from such abstention, those who are actually deprived of their civil liberties would not. But a decision in favor of civil liberty will stand as a precedent to regulate future actions of Congress and the executive branch in future wars. We must also ask whether in every case a ruling in favor of a claimed civil liberty is more desirable, more "just," than a contrary result.

The answer to this question will depend, in turn, on just what is meant by *civil* liberty. It is not simply "liberty" but civil liberty of which we speak. The word "civil," in turn, is derived from the Latin word *civis*, which means "citizen." A citizen is a person owing allegiance to some organized government, and not a person in an idealized "state of nature" free from any governmental restraint. Judge Learned Hand, in remarks entitled "The Spirit of Liberty," delivered during World War II, put it this way: "A society in which men recognize no check upon their freedom soon becomes a society where freedom is the possession of only a savage few."[3]

&)C&

In any civilized society the most important task is achieving a proper balance between freedom and order. In wartime, reason and history both suggest that this balance shifts to some degree in favor of order—in favor of the government's ability to deal with conditions that threaten the national well-being. It simply cannot be said, therefore, that in every conflict between individual liberty and governmental authority the former should prevail. And if we feel free to criticize court decisions that curtail civil liberty, we must also feel free to look critically at decisions favorable to civil liberty.

Was the dictum in the *Milligan* case, for example—saying that Congress could not authorize trials of civilians by military tribunals where civil courts were functioning and there was no invasion by hostile forces—a wise exercise of judicial power? The reasoning of the majority in that case would rule out not merely trials of civilians by military commissions but trials of civilians by a duly appointed federal judge without a jury. One may fully agree with the rather disparaging but nonetheless insightful argument of Jeremiah Black in the *Milligan* case—soldiers are no more occupationally trained to conduct trials than are sailors or sheep drovers—and yet believe that Congress should be able to provide for trial of defendants by a judge without a jury in a carefully limited class of cases dealing with national security in wartime.

The foregoing discussion deals with the judicial treatment of civil liberty claims. But this is only one part of the story during wartime. The . . . statement of Francis Biddle about Franklin Roosevelt's support for the internment of Issei and Nisei during World War II bears repeating here: "Nor do I think that the Constitutional difficulty plagued him. The Constitution has not greatly bothered any wartime President. That was a question of law, which ultimately the Supreme Court must decide. And meanwhile—probably a long meanwhile—we must get on with the war."[4]

Some executive actions in time of war will be reviewed by the courts only after the fact, if at all. Lincoln believed that the very survival of the Union could depend on getting troops from the north-east to Washington in April 1861. He also believed that the suspension of the writ of habeas corpus was necessary to guard against further destruction of the railroad route through Baltimore used to transport these troops. Should he have carefully weighed the pros and cons as to whether he was authorized by the Constitution to do this before acting? Should he, to paraphrase his own words, have risked losing the Union that gave life to the Constitution because that charter denied him the necessary authority to preserve the Union? Cast in these terms, it is difficult to quarrel with his decision.

But the same degree of necessity surely did not obtain in the suppression of the New York newspapers, or the trial of the Indianapolis defendants by a military commission. It is all too easy to slide from a case of genuine military necessity, where the power sought to be exercised is at least debatable, to one where the threat is not critical and the power either dubious or nonexistent.

One would think it likely, of course, that a Roman legal maxim which originated two millennia ago in a legal system with no written constitution, would have only the most general application to America. But the fact that the phrase *Inter arma silent leges* is quoted by modern writers suggests that it has validity at least in a descriptive way. As such, it may have several different levels of meaning. It speaks first simply as a truism: in time of war the government's authority to restrict civil liberty is greater than in peacetime. . . . But at another level, the maxim speaks to the attitude of wartime presidents such as Lincoln, Wilson, and Franklin Roosevelt, so well captured in Biddle's phrase "the Constitution has not greatly bothered any wartime President." Quite apart from the added authority that the law itself may give the president in time of war, presidents may act in ways that push their legal authority to its outer limits, if not beyond. Finally, the maxim speaks to the timing of a judicial decision on a question of civil liberty in wartime. If the decision is made after hostilities have ceased, it is more likely to favor civil liberty than if made while hostilities continue. The contrast between the *Quirin* and the Japanese internment decisions on the one hand and the *Milligan* and *Duncan* decisions on the other show that this, too, is a historically accurate observation about the American system.

An entirely separate and important philosophical question is whether occasional presidential excesses and judicial restraint in wartime are desirable or undesirable. In one sense, this question is very largely academic. There is no reason to think that future wartime presidents will act differently from Lincoln, Wilson, or Roosevelt, or that future justices of the Supreme Court will decide questions differently from their predecessors. But even though this be so, there is every reason to think that the historic trend against the least justified of the curtailments of civil liberty in wartime will continue in the future. It is neither desirable nor is it remotely likely that civil liberty will occupy as favored a position in wartime as it does in peacetime. But it is both desirable and likely that more careful attention will be paid by the courts to the basis for the government's claims of necessity as a basis for curtailing civil liberty. The laws will thus not be silent in time of war, but they will speak with a somewhat different voice.

NOTES

1. *The Prize Cases*, 67 US 635.

2. *Youngstown Sheet and Tool Company v. Sawyer*, 343 U.S. 579, 635–636 (1952).

3. Learned Hand, *The Spirit of Liberty* (New York: Alfred A. Knopf, 1952), p. 191.

4. Francis Biddle, *In Brief Authority* (Garden City, NY: Doubleday, 1962), p. 219.

2.

LOST LIBERTIES

ASHCROFT AND THE ASSAULT ON PERSONAL FREEDOM

Aryeh Neier

Within hours after the collapse of the World Trade Center and the destruction of a portion of the Pentagon, most of us knew that civil liberties would be under fire. After all, . . . we have been down this road before. The historical events of the past century that inspired the worst violations of civil liberties—aside from those that are endemic in our treatment of racial minorities—share certain characteristics.

The crackdown against pacifists and other opponents of World War I, against suspected anarchists and Reds after the war, against Japanese Americans during World War II, and against alleged Communists, sympathizers, and dupes during the early years of the Cold War all involved Americans thought to be aiding foreign conspiracies or undermining the country's resolve in a foreign conflict.

Though the consequences were not comparable in stifling dissent, an assault against civil liberties took place again during the Vietnam War. Hundreds of conscientious objectors were imprisoned; scores of thousands of peaceable demonstrators were arrested,

From the introduction to *Lost Liberties: Ashcroft and the Assault on Personal Freedom*, edited by Cytnhia Brown. Reprinted by permission of the New Press: (800) 233–4830.

and some of them were punitively reclassified in the draft to speed up their induction into the armed services; federal grand juries conducted wide-ranging investigations of critics of US foreign policy; prominent opponents of the war such as Dr. Benjamin Spock and the Reverend William Sloane Coffin were prosecuted for conspiring against the draft; President Richard Nixon established a personal secret police, "the Plumbers," operating outside the constraints of the law, to plug "leaks" such as the information that the United States had invaded Cambodia; the US Army was deployed to spy on civilians; the federal government sought to enjoin the *New York Times* and the *Washington Post* from publishing information about the origins of the war; and so on.

The anti-immigrant aspects of public policy since September 11, . . . and of some of the past century's most significant violations of civil liberties, had counterparts even earlier in American history. It is only necessary to mention the Alien and Sedition Acts of the end of the eighteenth century and the "Know-Nothing" movement of the middle of the nineteenth century. While Americans rightly celebrate our tradition of freedom, it is useful to recall that it is a tradition that has been sustained only because those committed to it have periodically fought back and overcome the forces in American society that—pretending to speak in the name of patriotism—would take the country in the opposite direction.

Though it is not surprising that the devastating events of September 11 should inspire a new round of attacks on civil liberties, it is nevertheless dismaying. As one looks back at the previous periods when rights were systematically violated, it is difficult to discern any resulting gain for national security. The prosecutions of critics of World War I did nothing for the war effort and did not hasten Germany's defeat and agreement to an armistice. So far as we know, none of those responsible for the letter bombs or the other terrorist *attentats* of the post–World War I era was netted by the Palmer raids. America's victory in the war in the Pacific was not hastened by the internment of the Japanese Americans. The loyalty and security investigations and purges of the late 1940s and the 1950s in Hollywood, the universities, and other sectors of public life appear not to have had an impact on the course of the Cold War. And, the efforts by the Johnson and Nixon administrations to curb dissent did nothing to stave off the ignominious end to the war in Vietnam.

That is not to say that governmental authorities are unjustified in taking certain steps to protect public safety in the current circumstances. It is a nuisance to take off one's shoes before boarding an airplane, but the longer wait to get through the security checks seems rationally related to our interest in enhanced safety aloft. One hopes that more safeguards are in place for the transport of hazardous materials, and that precautions are being taken against efforts to blow up the bridges and tunnels. Vaccinations against smallpox that could be lethal to some people seem an extreme measure. Yet if the government makes a case that the risk is real that bioterrorists could acquire the capacity to spread this dread disease, and appropriate steps are taken . . . to protect the vulnerable and to limit the availability of data on testing and screening, most of us would readily go along.

The case that has not been made, and probably cannot be made, is that abrogations of civil liberties make us safer. It did not happen in the past. What is it this time about the USA PATRIOT Act, John Poindexter's Total Information Awareness (TIA) proposal, John Ashcroft's secret detentions and immigration proceedings, or Donald Rumsfeld's denial of either prisoner-of-war status or of charges, attorneys, and hearings to the prisoners at Guantanamo that makes us more secure? Is it that the current generation of officials is wiser and more trustworthy than A. Mitchell Palmer, J. Edgar Hoover, Joseph McCarthy, Richard Nixon, and John Mitchell? What have they done to prove it? Or, as seems more likely, are some of these measures mainly intended to cover up government misconduct or incompetence? Closed-door immigration hearings merely hide the Justice Department's utter failure to connect those caught up in these proceedings to terrorism. Similarly, denying the prisoners at Guantanamo lawyers and hearings prevents us from finding out the absence of evidence justifying their detention. Until proven otherwise, these measures should be regarded as failures of the war against terrorism.

Looking back at what was done to curb civil liberties in earlier periods of national danger or perceived danger, one wonders whether the real purpose was in fact to increase security. No doubt this was the main consideration for many proponents of restrictions on rights, even if that was not the effect. Yet one also detects a punitive or vengeful strain in American history. That is, it is not only important to ensure safety, it also seems to be important to some that those living among us enjoying the fruits of American society whose presumed political sympathies or demographic characteristics are similar to those who have caused trouble for the country should pay a price. They are regarded as part of a wider conspiracy. Measures that violate civil liberties are inherently divisive. For those intent in separating not only the world but also Americans between those who are "with us" or "with the terrorists," such measures apparently serve a salutary purpose.

It is important, of course, to give credit where credit is due. President George W. Bush has made significant efforts to avoid violence along religious or ethnic lines. Were it not for his efforts against vigilantism starting immediately after the events of September 11, the situation undoubtedly would be far worse than it is today. One thinks of the horrendous carnage in Gujarat, India, after the episode in February 2002 in which a few harassed Muslim vendors set fire to a train carrying Hindu nationalists, causing some fifty-eight deaths. With Gujarati government officials standing by or egging them on, and with national leaders refusing to interfere, Hindu mobs destroyed Muslim shops and homes throughout the province, forcing scores of thousands to flee their homes. As many as two thousand Muslims were slaughtered, with no effort by the authorities to apprehend and punish the guilty. That no mass violence took place in the United States despite the vastly greater death toll of September 11 than on the train is due not only to differing traditions between the United States and India, it is also attributable to the president's leadership in steering the country away from communal strife.

Unfortunately, the president's praiseworthy and successful efforts to avoid ethnic and religious violence were not matched by a comparable attempt to protect constitutional rights. Major new violations of rights have already become a part of American law and practice. We are at risk of entering another of those dark periods of American history when the country abandons its proud tradition of respect for civil liberties.

To say that we are at risk, however, is not to say that the struggle to preserve our rights is hopeless. We have a chance to succeed again as we did three decades ago in beating back the assault on civil liberties that was aimed at suppressing dissent over the Vietnam War. In that era, not only did Americans continue to speak out about the war despite all efforts to silence them, the president of the United States was forced to resign for his violations of rights. Immediately following his resignation, Congress adopted such significant protections for civil liberties as the Privacy Act of 1974, the Federal Education Rights and Privacy Act (FERPA), and the 1974 amendments to the Freedom of Information Act (FOIA). Congress also adopted the main laws that continue today to commit the United States to promote human rights internationally, passing certain measures over President Gerald Ford's veto. Most important, in the latter part of the 1970s and the beginning of the 1980s, the federal courts dismantled much of the political surveillance system that had developed not only during the Vietnam War but since the early years of the twentieth century. These developments made the post-Vietnam era a high point for civil liberties protection in American history.

Several factors combined, I believe, to beat back the assault on civil liberties of the late 1960s and early 1970s. One of them was the availability of a large number of skilled advocates to represent those arrested and prosecuted for dissent or made targets of political surveillance. Some of the lawyers involved had played a part in the civil rights struggles of a slightly earlier period. Others were themselves of the generation that was most active in protesting the war. Many took on cases under the auspices of the American Civil Liberties Union or other civil liberties groups. In that period, literally thousands of lawyers were ready to take on the defense of First Amendment or due process rights without cost, an incommensurably greater number than had ever been available at any previous period.

Another factor was the receptivity of the judiciary, particularly in the federal courts, to efforts to protect civil liberties. This should not be overstated. Richard Nixon's imprint on the US Supreme Court was already evident by 1972, as when it considered *Laird v. Tatum*,[1] a challenge to the US Army's spying on civilians. In an opinion by one of Nixon's appointees, Chief Justice Warren Burger, that also reflected the views of his newest appointee, Justice William Rehnquist, the Court held that the targets of the spying lacked standing to bring the matter before the judiciary. Notwithstanding such significant setbacks, the courts did much to restrain excesses in the exercise of executive power, as in the Supreme Court's 1972 decision that warrants are required for all domestic security wiretaps,[2] and its 1971 decision rejecting the effort of the Nixon administration to prevent the *New York Times* and the *Washington Post* from publishing the Pentagon Papers.[3]

The discovery of the Watergate burglary by an alert security guard and the subsequent cover-up by President Nixon and his associates that gradually unraveled under probing by the press, the courts, and Congress was yet another factor that turned back the onslaught against civil liberties. Watergate gave its name to the entire panoply of Nixon's abuses, thereby tending to obscure the fact that, of itself, the bugging of the telephones at the headquarters of the Democratic National Committee was a relatively minor and peripheral example of what was going on during the Vietnam War era. Yet it did open the eyes of the country and helped to persuade most Americans that the Nixon administration was willing to resort to any means against those it saw as its critics and opponents. Thereby, it greatly strengthened public insistence that individual rights should be protected by legal process.

Perhaps the most important factor in safeguarding civil liberties during the Vietnam War era was the unwillingness of many millions of Americans to be intimidated. There was never a moment when wiretaps, grand jury investigations, arrests, prosecutions or convictions, and prison sentences stopped those critical of the war from speaking out. In that respect, the period differed markedly from earlier times when civil liberties were under attack. As one who attended college in the 1950s, I recall that we were known as "the silent generation." The term was justified. Though Joseph McCarthy's star was already fading when I entered my freshman year in September 1954—the Army-McCarthy hearings had taken place about three months earlier—we did not find our voice. It wasn't until the sit-ins and freedom rides of the civil rights movement took place several years later that college campuses began again to make themselves heard on matters of public policy.

Not all these factors are present today, of course. Nothing has happened or is likely to happen that is comparable to the fortuitous discovery of the Watergate break-in to discredit those promoting the violation of civil liberties. Whatever one thinks of the Bush administration's assaults on the rights of Americans, it is hard to imagine that it would engage in Nixon-style "dirty tricks," or that the president's men would stoop to burglaries to find information to discredit their opponents. Also, of course, the federal courts, while not a lost cause, have undergone major changes. Though probably still reliable where many freedom of expression issues are concerned, the courts cannot be counted upon for robust defense of civil liberties in a number of other areas where claims of national security are invoked. A crucial question for the courts will be to what extent they are ready to protect us against new forms of political surveillance made possible by advances in technology. Will they simply ratify the arrangements worked out in the complex interactions between corporate interests and government . . . ? Or, can we expect them to safeguard privacy as they did two decades ago? Unfortunately, if President Bush has a chance to make new appointments to the US Supreme Court, as seems likely, the situation is likely to worsen. As it is, the appointments he is making to the federal district and appellate judiciary with the advice and consent of a US Senate now controlled by his party are shifting the balance further against the protection of civil liberty.

On the other hand, even in a difficult judicial environment, the availability of skilled advocacy can mitigate abuses. As in the Vietnam War era, there is no shortage today of lawyers to take on civil liberties assignments. The defense of rights is as well organized at present as at any time previously. Moreover, although advocates for those denied their rights face a challenging task in the courts, that is not their only forum. The organizations that sponsor legal representation in civil liberties cases are also participants in broader public debates.

As always, the decisive factor in determining how badly the country fares in the current period of assault on civil liberties will be its effectiveness in cowing Americans into going along. Will universities turn their backs on students from the Middle East or South Asia? Will Muslim women fear to go in the streets wearing head scarves? Will the government's renewed passion to collect dossiers on Americans make us fearful of associations that could arouse suspicions? Will we balk if an attempt is made—as some have advocated—to require national identity cards? Is unfettered discussion and debate of sensitive topics such as the war in Afghanistan, the war against Iraq, and America's treatment of the Guantanamo detainees possible in the secondary schools?

The early signs are not consistent. It was distressing that only one United States senator, Russell Feingold of Wisconsin, voted against the USA PATRIOT Act that was passed in great haste just four weeks after the September 11 attacks and that . . . no major newspaper opposed it editorially before it was adopted. The act . . . is one of the most comprehensive assaults on civil liberties in American history. Similarly, it was sad to read in the *New York Times* in December 2001 that the publisher of the *Sacramento Bee* was booed off the stage as she tried to deliver a commencement address at California State University about the importance of preserving civil liberties even as the country wages the war against terrorism.[4] The widespread public support for racial profiling against Middle Easterners on national security grounds . . . is disturbing. On the other hand, it is reassuring to learn of the trend . . . in which local communities are adopting resolutions calling for the protection of civil liberties. As the *Times* reported a year after its account of the ugly incident in Sacramento, "Nearly two dozen cities around the country have passed resolutions urging federal authorities to respect the civil rights of local citizens when fighting terrorism. Efforts to pass similar measures are under way in more than 60 other places."[5]

Though lacking legal force, such resolutions nevertheless signify much about the public spirit. . . . Also, it is heartening to note . . . that the proposed Terrorism Information and Prevention System (TIPS) was dropped from the Homeland Security Act of 2002 in Congress at the insistence of conservative former House majority leader Richard Armey. If civil liberties are to be protected, those committed to constitutional rights on both sides of the political spectrum will have to be prominent in the struggle.

One argument that ought to carry weight with conservatives and liberals alike is . . . that the United States will be more effective in the fight against terrorism if it upholds human rights both at home and abroad. . . . We have long proclaimed to the world that our country stands for freedom, and President Bush has portrayed the terrorists as archenemies of the values that America represents. Yet unreadiness to uphold the standards of freedom at home, or in dealing with those apprehended in the struggle against terrorism overseas, or in relations with other governments that claim they, too, are engaged in the war against terrorism, inspires cynicism and the increased resentment against the United States. . . .

No one imagines that, by being more respectful of civil liberties domestically or more consistent in promoting human rights internationally, the United States will persuade would-be terrorists to undergo a change of heart and renounce violence. But the climate within which terrorists operate is important. As should be obvious, the struggle to defeat them or to thwart their intentions will be far more difficult if antagonism against the United States is pervasive in the societies in which they plan their attacks. . . . The international sympathy for the United States immediately following September 11 was quickly squandered. Yet it can be recaptured, but not by pursuing a course that makes the United States seem duplicitous when it asserts its commitment to freedom. The image of prisoners held incommunicado at Guantanamo beyond the reach of any court, perhaps forever . . . clashes sharply with such assertions.

United States attorney general John Ashcroft has portrayed the effort to protect civil liberties as support for the terrorists. He told the United States Senate Judiciary Committee that "to those who scare peace-loving people with phantoms of lost liberty my message is this: Your tactics only aid terrorists, for they erode our national unity and diminish our resolve. They give ammunition to America's enemies and pause to America's friends."[6] It is a statement that echoes similar comments uttered over the course of the past century by such officials as J. Edgar Hoover, Joseph McCarthy, and Richard Nixon who led earlier assaults on civil liberty. Over time, Americans rejected such efforts to smear the proponents of rights. "McCarthyism" is now a term of opprobrium used by those across the political spectrum to denote such assertions as these by Ashcroft that attempt to link those who uphold constitutional principles with those out to destroy the United States.

Subsequent to this December 2001 Senate Judiciary Committee testimony, the Bush administration seemed to exercise tighter control over Attorney General Ashcroft, the leading present-day embodiment of what historian Richard Hofstadter referred to as "the paranoid style in American politics."[7] Ashcroft's public appearances during 2002 were less frequent and more circumscribed. It appeared that the White House recognized his potential for becoming a political liability to the president. Yet the failure of the president to repudiate publicly such comments, the leeway given to Vice Admiral John Poindexter to develop his appalling Total Information Awareness program, and the many violations of constitutional principles that characterize the policies and practices of the Bush administration suggest that it considers that attacks on civil liberties will secure broad public support only if they are not accompanied by the rhetorical extremes to which Ashcroft would take them. As the Bush administration seems to have its ear close to the ground and has demonstrated its acute sensitivity to public opinion, its judgment on this matter is especially disturbing. It may be that the only way to alter its policies is to ensure that Americans are more outspoken in demanding that their rights, and the rights of others, should be respected.

NOTES

1. *Laird v. Tatum*, 408 US 1 (1972).

2. *United States v. United States District Court*, 407 US 297 (1972).

3. *New York Times Co. v. United States*, 403 US 713 (1971).

4. Timothy Egan, "In Sacramento, a Publisher's Questions Draw the Wrath of the Crowd," *New York Times*, December 21, 2001.

5. Michael Janofsky, "Cities Wary of Anti-terror Tactics Pass Civil Liberties Resolutions," *New York Times*, December 23, 2002.

6. John Ashcroft, Testimony before the Senate Committee on the Judiciary, *Hearings on the USA PATRIOT ACT*, December 6, 2001.

7. Richard Hofstadter, *The Paranoid Style in American Politics and Other Essays* (New York: Vintage Books, 1967).

3.

SELECTIONS FROM THE US CONSTITUTION

The following brief selections from the US Constitution relate to the separation of powers and are particularly relevant to the *Padilla v. Rumsfeld* and *Hamdi v. Rumsfeld* opinions, which are included in parts five and six of this volume. Also included are three constitutional amendments that do not relate to the separation of powers, but are relevant to other issues raised in this book.

Editors' Note

We the People of the United States, in Order to form a more perfect Union, establish Justice, insure domestic Tranquility, provide for the common defence, promote the general Welfare, and secure the Blessings of Liberty to ourselves and our Posterity, do ordain and establish this Constitution for the United States of America.

ARTICLE I

Section 1

All legislative Powers herein granted shall be vested in a Congress of the United States, which shall consist of a Senate and House of Representatives. . . .

Section 8

Clause 1: The Congress shall have Power to lay and collect Taxes, Duties, Imposts and Excises, to pay the Debts and provide for the common Defence and general Welfare of the United States; but all Duties, Imposts and Excises shall be uniform throughout the United States; . . .

Clause 9: To constitute Tribunals inferior to the supreme Court;

Clause 10: To define and punish Piracies and Felonies committed on the high Seas, and Offences against the Law of Nations;

Clause 11: To declare War, grant Letters of Marque and Reprisal, and make Rules concerning Captures on Land and Water;

Clause 12: To raise and support Armies, but no Appropriation of Money to that Use shall be for a longer Term than two Years;

Clause 13: To provide and maintain a Navy;

Clause 14: To make Rules for the Government and Regulation of the land and naval Forces;

Clause 15: To provide for calling forth the Militia to execute the Laws of the Union, suppress Insurrections and repel Invasions;

Clause 16: To provide for organizing, arming, and disciplining, the Militia, and for governing such Part of them as may be employed in the Service of the United States, reserving to the States respectively, the Appointment of the Officers, and the Authority of training the Militia according to the discipline prescribed by Congress; . . .

Clause 18: To make all Laws which shall be necessary and proper for carrying into Execution the foregoing Powers, and all other Powers vested by this Constitution in the Government of the United States, or in any Department or Officer thereof.

Section 9

Clause 2: The Privilege of the Writ of Habeas Corpus shall not be suspended, unless when in Cases of Rebellion or Invasion the public Safety may require it. . . .

ARTICLE II

Section 1

Clause 1: The executive Power shall be vested in a President of the United States of America. He shall hold his Office during the Term of four Years, and, together with the Vice President, chosen for the same Term, be elected. . . .

Section 2

Clause 1: The President shall be Commander in Chief of the Army and Navy of the United, and of the Militia of the several States, when called into the actual Service of the United States. . . .

Section 3

He shall . . . take Care that the Laws be faithfully executed, and shall Commission all the Officers of the United States. . . .

ARTICLE III

Section 1

The judicial Power of the United States, shall be vested in one supreme Court, and in such inferior Courts as the Congress may from time to time ordain and establish. . . .

Section 2

Clause 1: The judicial Power shall extend to all Cases, in Law and Equity, arising under this Constitution, the Laws of the United States, and Treaties made, or which shall be made, under their Authority. . . .

Section 3

Clause 1: Treason against the United States, shall consist only in levying War against them, or in adhering to their Enemies, giving them Aid and Comfort. No Person shall be convicted of Treason unless on the Testimony of two Witnesses to the same overt Act, or on Confession in open Court.

Clause 2: The Congress shall have Power to declare the Punishment of Treason, but no Attainder of Treason shall work Corruption of Blood, or Forfeiture except during the Life of the Person attainted.

BILL OF RIGHTS

Amendment IV

The right of the people to be secure in their persons, houses, papers, and effects, against unreasonable searches and seizures, shall not be violated, and no Warrants shall issue, but upon probable cause, supported by Oath or affirmation, and particularly describing the place to be searched, and the persons or things to be seized.

Amendment V

No person shall be held to answer for a capital, or otherwise infamous crime, unless on a presentment or indictment of a Grand Jury, except in cases arising in the land or naval forces, or in the Militia, when in actual service in time of War or public danger; nor shall any person be subject for the same offense to be twice put in jeopardy of life or limb; nor shall be compelled in any criminal case to be a witness against himself, nor be deprived of life, liberty, or property, without due process of law; nor shall private property be taken for public use, without just compensation.

Amendment VI

In all criminal prosecutions, the accused shall enjoy the right to a speedy and public trial, by an impartial jury of the State and district wherein the crime shall have been committed, which district shall have been previously ascertained by law, and to be informed of the nature and cause of the accusation; to be confronted with the witnesses against him; to have compulsory process for obtaining witnesses in his favor, and to have the Assistance of Counsel for his defense.

4.

HABEAS CORPUS STATUTE

28 United States Code, Section 2241. Power to Grant Writ

(a) Writs of habeas corpus may be granted by the Supreme Court, any justice thereof, the district courts and any circuit judge within their respective jurisdictions. The order of a circuit judge shall be entered in the records of the district court of the district wherein the restraint complained of is had.

(b) The Supreme Court, any justice thereof, and any circuit judge may decline to entertain an application for a writ of habeas corpus and may transfer the application for hearing and determination to the district court having jurisdiction to entertain it.

(c) The writ of habeas corpus shall not extend to a prisoner unless—

   (1) He is in custody under or by color of the authority of the United States or is committed for trial before some court thereof; or

   (2) He is in custody for an act done or omitted in pursuance of an Act of Congress, or an order, process, judgment or decree of a court or judge of the United States; or

   (3) He is in custody in violation of the Constitution or laws or treaties of the United States; or

(4) He, being a citizen of a foreign state and domiciled therein is in custody for an act done or omitted under any alleged right, title, authority, privilege, protection, or exemption claimed under the commission, order or sanction of any foreign state, or under color thereof, the validity and effect of which depend upon the law of nations; or

(5) It is necessary to bring him into court to testify or for trial.

(d) Where an application for a writ of habeas corpus is made by a person in custody under the judgment and sentence of a State court of a State which contains two or more Federal judicial districts, the application may be filed in the district court for the district wherein such person is in custody or in the district court for the district within which the State court was held which convicted and sentenced him and each of such district courts shall have concurrent jurisdiction to entertain the application. The district court for the district wherein such an application is filed in the exercise of its discretion and in furtherance of justice may transfer the application to the other district court for hearing and determination.

PART 2.

DOMESTIC SURVEILLANCE

5.

BIGGER MONSTER, WEAKER CHAINS
THE GROWTH OF AN AMERICAN SURVEILLANCE SOCIETY

Jay Stanley and Barry Steinhardt

PREFACE

There is no shortage of stories in the media today about the continuing assault on our privacy. But while the latest surveillance program or privacy-invading gadget always receives ample coverage, it is much rarer to find stories that connect the dots and describe the overall impact on privacy in the United States. And without that big picture, the importance of the individual pieces often gets lost.

This new report from the American Civil Liberties Union seeks to provide greater understanding of how our activities are increasingly being tracked and recorded, and how all that data could be drawn together from different sources to create a single high-resolution image of our private lives.

For decades, the notion of a "surveillance society," where every facet of our private lives is monitored and recorded, has sounded abstract, paranoid, or far-fetched to many people.

No more! The public's recent introduction to the Pentagon's

"Total Information Awareness" project, which seeks to tie together every facet of our private lives in one big surveillance scheme, has provided a stunning lesson in the realities of the new world in which we live. The revelations about the Total Information Awareness program have given the public a sudden introduction to the concept of "data surveillance," and an early glimmer of the technological potential for a surveillance society. It has also confirmed the national security and law enforcement establishments' hunger for such surveillance.

Yet too many people still do not understand the danger, do not grasp just how radical an increase in surveillance by both the government and the private sector is becoming possible, or do not see that the danger stems not just from a single government program, but from a number of parallel developments in the worlds of technology, law, and politics. In this report, the ACLU seeks to flesh out these trends, and, by setting down various developments together in one place, to illuminate the overall danger and what can be done to eliminate it.

The surveillance monster is getting bigger and stronger by the day. But the American Civil Liberties Union believes that it is not too late to build a system of law that can chain it. It is not too late to take back our data.

INTRODUCTION

Privacy and liberty in the United States are at risk. A combination of lightning-fast technological innovation and the erosion of privacy protections threatens to transform Big Brother from an oft-cited but remote threat into a very real part of American life. We are at risk of turning into a Surveillance Society.

The explosion of computers, cameras, sensors, wireless communication, GPS, biometrics, and other technologies in just the last ten years is feeding a surveillance monster that is growing silently in our midst. Scarcely a month goes by in which we don't read about some new high-tech way to invade people's privacy, from face recognition to implantable microchips, data-mining, DNA chips, and even "brain wave fingerprinting." The fact is, there are no longer any technical barriers to the Big Brother regime portrayed by George Orwell.

Even as this surveillance monster grows in power, we are weakening the legal chains that keep it from trampling our lives. We should be responding to intrusive new technologies by building stronger restraints to protect our privacy; instead, we are doing the opposite—loosening regulations on government surveillance, watching passively as private surveillance grows unchecked, and contemplating the introduction of tremendously powerful new surveillance infrastructures that will tie all this information together.

A gradual weakening of our privacy rights has been underway for decades, but many of the most startling developments have come in response to the terrorist attacks of September 11. But few of these hastily enacted measures are likely to increase our protection against terrorism. More often than not, September 11 has been used as a pretext to loosen constraints that law enforcement has been chafing under for years.

It doesn't require some apocalyptic vision of American democracy being replaced by dictatorship to worry about a surveillance society. There is a lot of room for the United States to become a meaner, less open, and less just place without any radical change in government. All that's required is the continued construction of new surveillance technologies and the simultaneous erosion of privacy protections.

It's not hard to imagine how in the near future we might see scenarios like the following:

- An African American man from the central city visits an affluent white suburb to attend a coworker's barbeque. Later that night, a crime takes place elsewhere in the neighborhood. The police review surveillance camera images, use face recognition to identify the man, and pay him a visit at home the next day. His trip to the suburbs where he "didn't belong" has earned him an interrogation from suspicious police.
- A tourist walking through an unfamiliar city happens upon a

sex shop. She stops to gaze at several curious items in the store's window before moving along. Unbeknownst to her, the store has set up the newly available "Customer Identification System," which detects a signal being emitted by a computer chip in her driver's license and records her identity and the date, time, and duration of her brief look inside the window. A week later, she gets a solicitation in the mail mentioning her "visit" and embarrassing her in front of her family.

Such possibilities are only the tip of the iceberg. The media faithfully reports the latest surveillance gadgets and the latest moves to soften the rules on government spying, but rarely provides the big picture. That is unfortunate, because each new threat to our privacy is much more significant as part of the overall trend than it seems when viewed in isolation. When these monitoring technologies and techniques are combined, they can create a surveillance network far more powerful than any single one would create on its own.

The good news is that these trends can be stopped. As the American people realize that each new development is part of this larger story, they will give more and more weight to protecting privacy, and support the measures we need to preserve our freedom.

THE GROWING SURVEILLANCE MONSTER

In the film *Minority Report*, which takes place in the United States in the year 2050, people called "Pre-cogs" can supposedly predict future crimes, and the nation has become a perfect surveillance society. The frightening thing is that except for the psychic Pre-cogs, the technologies of surveillance portrayed in the film already exist or are in the pipeline. Replace the Pre-cogs with "brain fingerprinting"—the supposed ability to ferret out dangerous tendencies by reading brain waves—and the film's entire vision no longer lies far in the future. Other new privacy invasions are coming at us from all directions, from video and data surveillance to DNA scanning to new data-gathering gadgets.

Video Surveillance

Surveillance video cameras are rapidly spreading throughout the public arena. A survey of surveillance cameras in Manhattan, for example, found that it is impossible to walk around the city without being recorded nearly every step of the way. And since September 11 the pace has quickened, with new cameras being placed not only in some of our most sacred public spaces, such as the National Mall in Washington and the Statue of Liberty in New York harbor, but on ordinary public streets all over America.

As common as video cameras have become, there are strong signs that, without public action, video surveillance may be on the verge of a revolutionary expansion in American life. There are three factors propelling this revolution:

1. Improved technology. Advances such as the digitization of video mean cheaper cameras, cheaper transmission of far-flung video feeds, and cheaper storage and retrieval of images.

2. Centralized surveillance. A new centralized surveillance center in Washington, DC, is an early indicator of what technology may bring. It allows officers to view images from video cameras across the city—public buildings and streets, neighborhoods, Metro stations, and even schools. With the flip of a switch, officers can zoom in on people from cameras a half-mile away.[1]

3. Unexamined assumptions that cameras provide security. In the wake of the September 11 attacks, many embraced surveillance as the way to prevent future attacks and prevent crime. But it is far from clear how cameras will increase security. US government experts on security technology, noting that "monitoring video screens is both boring and mesmerizing," have found in experiments that after only twenty minutes of watching video monitors, "the attention of most individuals has degenerated to well below acceptable levels."[2] In addition, studies of cameras' effect on crime in

Britain, where they have been extensively deployed, have found no conclusive evidence that they have reduced crime.[3]

These developments are creating powerful momentum toward pervasive video surveillance of our public spaces. If centralized video facilities are permitted in Washington and around the nation, it is inevitable that they will be expanded—not only in the number of cameras but also in their power and ability. It is easy to foresee inexpensive, one-dollar cameras being distributed throughout our cities and tied via wireless technology into a centralized police facility where the life of the city can be monitored. Those video signals could be stored indefinitely in digital form in giant but inexpensive databases, and called up with the click of a mouse at any time. With face recognition, the video records could even be indexed and searched based on who the systems identify—correctly, or all too often, incorrectly.

Several airports around the nation, a handful of cities, and even the National Park Service at the Statue of Liberty have installed face recognition. While not nearly reliable enough to be effective as a security application,[4] such a system could still violate the privacy of a significant percentage of the citizens who appeared before it (as well as the privacy of those who do not appear before it but are falsely identified as having done so). Unlike, say, an iris scan, face recognition doesn't require the knowledge, consent, or participation of the subject; modern cameras can easily view faces from over one hundred yards away.

Further possibilities for the expansion of video surveillance lie with unmanned aircraft, or drones, which have been used by the military and the CIA overseas for reconnaissance, surveillance, and targeting. Controlled from the ground, they can stay airborne for days at a time. Now there is talk of deploying them domestically. Senate Armed Services Committee chairman John Warner (R-VA) said in December 2002 that he wants to explore their use in Homeland Security, and a number of domestic government agencies have expressed interest in deploying them. Drones are likely to be just one of many ways in which improving robotics technology will be applied to surveillance.[5]

The bottom line is that surveillance systems, once installed, rarely remain confined to their original purpose. Once the nation decides to go down the path of seeking security through video surveillance, the imperative to make it work will become overwhelming, and the monitoring of citizens in public places will quickly become pervasive.

Data Surveillance

An insidious new type of surveillance is becoming possible that is just as intrusive as video surveillance—what we might call "data surveillance." Data surveillance is the collection of information about an identifiable individual, often from multiple sources, that can be assembled into a portrait of that person's activities.[6] Most computers are programmed to automatically store and track usage data, and the spread of computer chips in our daily lives means that more and more of our activities leave behind "data trails." It will soon be possible to combine information from different sources to recreate an individual's activities with such detail that it becomes no different from being followed around all day by a detective with a video camera.

Some think comprehensive public tracking will make no difference, since life in public places is not "private" in the same way as life inside the home. This is wrong; such tracking would represent a radical change in American life. A woman who leaves her house, drives to a store, meets a friend for coffee, visits a museum, and then returns home may be in public all day, but her life is still private in that she is the only one who has an overall view of how she spent her day. In America, she does not expect that her activities are being watched or tracked in any systematic way—she expects to be left alone. But if current trends continue, it will be impossible to have any contact with the outside world that is not watched and recorded.

The Commodification of Information

A major factor driving the trend toward data surveillance forward is the commodification of personal information by corporations. As computer technology exploded in recent decades, making it much easier to collect information about what Americans buy and do, companies came to realize that such data is often very valuable. The expense of marketing efforts gives businesses a strong incentive to know as much about consumers as possible so they can focus on the most likely new customers. Surveys, sweepstakes questionnaires, loyalty programs, and detailed product registration forms have proliferated in American life—all aimed at gathering information about consumers. Today, any consumer activity that is not being tracked and recorded is increasingly being viewed by businesses as money left on the table.

On the Internet, where every mouse click can be recorded, the tracking and profiling of consumers is even more prevalent. Web sites cannot only track what consumers buy, but what they look at—and for how long, and in what order. With the end of the dot-com era, personal information has become an even more precious source of hard cash for those Internet ventures that survive. And of course Americans use the Internet not just as a shopping mall, but to research topics of interest, debate political issues, seek support for personal problems, and many other purposes that can generate deeply private information about their thoughts, interests, lifestyles, habits, and activities. . . .

New Data-Gathering Technologies

The discovery by businesses of the monetary value of personal information and the vast new project of tracking the habits of consumers has been made possible by advances in computers, databases, and the Internet. In the near future, other new technologies will continue to fill out the mosaic of information it is possible to collect on every individual. Examples include:

- **Cell phone location data.** The government has mandated that manufacturers make cell phones capable of automatically reporting their location when an owner dials 911. Of course, those phones are capable of tracking their location at other times as well. And in applying the rules that protect the privacy of telephone records to this location data, the government is weakening those rules in a way that allows phone companies to collect and share data about the location and movements of their customers.

- **Biometrics.** Technologies that identify us by unique bodily attributes such as our fingerprints, faces, iris patterns, or DNA are already being proposed for inclusion on national ID cards and to identify airline passengers. Face recognition is spreading. Fingerprint scanners have been introduced as security or payment mechanisms in office buildings, college campuses, grocery stores, and even fast-food restaurants. And several companies are working on DNA chips that will be able to instantly identify individuals by the DNA we leave behind everywhere we go.

- **Black boxes.** All cars built today contain computers, and some of those computers are being programmed in ways that are not necessarily in the interest of owners. An increasing number of cars contain devices akin to the "black boxes" on aircraft that record details about a vehicle's operation and movement. Those devices can "tattle" on car owners to the police or insurance investigators. Already, one car rental agency tried to charge a customer for speeding after a GPS device in the car reported the transgression back to the company. And cars are just one example of how products and possessions can be programmed to spy and inform on their owners.

- **RFID chips.** RFID chips, which are already used in such applications as toll booth speed passes, emit a short-range radio signal containing a unique code that identifies each chip. Once the cost of these chips falls to a few pennies each, plans are underway to affix them to products in stores, down to every can of soup and tube of toothpaste. They will allow everyday objects to "talk" to each other—or to anyone else who is listening. For example, they could let market researchers scan the contents of your purse or car from five feet away, or let police officers scan your identification when they pass you on the street.

- **Implantable GPS chips.** Computer chips that can record and broadcast their location have also been developed. In addition to practical uses such as building them into shipping containers, they can also serve as location "bugs" when, for example, hidden by a suspicious husband in a wife's purse. And they can be implanted under the skin (as can RFID chips).

If we do not act to reverse the current trend, data surveillance—like video surveillance—will allow corporations or the government to constantly monitor what individual Americans do every day. Data surveillance would cover everyone, with records of every transaction and activity squirreled away until they are sucked up by powerful search engines, whether as part of routine security checks, a general sweep for suspects in an unsolved crime, or a program of harassment against some future Martin Luther King Jr.

Government Surveillance

Data surveillance is made possible by the growing ocean of privately collected personal data. But who would conduct that surveillance? There are certainly business incentives for doing so; companies called data aggregators (such as Acxiom and ChoicePoint) are in the business of compiling detailed databases on individuals and then selling that information to others. Although these companies are invisible to the average person, data aggregation is an enormous, multibillion-dollar industry. Some databases are even "co-ops" where participants agree to contribute data about their customers in return for the ability to pull out cross-merchant profiles of customers' activities.

The biggest threat to privacy, however, comes from the government. Many Americans are naturally concerned about corporate surveillance, but only the government has the power to take away liberty—as has been demonstrated starkly by the post–September 11 detention of suspects without trial as "enemy combatants."

In addition, the government has unmatched power to centralize all the private-sector data that is being generated. In fact, the distinction between government and private-sector privacy invasions is fading quickly. The Justice Department, for example, reportedly has an $8 million contract with data aggregator ChoicePoint that allows government agents to tap into the company's vast database of personal information on individuals.[7] Although the Privacy Act of 1974 banned the government from maintaining information on citizens who are not the targets of investigations, the FBI can now evade that requirement by simply purchasing information that has been collected by the private sector. Other proposals—such as the Pentagon's "Total Information Awareness" project and airline passenger profiling programs—would institutionalize government access to consumer data in even more far-reaching ways (see below).

Government Databases

The government's access to personal information begins with the thousands of databases it maintains on the lives of Americans and others. For instance:

- The FBI maintains a giant database that contains millions of records covering everything from criminal records to stolen boats and databases with millions of computerized fingerprints and DNA records.
- The Treasury Department runs a database that collects financial information reported to the government by thousands of banks and other financial institutions.
- A "new hires" database maintained by the Department of Health and Human Services, which contains the name, address, social security number, and quarterly wages of every working person in the United States.
- The federal Department of Education maintains an enormous information bank holding years worth of educational records on individuals stretching from their primary school years through higher education. After September 11, Con-

gress gave the FBI permission to access the database without probable cause.

- State departments of motor vehicles, of course, possess millions of up-to-date files containing a variety of personal data, including photographs of most adults living in the United States.

Communications Surveillance

The government also performs an increasing amount of eavesdropping on electronic communications. While technologies like telephone wiretapping have been around for decades, today's technologies cast a far broader net. The FBI's controversial "Carnivore" program, for example, is supposed to be used to tap into the e-mail traffic of a particular individual. Unlike a telephone wiretap, however, it doesn't cover just one device but (because of how the Internet is built) filters through all the traffic on the Internet Service Provider to which it has been attached. The only thing keeping the government from trolling through all this traffic is software instructions that are written by the government itself. (Despite that clear conflict of interest, the FBI has refused to allow independent inspection and oversight of the device's operation.)

Another example is the international eavesdropping program code-named Echelon. Operated by a partnership consisting of the United States, Britain, Canada, Australia, and New Zealand, Echelon reportedly grabs e-mail, phone calls, and other electronic communications from its far-flung listening posts across most of the earth. (US eavesdroppers are not supposed to listen in on the conversations of Americans, but the question about Echelon has always been whether the intelligence agencies of participating nations can set up reciprocal, back-scratching arrangements to spy on each others' citizens.) Like Carnivore, Echelon may be used against particular targets, but to do so its operators must sort through massive amounts of information about potentially millions of people. That is worlds away from the popular conception of the old wiretap where an FBI agent listens to one line. Not only the volume of intercepts but the potential for abuse is now exponentially higher.

The "PATRIOT" Act

The potential for the abuse of surveillance powers has also risen sharply due to a dramatic post-9/11 erosion of legal protections against government surveillance of citizens. Just six weeks after the September 11 attacks, a panicked Congress passed the "USA PATRIOT Act," an overnight revision of the nation's surveillance laws that vastly expanded the government's authority to spy on its own citizens and reduced checks and balances on those powers, such as judicial oversight. The government never demonstrated that restraints on surveillance had contributed to the attack, and indeed much of the new legislation had nothing to do with fighting terrorism. Rather, the bill represented a successful use of the terrorist attacks by the FBI to roll back unwanted checks on its power. The most powerful provisions of the law allow for:

- **Easy access to records.** Under the PATRIOT Act, the FBI can force anyone to turn over records on their customers or clients, giving the government unchecked power to rifle through individuals' financial records, medical histories, Internet usage, travel patterns, or any other records. Some of the most invasive and disturbing uses permitted by the act involve government access to citizens' reading habits from libraries and bookstores. The FBI does not have to show suspicion of a crime, can gag the recipient of a search order from disclosing the search to anyone, and is subject to no meaningful judicial oversight.
- **Expansion of the "pen register" exception in wiretap law.** The PATRIOT Act expands exceptions to the normal requirement for probable cause in wiretap law.[8] As with its new power to search records, the FBI need not show probable cause or even reasonable suspicion of criminal activity, and judicial oversight is essentially nil.
- **Expansion of the intelligence exception in wiretap law.** The PATRIOT Act also loosens the evidence needed by the government to justify an intelligence wiretap or physical search. Previously the law allowed exceptions to the Fourth Amendment

for these kinds of searches only if "the purpose" of the search was to gather foreign intelligence. But the act changes "the purpose" to "a significant purpose," which lets the government circumvent the Constitution's probable cause requirement even when its main goal is ordinary law enforcement.[9]

- **More secret searches.** Except in rare cases, the law has always required that the subject of a search be notified that a search is taking place. Such notice is a crucial check on the government's power because it forces the authorities to operate in the open and allows the subject of searches to challenge their validity in court. But the PATRIOT Act allows the government to conduct searches without notifying the subjects until long after the search has been executed.

Under these changes and other authorities asserted by the Bush administration, US intelligence agents could conduct a secret search of an American citizen's home, use evidence found there to declare him an "enemy combatant," and imprison him without trial. The courts would have no chance to review these decisions—indeed, they might never even find out about them.

The "TIPS" Program

In the name of fighting terrorism, the Bush administration has also proposed a program that would encourage citizens to spy on each other. The administration initially planned to recruit people such as letter carriers and utility technicians, who, the White House said, are "well-positioned to recognize unusual events." In the face of fierce public criticism, the administration scaled back the program, but continued to enlist workers involved in certain key industries. In November 2002, Congress included a provision in the Homeland Security Act prohibiting the Bush administration from moving forward with TIPS.

Although Congress killed TIPS, the fact that the administration would pursue such a program reveals a disturbing disconnect with American values and a disturbing lack of awareness of the history of governmental abuses of power. Dividing citizen from citizen by encouraging mutual suspicion and reporting to the government would dramatically increase the government's power by extending surveillance into every nook and cranny of American society. Such a strategy was central to the Soviet Union and other totalitarian regimes.

Loosened Domestic Spying Regulations

In May 2002, Attorney General John Ashcroft issued new guidelines on domestic spying that significantly increase the freedom of federal agents to conduct surveillance on American individuals and organizations. Under the new guidelines, FBI agents can infiltrate "any event that is open to the public," from public meetings and demonstrations to political conventions to church services to twelve-step programs. This was the same basis upon which abuses were carried out by the FBI in the 1950s and 1960s, including surveillance of political groups that disagreed with the government, anonymous letters sent to the spouses of targets to try to ruin their marriages, and the infamous campaign against Martin Luther King Jr., who was investigated and harassed for decades. The new guidelines are purely for spying on Americans; there is a separate set of Foreign Guidelines that cover investigations inside the United States of foreign powers and terrorist organizations such as al Qaeda.

Like the TIPS program, Ashcroft's guidelines sow suspicion among citizens and extend the government's surveillance power into the capillaries of American life. It is not just the reality of government surveillance that chills free expression and the freedom that Americans enjoy. The same negative effects come when we are constantly forced to wonder whether we might be under observation— whether the person sitting next to us is secretly informing the government that we are "suspicious."

THE SYNERGIES OF SURVEILLANCE

Multiple surveillance techniques added together are greater than the sum of their parts. One example is face recognition, which combines the power of computerized software analysis, cameras, and data-bases to seek matches between facial images. But the real synergies of surveillance come into play with data collection.

The growing piles of data being collected on Americans represent an enormous invasion of privacy, but our privacy has actually been protected by the fact that all this information still remains scattered across many different databases. As a result, there exists a pent-up capacity for surveillance in American life today—a capacity that will be fully realized if the government, landlords, employers, or other powerful forces gain the ability to draw together all this information. A particular piece of data about you—such as the fact that you entered your office at 10:29 AM on July 5, 2001—is normally innocuous. But when enough pieces of that kind of data are assembled together, they add up to an extremely detailed and intrusive picture of an individual's life and habits.

Data Profiling and "Total Information Awareness"

Just how real this scenario is has been demonstrated by another ominous surveillance plan to emerge from the effort against terrorism: the Pentagon's "Total Information Awareness" program. The aim of this program is to give officials easy, unified access to every possible government and commercial database in the world.[11] According to program director John Poindexter, the program's goal is to develop "ultra-large-scale" database technologies with the goal of "treating the worldwide, distributed, legacy databases as if they were one centralized database." The program envisions a "full-coverage database containing all information relevant to identifying" potential terrorists and their supporters. As we have seen, the amount of available information is mushrooming by the day, and will soon be rich enough to reveal much of our lives.

The TIA program, which is run by the Defense Advanced Research Projects Agency (DARPA), not only seeks to bring together the oceans of data that are already being collected on people, but would be designed to afford what DARPA calls "easy future scaling" to embrace new sources of data as they become available. It would also incorporate other work being done by the military, such as their "Human Identification at a Distance" program, which seeks to allow identification and tracking of people from a distance, and therefore without their permission or knowledge.[12]

Although it has not received nearly as much media attention, a close cousin of TIA is also being created in the context of airline security. This plan involves the creation of a system for conducting background checks on individuals who wish to fly and then separating out either those who appear to be the most trustworthy passengers (proposals known as "trusted traveler") or flagging the least trustworthy (a proposal known as CAPS II, for Computer Assisted Passenger Screening) for special attention.

The *Washington Post* has reported that work is being done on CAPS II with the goal of creating a "vast air security screening system designed to instantly pull together every passenger's travel history and living arrangements, plus a wealth of other personal and demographic information" in the hopes that the authorities will be able to "profile passenger activity and intuit obscure clues about potential threats." The government program would reportedly draw on enormous stores of personal information from data aggregators and other sources, including travel records, real estate histories, personal associations, credit card records, and telephone records. Plans call for using complex computer algorithms, including highly experimental technologies such as "neural networks," to sort through the reams of new personal information and identify "suspicious" people.[13]

The dubious premise of programs like TIA and CAPS II—that "terrorist patterns" can be ferreted out from the enormous mass of American lives, many of which will inevitably be quirky, eccentric, or riddled with suspicious coincidences—probably dooms them to failure. But failure is not likely to lead these programs to be shut down—instead, the government will begin feeding its computers more and more personal information in a vain effort to make the concept work. We will then have the worst of both worlds: poor security and a supercharged surveillance tool that would destroy Americans' privacy and threaten our freedom.

It is easy to imagine these systems being expanded in the future to share their risk assessments with other security systems. For example, CAPS II could be linked to a photographic database and surveillance cameras equipped with face recognition software. Such a system might sound an alarm when a subject who has been designated as "suspicious" appears in public. The suspicious citizen could then be watched from a centralized video monitoring facility as he moves around the city.

In short, the government is working furiously to bring disparate sources of information about us together into one view, just as privacy advocates have been warning about for years. That would represent a radical branching off from the centuries-old Anglo-American tradition that the police conduct surveillance only where there is evidence of involvement in wrongdoing. It would seek to protect us by monitoring everyone for signs of wrongdoing—in short, by instituting a giant dragnet capable of sifting through the personal lives of Americans in search of "suspicious" patterns. The potential for abuse of such a system is staggering.

The massive defense research capabilities of the United States have always involved the search for ways of outwardly defending our nation. Programs like TIA[14] involve turning those capabilities inward and applying them to the American people—something that should be done, if at all, only with extreme caution and plenty of public input, political debate, checks and balances, and congressional oversight. So far, none of those things have been present with TIA or CAPS II.

National ID Cards

If Americans allow it, another convergence of surveillance technologies will probably center around a national ID card. A national ID would immediately combine new technologies such as biometrics and RFID chips along with an enormously powerful database (possibly distributed among the fifty states). Before long, it would become an overarching means of facilitating surveillance by allowing far-flung pools of information to be pulled together into a single, incredibly rich dossier or profile of our lives. Before long, office buildings, doctors' offices, gas stations, highway tolls, subways, and buses would incorporate the ID card into their security or payment systems for greater efficiency, and data that is currently scattered and disconnected will get organized around the ID and lead to the creation of what amounts to a national database of sensitive information about American citizens.

History has shown that databases created for one purpose are almost inevitably expanded to other uses; Social Security, which was prohibited by federal law from being used as an identifier when it was first created, is a prime example. Over time, a national ID database would inevitably contain a wider and wider range of information and become accessible to more and more people for more and more purposes that are further and further removed from its original justification.

The most likely route to a national ID is through our driver's licenses. Since September 11, the American Association of Motor Vehicle Administrators has been forcefully lobbying Congress for funds to establish nationwide uniformity in the design and content of driver's licenses—and more importantly, for tightly interconnecting the databases that lie behind the physical licenses themselves.

An attempt to retrofit driver's licenses into national ID cards will launch a predictable series of events bringing us toward a surveillance society:

- Proponents will promise that the IDs will be implemented in limited ways that won't devastate privacy and other liberties.
- Once a limited version of the proposal is put in place, its limits as an antiterrorism measure will quickly become apparent. Like a dam built halfway across a river, the IDs cannot possibly be effective unless their coverage is total.
- The scheme's ineffectiveness—starkly demonstrated, perhaps, by a new terrorist attack—will create an overwhelming imperative to "fix" and "complete" it, which will turn it into the totalitarian tool that proponents promised it would never become.

A perfect example of that dynamic is the requirement that travelers present driver's licenses when boarding airplanes, instituted after the explosion (now believed to have been mechanical in cause) that brought down TWA Flight 800 in 1996. On its own, the requirement was meaningless as a security measure, but after September 11 its existence quickly led to calls to begin tracking and identifying citizens on the theory that "we already have to show ID, we might as well make it mean something."

Once in place, it is easy to imagine how national IDs could be combined with an RFID chip to allow for convenient, at-a-distance verification of ID. The IDs could then be tied to access control points around our public places, so that the unauthorized could be kept out of office buildings, apartments, public transit, and secure public buildings. Citizens with criminal records, poor CAPS ratings, or low incomes could be barred from accessing airports, sports arenas, stores, or other facilities. Retailers might add RFID readers to find out exactly who is browsing their aisles, gawking at their window displays from the sidewalk, or passing by without looking. A network of automated RFID listening posts on the sidewalks and roads could even reveal the location of all citizens at all times. Pocket ID readers could be used by FBI agents to sweep up the identities of everyone at a political meeting, protest march, or Islamic prayer service.

CONCLUSION

If we do not take steps to control and regulate surveillance to bring it into conformity with our values, we will find ourselves being tracked, analyzed, profiled, and flagged in our daily lives to a degree we can scarcely imagine today. We will be forced into an impossible struggle to conform to the letter of every rule, law, and guideline, lest we create ammunition for enemies in the government or elsewhere. Our transgressions will become permanent scarlet letters that follow us throughout our lives, visible to all and used by the government, landlords, employers, insurance companies, and other powerful parties to increase their leverage over average people. Americans will not be able to engage in political protest or go about their daily lives without the constant awareness that we are—or could be—under surveillance. We will be forced to constantly ask of even the smallest action taken in public, "Will this make me look suspicious? Will this hurt my chances for future employment? Will this reduce my ability to get insurance?" The exercise of free speech will be chilled as Americans become conscious that their every word may be reported to the government by FBI infiltrators, suspicious fellow citizens, or an Internet Service Provider.

Many well-known commentators like Sun Microsystems CEO Scott McNealy have already pronounced privacy dead. The truth is that a surveillance society does loom over us, and privacy, while not yet dead, is on life support.

Heroic Measures Are Required to Save It

Four main goals need to be attained to prevent this dark potential from being realized: a change in the terms of the debate, passage of comprehensive privacy laws, passage of new laws to regulate the powerful and invasive new technologies that have and will continue to appear, and a revival of the Fourth Amendment to the US Constitution.

1. Changing the Terms of the Debate

In the public debates over every new surveillance technology, the forest too often gets lost for the trees, and we lose sight of the larger trend: the seemingly inexorable movement toward a surveillance society. It will always be important to understand and publicly debate every new technology and every new technique for spying on people. But unless each new development is also understood as just one piece of the larger surveillance mosaic that is rapidly being constructed around us, Americans are not likely to get excited about a given incremental loss of privacy like the tracking of cars through tollbooths or the growing practice of tracking consumers' supermarket purchases.

We are being confronted with fundamental choices about what

sort of society we want to live in. But unless the terms of the debate are changed to focus on the forest instead of individual trees, too many Americans will never even recognize the choice we face, and a decision against preserving privacy will be made by default.

2. Comprehensive Privacy Laws

Although broad-based protections against government surveillance, such as the wiretap laws, are being weakened, at least they exist. But surveillance is increasingly being carried out by the private sector—frequently at the behest of government—and the laws protecting Americans against non-governmental privacy invasions are pitifully weak.

In contrast to the rest of the developed world, the United States has no strong, comprehensive law protecting privacy—only a patchwork of largely inadequate protections. For example, as a result of many legislators' discomfort over the disclosure of Judge Robert Bork's video rental choices during his Supreme Court confirmation battle, video records are now protected by a strong privacy law. Medical records are governed by a separate, far weaker law that allows for widespread access to extremely personal information. Financial data is governed by yet another "privacy" law—Gramm-Leach—which as we have seen really amounts to a license to share financial information. Another law protects only the privacy of children under age thirteen on the Internet. And layered on top of this sectoral approach to privacy by the federal government is a geographical patchwork of constitutional and statutory privacy protections in the states.

The patchwork approach to privacy is grossly inadequate. As invasive practices grow, Americans will face constant uncertainty about when and how these complex laws protect them, contributing to a pervasive sense of insecurity. With the glaring exception of the United States, every advanced industrialized nation in the world has enacted overarching privacy laws that protect citizens against private-sector abuses. When it comes to this fundamental human value, the United States is an outlaw nation. For example, the European Union bars companies from evading privacy rules by transferring personal information to other nations whose data-protection policies are "inadequate." That is the kind of law that is usually applied to third world countries, but the European Union counts the United States in this category.

We need to develop a baseline of simple and clear privacy protections that crosses all sectors of our lives and give it the force of law. Only then can Americans act with a confident knowledge of when they can and cannot be monitored.

3. New Technologies and New Laws

The technologies of surveillance are developing at the speed of light, but the body of law that protects us is stuck back in the Stone Age. In the past, new technologies that threatened our privacy, such as telephone wiretapping, were assimilated over time into our society. The legal system had time to adapt and reinterpret existing laws, the political system had time to consider and enact new laws or regulations, and the culture had time to absorb the implications of the new technology for daily life. Today, however, change is happening so fast that none of this adaptation has time to take place—a problem that is being intensified by the scramble to enact unexamined antiterrorism measures. The result is a significant danger that surveillance practices will become entrenched in American life that would never be accepted if we had more time to digest them.

Since a comprehensive privacy law may never be passed in the United States—and certainly not in the near future—law and legal principles must be developed or adapted to rein in particular new technologies such as surveillance cameras, location-tracking devices, and biometrics. Surveillance cameras, for example, must be subject to force-of-law rules covering important details like when they will be used, how long images will be stored, and when and with whom they will be shared.

4. Reviving the Fourth Amendment

The right of the people to be secure in their persons, houses, papers, and effects, against unreasonable searches and seizures, shall not be

violated, and no warrants shall issue, but upon probable cause, supported by oath or affirmation, and particularly describing the place to be searched, and the persons or things to be seized.
—Fourth Amendment to the US Constitution

The Fourth Amendment, the primary constitutional bulwark against government invasion of our privacy, was a direct response to the British authorities' use of "general warrants" to conduct broad searches of the rebellious colonists.

Historically, the courts have been slow to adapt the Fourth Amendment to the realities of developing technologies. It took almost forty years for the US Supreme Court to recognize that the Constitution applies to the wiretapping of telephone conversations.[15]

In recent years—in no small part as the result of the failed "war on drugs"—Fourth Amendment principles have been steadily eroding. The circumstances under which police and other government officials may conduct warrantless searches has been rapidly expanding. The courts have allowed for increased surveillance and searches on the nation's highways and at our "borders" (the legal definition of which actually extends hundreds of miles inland from the actual border). And despite the Constitution's plain language covering "persons" and "effects," the courts have increasingly allowed for warrantless searches when we are outside of our homes and "in public." Here the courts have increasingly found we have no "reasonable expectation" of privacy and that therefore the Fourth Amendment does not apply.

But like other constitutional provisions, the Fourth Amendment needs to be understood in contemporary terms. New technologies are endowing the government with the twenty-first century equivalent of Superman's x-ray vision. Using everything from powerful video technologies that can literally see in the dark, to biometric identification techniques like face recognition, to "brain fingerprinting" that can purportedly read our thoughts, the government is now capable of conducting broad searches of our "persons and effects" while we are going about our daily lives—even while we are in "public."

The Fourth Amendment is in desperate need of a revival. The reasonable expectation of privacy cannot be defined by the power that technology affords the government to spy on us. Since that power is increasingly limitless, the "reasonable expectation" standard will leave our privacy dead indeed.

But all is not yet lost. There is some reason for hope. In an important pre-9/11 case, *Kyllo v. United States*,[16] the Supreme Court held that the reasonable expectation of privacy could not be determined by the power of new technologies. In a remarkable opinion written by conservative Justice Antonin Scalia, the Court held that without a warrant the police could not use a new thermal-imaging device that searches for heat sources to conduct what was the functional equivalent of a warrantless search for marijuana cultivation in Danny Kyllo's home.

The Court specifically declined to leave *Kyllo* "at the mercy of advancing technology." While *Kyllo* involved a search of a home, it enunciates an important principle: the Fourth Amendment must adapt to new technologies. That principle can and should be expanded to general use. The framers never expected the Constitution to be read exclusively in terms of the circumstances of 1791.

NOTES

1. Jess Bravin, "Washington Police to Play 'I Spy' with Cameras, Raising Concerns," *Wall Street Journal*, February 13, 2002.

2. See National Criminal Justice Reference Service, http://www.ncjrs.org/school/ch2a_5.html.

3. See Scottish Centre for Criminology, http://www.scotcrim.u-net.com/researchc.htm.

4. The success rate of face recognition technology has been dismal. The many independent findings to that effect include a trial conducted by the US military in 2002, which found that with a reasonably low false-positive rate, the technology had less than a 20 percent chance of successfully identifying a person in its database who appeared before the camera. See American Civil Liberties Union, http://www.aclu.org/issues/privacy/FINAL_1_Final_Steve_King.pdf, 17th slide.

5. Richard H. P. Sia, "Pilotless Aircraft Makers Seek Role for Domestic Uses," *CongressDaily*, December 17, 2002.

6. Data surveillance is often loosely referred to as "data mining." Strictly speaking, however, data mining refers to the search for hidden patterns in large, preexisting collections of data (such as finding that sales of both beer and diapers rise on Friday nights). Data mining need not involve personally identifiable information. Data surveillance, on the other hand, involves the collection of information about an identifiable individual. Note, however, that when data surveillance is carried out on a mass scale, a search for patterns in people's activities—data mining—can then be conducted as well. This is what appears to be contemplated in the Total Information Awareness and CAPS II programs.

7. Glenn R. Simpson, "Big Brother-in-Law: If the FBI Hopes to Get the Goods on You, It May Ask ChoicePoint," *Wall Street Journal*, April 13, 2001.

8. The expanded exception involves what are called "pen register/ trap & trace" warrants that collect "addressing information" but not the content of a communication. Those searches are named after devices that were used on telephones to show a list of telephone numbers dialed and received (as opposed to tapping into actual conversations). The PATRIOT Act expands the pen register exception onto the Internet in ways that will probably be used by the government to collect the actual content of communications and that allow nonspecific "nationwide" warrants in violation of the Fourth Amendment's explicit requirement that warrants "must specify the place to be searched."

9. In August, the secret "FISA" court that oversees domestic intelligence spying released an opinion rejecting a Bush administration attempt to allow criminal prosecutors to use intelligence warrants to evade the Fourth Amendment entirely. The court noted that agents applying for warrants had regularly filed false and misleading information. In November 2002, however, the FISA appeals court (three judges chosen by Chief Justice William Rehnquist), meeting for the first time ever, ruled in favor of the government.

10. See Charles Lane, "In Terror War, 2nd Track for Suspects," *Washington Post*, December 1, 2002, http:// www.washingtonpost.com/wp-dyn/ articles/A58308-2002Nov30.html.

11. See "Pentagon Plans a Computer System That Would Peek at Personal Data of Americans," *New York Times*, November 9, 2002; "U.S. Hopes to Check Computers Globally," *Washington Post*, November 12, 2002; "The Poindexter Plan," *National Journal*, September 7, 2002.

12. Quotes are from the TIA homepage at Defense Advanced Research Projects Agency, http://www.darpa.mil/iao/index.htm, and from public, August 2, 2002, remarks by Poindexter, online at Federation of American Scientists, http://www.fas.org/irp/agency/dod/poindexter.html.

13. Robert O'Harrow Jr., "Intricate Screening of Fliers in Works," *Washington Post*, February 1, 2002.

14. The TIA is just one part of a larger post-9/11 expansion of federal research and development efforts. The budget for military R&D spending alone has been increased by 18 percent in the current fiscal year to a record $58.8 billion. Bob Davis, "Massive Federal R&D Initiative to Fight Terror Is Under Way," *Wall Street Journal*, November 25, 2002.

15. In 1967 the Supreme Court finally recognized the right to privacy in telephone conversations in the case *Katz v. United States*, 389 US 347 (1967), reversing the 1928 opinion *Olmstead v. United States*, 277 US 438 (1928).

16. *Kyllo v. United States*, 190 F.3d 1041 (2001) (No. 99-8508).

6.

KYLLO V. UNITED STATES

US Supreme Court

Danny Lee KYLLO, Petitioner

v.

United States

Decided June 11, 2001.

J ustice Scalia delivered the opinion of the Court.

This case presents the question whether the use of a thermal-imaging device aimed at a private home from a public street to detect relative amounts of heat within the home constitutes a "search" within the meaning of the Fourth Amendment.

I

In 1991 Agent William Elliott of the United States Department of the Interior came to suspect that marijuana was being grown in the home belonging to petitioner Danny Kyllo, part of a triplex on

Rhododendron Drive in Florence, Oregon. Indoor marijuana growth typically requires high-intensity lamps. In order to determine whether an amount of heat was emanating from petitioner's home consistent with the use of such lamps, at 3:20 AM on January 16, 1992, Agent Elliott and Dan Haas used an Agema Thermovision 210 thermal imager to scan the triplex. Thermal imagers detect infrared radiation, which virtually all objects emit but which is not visible to the naked eye. The imager converts radiation into images based on relative warmth—black is cool, white is hot, shades of gray connote relative differences; in that respect, it operates somewhat like a video camera showing heat images. The scan of Kyllo's home took only a few minutes and was performed from the passenger seat of Agent Elliott's vehicle across the street from the front of the house and also from the street in back of the house. The scan showed that the roof over the garage and a side wall of petitioner's home were relatively hot compared to the rest of the home and substantially warmer than neighboring homes in the triplex. Agent Elliott concluded that petitioner was using halide lights to grow marijuana in his house, which indeed he was. Based on tips from informants, utility bills, and the thermal imaging, a federal magistrate judge issued a warrant authorizing a search of petitioner's home, and the agents found an indoor growing operation involving more than one hundred plants. Petitioner was indicted on one count of manufacturing marijuana. . . . He unsuccessfully moved to suppress the evidence seized from his home and then entered a conditional guilty plea.

The Court of Appeals for the Ninth Circuit remanded the case for an evidentiary hearing regarding the intrusiveness of thermal imaging. On remand the District Court found that the Agema 210 "is a nonintrusive device which emits no rays or beams and shows a crude visual image of the heat being radiated from the outside of the house"; it "did not show any people or activity within the walls of the structure"; "[t]he device used cannot penetrate walls or windows to reveal conversations or human activities"; and "[n]o intimate details of the home were observed based on these findings, the District Court upheld the validity of the warrant that relied in part upon the thermal imaging, and reaffirmed its denial of the motion to suppress. A divided Court of Appeals [ultimately] . . . affirmed, with Judge Noonan dissenting. The court held that petitioner had shown no subjective expectation of privacy because he had made no attempt to conceal the heat escaping from his home, and even if he had, there was no objectively reasonable expectation of privacy because the imager "did not expose any intimate details of Kyllo's life," only "amorphous 'hot spots' on the roof and exterior wall." We granted certiorari.

II

The Fourth Amendment provides that "[t]he right of the people to be secure in their persons, houses, papers, and effects, against unreasonable searches and seizures, shall not be violated." "At the very core" of the Fourth Amendment "stands the right of a man to retreat into his own home and there be free from unreasonable governmental intrusion." *Silverman v. United States* (1961). With few exceptions, the question whether a warrantless search of a home is reasonable and hence constitutional must be answered no.

On the other hand, the antecedent question of whether or not a Fourth Amendment "search" has occurred is not so simple under our precedent. The permissibility of ordinary visual surveillance of a home used to be clear because, well into the twentieth century, our Fourth Amendment jurisprudence was tied to common-law trespass. Visual surveillance was unquestionably lawful because "'the eye cannot by the laws of England be guilty of a trespass.'" *Boyd v. United States* (1866). We have since decoupled violation of a person's Fourth Amendment rights from trespassory violation of his property, but the lawfulness of warrantless visual surveillance of a home has still been preserved. As we observed in *California v. Ciraolo,* "[t]he Fourth Amendment protection of the home has never been extended to require law enforcement officers to shield their eyes when passing by a home on public thoroughfares."

One might think that the new validating rationale would be that examining the portion of a house that is in plain public view, while it is a "search" despite the absence of trespass, is not an "unreasonable" one under the Fourth Amendment. But in fact we have held that visual observation is no "search" at all—perhaps in order to preserve somewhat more intact our doctrine that warrantless searches are presumptively unconstitutional. In assessing when a search is not a search, we have applied somewhat in reverse the principle first enunciated in *Katz v. United States*. *Katz* involved eavesdropping by means of an electronic listening device placed on the outside of a telephone booth—a location not within the catalog ("persons, houses, papers, and effects") that the Fourth Amendment protects against unreasonable searches. We held that the Fourth Amendment nonetheless protected Katz from the warrantless eavesdropping because he "justifiably relied" upon the privacy of the telephone booth. As Justice Harlan's oft-quoted concurrence described it, a Fourth Amendment search occurs when the government violates a subjective expectation of privacy that society recognizes as reasonable. . . . We have applied this test in holding that it is not a search for the police to use a pen register at the phone company to determine what numbers were dialed in a private home, *Smith v. Maryland* (1979), and we have applied the test on two different occasions in holding that aerial surveillance of private homes and surrounding areas does not constitute a search, *Ciraolo, supra; Florida v. Riley* (1989).

The present case involves officers on a public street engaged in more than naked-eye surveillance of a home. We have previously reserved judgment as to how much technological enhancement of ordinary perception from such a vantage point, if any, is too much. While we upheld enhanced aerial photography of an industrial complex in *Dow Chemical*, we noted that we found "it important that this is *not* an area immediately adjacent to a private home, where privacy expectations are most heightened."

III

It would be foolish to contend that the degree of privacy secured to citizens by the Fourth Amendment has been entirely unaffected by the advance of technology. For example . . . the technology enabling human flight has exposed to public view (and hence, we have said, to official observation) uncovered portions of the house and its curtilage that once were private. The question we confront today is what limits there are upon this power of technology to shrink the realm of guaranteed privacy.

The *Katz* test—whether the individual has an expectation of privacy that society is prepared to recognize as reasonable—has often been criticized as circular, and hence subjective and unpredictable. While it may be difficult to refine *Katz* when the search of areas such as telephone booths, automobiles, or even the curtilage and uncovered portions of residences are at issue, in the case of the search of the interior of homes—the prototypical and hence most commonly litigated area of protected privacy—there is a ready criterion, with roots deep in the common law, of the minimal expectation of privacy that exists, and that is acknowledged to be reasonable. To withdraw protection of this minimum expectation would be to permit police technology to erode the privacy guaranteed by the Fourth Amendment. We think that obtaining by sense-enhancing technology any information regarding the interior of the home that could not otherwise have been obtained without physical "intrusion into a constitutionally protected area," *Silverman*, constitutes a search—at least where (as here) the technology in question is not in general public use. This assures preservation of that degree of privacy against government that existed when the Fourth Amendment was adopted. On the basis of this criterion, the information obtained by the thermal imager in this case was the product of a search.

The Government maintains, however, that the thermal imaging must be upheld because it detected "only heat radiating from the external surface of the house." The dissent makes this its leading point, contending that there is a fundamental difference between what it calls "off-the-wall" observations and "through-the-wall surveillance." But just as a thermal imager captures only heat emanating from a house, so also a powerful directional microphone picks up only sound emanating from a house—and a satellite capable of scanning from many miles away would pick up only visible light emanating from a house. We rejected such a mechanical interpretation of the Fourth Amendment in *Katz*, where the eavesdropping device picked up only sound waves that reached the exterior of the phone booth. Reversing that approach would leave the homeowner at the mercy of advancing technology—including imaging technology that could discern all human activity in the home. While the technology used in the present case was relatively crude, the rule we adopt must take account of more sophisticated systems that are already in use or in development. . . .

The Government also contends that the thermal imaging was constitutional because it did not "detect private activities occurring in private areas." It points out that in *Dow Chemical* we observed that the enhanced aerial photography did not reveal any "intimate details." *Dow Chemical*, however, involved enhanced aerial photography of an industrial complex, which does not share the Fourth Amendment sanctity of the home. The Fourth Amendment's protection of the home has never been tied to measurement of the quality or quantity of information obtained. In *Silverman*, for example, we made clear that any physical invasion of the structure of the home, "by even a fraction of an inch," was too much, and there is certainly no exception to the warrant requirement for the officer who barely cracks open the front door and sees nothing but the nonintimate rug on the vestibule floor. In the home, our cases show, *all* details are intimate details, because the entire area is held safe from prying government eyes. . . .

Limiting the prohibition of thermal imaging to "intimate details" would not only be wrong in principle; it would be impractical in application, failing to provide "a workable accommodation between the needs of law enforcement and the interests protected by the Fourth Amendment," *Oliver v. United States* (1984). To begin with, there is no necessary connection between the sophistication of the surveillance equipment and the "intimacy" of the details that it observes—which means that one cannot say (and the police cannot be assured) that use of the relatively crude equipment at issue here will always be lawful. The Agema Thermovision 210 might disclose, for example, at what hour each night the lady of the house takes her daily sauna and bath—a detail that many would consider "inti-mate"; and a much more sophisticated system might detect nothing more intimate than the fact that someone left a closet light on. We could not, in other words, develop a rule approving only that through-the-wall surveillance which identifies objects no smaller than 36 by 36 inches, but would have to develop a jurisprudence specifying which home activities are "intimate" and which are not. And even when (if ever) that jurisprudence were fully developed, no police officer would be able to know *in advance* whether his through-the-wall surveillance picks up "intimate" details—and thus would be unable to know in advance whether it is constitutional. . . .

We have said that the Fourth Amendment draws "a firm line at the entrance to the house." *Payton v. New York* (1980). That line, we think, must be not only firm but also bright—which requires clear specifica-tion of those methods of surveillance that require a warrant. While it is certainly possible to conclude from the videotape of the thermal imaging that occurred in this case that no "significant" compromise of the homeowner's privacy has occurred, we must take the long view, from the original meaning of the Fourth Amendment forward. . . .

Where, as here, the Government uses a device that is not in gen-eral public use, to explore details of the home that would previously have been unknowable without physical intrusion, the surveillance is a "search" and is presumptively unreasonable without a warrant. . . .

The judgment of the Court of Appeals is reversed; the case is remanded for further proceedings consistent with this opinion.

It is so ordered.
[June 11, 2001]

Justice Stevens, with whom the Chief Justice, Justice O'Connor, and Justice Kennedy join, dissenting.

There is, in my judgment, a distinction of constitutional magni-tude between "through-the-wall surveillance" that gives the observer or listener direct access to information in a private area, on the one hand, and the thought processes used to draw inferences from infor-mation in the public domain, on the other hand. The Court has crafted a rule that purports to deal with direct observations of the inside of the home, but the case before us merely involves indirect deductions from "off-the-wall" surveillance, that is, observations of the exterior of the home. Those observations were made with a fairly primitive thermal imager that gathered data exposed on the outside of petitioner's home but did not invade any constitutionally protected interest in privacy. Moreover, I believe that the supposedly "bright-line" rule the Court has created in response to its concerns about future technological developments is unnecessary, unwise, and inconsistent with the Fourth Amendment.

7.

NO CHECKS, NO BALANCES

DISCARDING BEDROCK CONSTITUTIONAL PRINCIPLES

Stephen J. Schulhofer

As expected, September 11 has prompted an expansion of law enforcement powers at almost every level. The domain of individual rights has contracted. And who would have it otherwise? For those of us who live and work in Manhattan, September 11 was not just a single horrific day but an extended nightmare. For weeks, kiosks, store windows, and parks displayed flyers by the thousands, pleading for information about loved ones still missing. National Guard units seemed to be everywhere. Day after day, the air, gray and acrid, carried the smell of burning flesh.

No, the "war" metaphor is not just convenient political spin. And despite shameless hyping of so-called sleeper cells and color-coded threat levels, no responsible person can dismiss the danger of devastating future attacks. Actions to strengthen law enforcement are not simply the product of panic or paranoia.

But the particulars are troubling—and worse. Predictably, there has been overreaction and political grandstanding. More surprising is

Reprinted from *The War on Our Freedoms: Civil Liberties in an Age of Terrorism*, by Richard C. Leone and Greg Anrig Jr., with permission from the Century Foundation, Inc. Copyright © 2003.

the neglect. Inexcusably, the administration of George W. Bush has swept aside urgent security needs while it continues to win public acclaim for toughness by targeting and scapegoating civil liberties.

An accounting of the state of our liberties should begin with the positives. To his credit, President Bush has preached tolerance and respect for our Muslim neighbors. Unlike previous wartime governments, this administration has not sought to prosecute dissenters for political speech, has not attempted anything comparable to the internment of Japanese Americans during World War II, and (technically, at least) has not tried to suspend the writ of habeas corpus.

But to measure performance by these standards is to set the bar terribly low; these were sorry historical embarrassments. And 9/11 has already produced several comparable missteps. The administration's efforts to stymie habeas corpus rival the civil liberties low points of prior wars, as does its determination (wholly without precedent) to hold American citizens indefinitely on disputed charges without affording them a trial in any forum whatsoever. Likewise without precedent are the oddly imbalanced means chosen to fight this war. Never before in American history has an administration claimed emergency powers while stinting on urgent national security expenditures and making tax cuts its top wartime priority. Conventional wisdom about "striking a balance" between liberty and security obscures the fact that responses to 9/11 are deeply flawed from both perspectives.

Specifically, the domestic security policies of this administration encroach on three principles that are fundamental to the preservation of freedom: accountability, checks and balances, and narrow tailoring of government's power to intrude into the lives of citizens. In each case, the administration has overlooked or dismissed alternative approaches that would strengthen the nation's security at least as effectively without weakening fundamental freedoms. The encroachments on bedrock principles, altogether unnecessary even in this perilous time, are especially evident in four realms of policy: domestic surveillance, new guidelines governing the Federal Bureau of Investigation, the detention of foreign nationals, and the erosion of habeas corpus.

DOMESTIC SURVEILLANCE

Expanded surveillance powers have reduced privacy rights that most of us took for granted before September 11. Yet even without knowing the details, many Americans see no need to worry about the civil liberties impact of the new laws. They feel that law-abiding citizens should have nothing to hide, and they welcome rather than fear this enhancement of government surveillance powers. Others (a relatively small minority) argue that sacrificing any of our pre-9/11 privacy rights will simply make us less free without making us more secure and will amount to destroying our freedom in order to defend it. Neither of these positions captures the complex reality of the expanded surveillance powers.

Some of the provisions included in the October 2001 USA PATRIOT Act simply correct oversights in prior law or adapt technically worded statutes to new technologies and practices. For example, the authority included in the act for judges to permit surveillance of mobile phones in foreign intelligence investigations (a power long permitted in domestic law enforcement) and to issue search warrants with nationwide effect reflect legitimate law enforcement needs that raise no new privacy concerns.

But other new powers are more problematic. The PATRIOT Act undermines checks and balances by giving investigators new authority to track Internet usage and to obtain previously confidential financial records without having to demonstrate probable cause or obtain a judicial warrant. The Treasury Department expanded its authority to require banks, brokers, and other businesses to report cash transactions and "suspicious activities," which include any transaction that differs from ones the customer typically conducts. Though the Justice Department created a furor with its proposal for Operation TIPS to encourage voluntary snooping by private citizens, the Treasury Department's regulations require private citizens and businesses to become eyes and ears for the government—again without any oversight by the judicial branch. Compounding this problem, the new FBI and Treasury Department powers are not narrowly tailored to investigations potentially related to terrorism; the government can invoke most of these new powers even when it seeks only to investigate routine criminal offenses.

The PATRIOT Act also made especially important changes in the complex Foreign Intelligence Surveillance Act (FISA). The expanded FISA provisions now allow FBI agents to obtain business and educational records, without any need to certify that the targeted customer or student is considered a foreign agent or a suspect in any way. Before 9/11, FISA gave investigators access to the records of a narrow category of travel-industry businesses, provided that the person targeted was a foreign agent. The PATRIOT Act now permits FBI access to all the records of any business and any nonbusiness entity, apparently including noncommercial entities such as a synagogue or mosque. And the new authority (like that for financial and educational records) drops the requirement that the records pertain to a suspected foreign agent. Formerly confidential records concerning any American citizen are now available for FBI inspection on a clandestine basis whenever an investigator thinks they may be relevant to a terrorism investigation, whether or not the person concerned is a foreign agent or a suspected criminal offender. Again, this is the antithesis of government restraint: judicial oversight is allowed no role as a check on the executive branch, and the powers granted extend far beyond the international terrorism suspects that are the legitimate targets of concern.

The PATRIOT Act also eliminated a technical but highly significant limitation on FISA's reach. Prior to 9/11, FISA was not considered a law enforcement tool; its function was exclusively preventative. FISA surveillance powers were available only when the primary purpose of an investigation was to obtain foreign intelligence, including counterespionage and counterterrorism information. In that unique setting, FISA authorized surveillance under flexible conditions that are considered unacceptable when the government's objective is to gather evidence for criminal prosecution. In a criminal investigation, the Fourth Amendment prohibits searches except when investigators have "probable cause" to believe that a search will reveal evidence of criminal activity. A neutral judicial officer, concurring in that assessment, must authorize the search in a court order that "particularly describ[es] the place to be searched, and the persons or things to be seized." In electronic surveillance and wiretaps, this particularity requirement in effect mandates narrow tailoring of the time, place, and duration of the surveillance—all subject to close judicial oversight.

This constitutional regime is a concrete expression of our commitment to effective checks and balances. The framers of the US Constitution knew that without some outside control well-intentioned investigators in the executive branch would too quickly find "probable cause" and too easily abuse their power to search. The Fourth Amendment therefore requires that the judgment about probable cause ordinarily be made by a neutral judicial officer, who will narrowly define the permissible scope of a search before it occurs.

This centuries-old requirement of independent judicial approval obviously casts no doubt on the wisdom and decency of our current president and attorney general. As most attorneys general have themselves understood, checks and balances—and the warrant requirement in particular—reflect the consistent verdict of history that grave abuses are all too likely if investigators—even conscientious, well-trained investigators—are permitted to search without judicial approval.

Foreign intelligence surveillance, because of its predominantly preventive purpose, traditionally has been allowed more leeway. The differences from the regime applicable to criminal investigations are important to notice:

- FISA surveillance is permitted after showing only a diluted form of suspicion not equivalent to the traditional criminal standard of probable cause.
- FISA authorizes intrusive investigative techniques, such as clandestine physical searches, that are normally impermissible in criminal investigations.
- Surveillance and physical searches can continue over more extensive periods of time, with less judicial supervision.
- The person targeted normally is never notified that he was subjected to surveillance.
- If that person is prosecuted, his attorneys normally cannot

review the surveillance documents for purposes of his defense, as they could if surveillance had been conducted under conventional law enforcement standards.

The PATRIOT Act gives prosecutors, for the first time, the ability to use these broad FISA powers when their primary objective is not preventative but is rather to gather evidence for criminal prosecution. Moreover, FISA does not require that the person targeted be a foreign spy or an international terrorist. Foreign nationals and US citizens qualify as "foreign agents" subject to clandestine searches and broad FISA surveillance when they are merely suspected of having ties to foreign organizations or governments, and even when they are merely employed by various *legitimate* foreign organizations. The PATRIOT Act permits prosecutors to subject these individuals to surveillance that would be unconstitutional if based only on probable cause to believe that the target was a serial killer or rapist.

Concern about the broad reach of these FISA amendments, and their potential to undermine the traditional wall between law enforcement and preventive counterintelligence, led to unique litigation and two historic judicial decisions. FISA has long required the FBI and the Justice Department to establish "minimization" procedures to protect the privacy rights of American citizens by maintaining "rigorous and strict controls" over the use of information about Americans gathered under FISA's exceptional powers. When a foreign intelligence operation uncovers evidence of crime, those procedures authorize agents, with appropriate approval, to discuss their investigation with federal prosecutors and to turn over to them leads they have uncovered. But until 9/11, the regulations barred prosecutors from intentionally or inadvertently "directing or controlling the [foreign intelligence] investigation toward law enforcement objectives." The concern, of course, was that prosecutors lacking grounds for a conventional warrant might otherwise instruct FISA teams to conduct expanded surveillance of American citizens as part of a fishing expedition seeking to build a criminal case.

In a memorandum dated March 6, 2002, Attorney General John Ashcroft initiated a significant change in these minimization procedures. The memorandum instructed FBI and Justice Department officials that FISA powers could now "be used primarily for a law enforcement purpose, so long as a significant foreign intelligence purpose remains." To this end, Ashcroft authorized prosecutors pursuing criminal cases to give advice to foreign intelligence investigators concerning the "initiation or expansion of FISA searches or surveillance," and he deleted the previous caveat that barred prosecutors from "directing or controlling" the scope of FISA surveillance.

The March 6 memorandum drew attention to an obscure body known as the Foreign Intelligence Surveillance Court. Composed of sitting federal judges, the FISA court meets in secret to consider applications for FISA surveillance warrants. From 1979 to 2001, the FISA court approved without modification all but five of more than fourteen thousand surveillance applications. Its judges have detailed familiarity with foreign intelligence operations and with the workability and shortcomings of the minimization procedures in place before 9/11. And there is little reason to doubt their appreciation for legitimate law enforcement needs. The presiding judge, Royce C. Lamberth, was named to the federal bench by President Ronald Reagan, and five of the six judges who comprised the remainder of the panel in March 2002 were likewise appointed by Republican presidents. All of the FISA judges had been selected for the assignment by Chief Justice William Rehnquist.

Nonetheless, the FISA court unanimously rejected key provisions of the Ashcroft memorandum. In a secret ruling on May 17 (made public in late August), the court specified that "law enforcement officials shall not make recommendations to intelligence officials concerning the initiation . . . or expansion of FISA searches or surveillance," and it insisted on rules to ensure that prosecutors "do not direct or control the use of the FISA procedures to enhance criminal prosecution." The court noted tartly that any need for prosecutors to direct "the use of highly intrusive FISA surveillances . . . is yet to be explained."

The FISA court did not have the last word, however. The FISA statute gives the Justice Department the right, never before invoked, to appeal an adverse ruling to the Foreign Intelligence Surveillance

Court of Review; comprised of three federal judges also selected by Chief Justice Rehnquist. The FISA court of review had never before met, and it heard arguments only from the Justice Department, technically the only party to the case.[1] The court of review concluded that the PATRIOT Act amendments did indeed permit prosecutors to use FISA in criminal investigations, without complying with conventional statutory and constitutional limits on law enforcement surveillance, as long as foreign intelligence gathering was a primary or *subsidiary* purpose of the surveillance. And the court of review ruled that given the importance of the counterterrorism effort, use of these exceptional powers was not unconstitutional. For now, the conclusions of the court of review are final because the only party to the case, the Justice Department, prevailed. There are apparently no means to bring the issue before the Supreme Court, unless and until evidence acquired by expanded FISA surveillance is introduced against a defendant in a criminal prosecution.

This controversy about the wall that traditionally separated intelligence gathering from law enforcement poses one of the most difficult problems arising out of the 9/11 attacks. September 11 made clear that a rigid division between law enforcement and foreign intelligence operations can be artificial and counterproductive in the context of fighting international terrorist groups like al Qaeda. The court of review rightly stressed this point, but then, in a non sequitur, concluded that it was either impossible or too dangerous to attempt any separation of these functions. Yet law enforcement and counterterrorism operations are not always inextricable. And law enforcement can easily slide into prosecutorial fishing expeditions and other dangers to a free society, when it operates free from close judicial scrutiny.

The importance of containing both dangers—the danger of international terrorism and the less obvious, less acute, but still significant danger of prosecutorial abuse—suggests the need to avoid the court of review's all-or-nothing approach. Flexibility for FISA teams to share evidence of crime obtained in foreign intelligence operations was always part of the FISA system and can be enhanced without significant danger to basic Fourth Amendment values. The risk of overreaching arises when the same team uses broad FISA tools to pursue both intelligence and law enforcement goals. In a world of unlimited resources, therefore, we would surely insist that law enforcement and counterterrorism investigators be confined to distinct teams.

The difficulty here, as the court of review recognized, is that resources are limited. At the highest levels of the FBI and the Justice Department, senior executives will almost inevitably have responsibility for both functions. And barriers to a blending of roles could (rightly or out of excess caution) inhibit efforts to use criminal investigators in the field for vital counterterrorism measures.

What seems hard to justify, even against this background, is the core of the Ashcroft innovation: the provision granting the department's litigating lawyers the power to *initiate* FISA surveillance, and to *enlarge* its scope, in order to develop evidence for a criminal prosecution. Here, as the initial FISA court decision stressed, flexibility and appropriate coordination are no longer at issue. Rather, the remedy has expanded to encompass rules making FISA's highly intrusive, lightly restricted surveillance powers available for objectives not primarily concerned with preventive intelligence gathering. The need for some blending of functions does not come close to justifying the Ashcroft innovation that grants prosecutors primacy in initiating and directing the use of broad FISA powers. As the FISA court's initial decision recognized, the need for prosecutors to control the scope of FISA surveillance has never been explained.

The FISA changes, of course, are just one part of the multidimensional expansion of government surveillance powers, an expansion that encompasses the many new FBI and Treasury Department capabilities just mentioned. An overall assessment of these developments must begin by acknowledging that the counterterrorism payoff from the new powers, though not scientifically measurable, can't be dismissed as insignificant. And many Americans probably feel ready to sacrifice all the privacy interests that these new powers affect, if only to obtain even a small nugget of information about al Qaeda's plans. Nonetheless, the rollback of privacy rights has three flaws that should trouble us all.

First, worries about terrorism provide no reason to expand law enforcement power across the board. Yet FBI and Treasury agents can use most of their new powers to investigate allegations of prostitution, gambling, insider trading, and any other offense. Prosecutors can now use open-ended FISA surveillance powers to gather evidence for a conventional fraud or income-tax prosecution. Treasury regulations impose reporting obligations that can even be used to police compliance with ordinary government regulations. Far from respecting the imperative to tailor government power narrowly, even in times of peril, we have seen inexcusable opportunism on the part of the law enforcement establishment, which has exploited the momentum of 9/11 to expand government power to intrude on privacy in pursuit of wholly unrelated goals.

Second, accountability measures, though neglected in the rush to pass the PATRIOT Act, need not impair the usefulness of the new powers and, if well designed, will enhance them. The new provisions not only dilute traditional checks and balances; they neglect many of the internal supervision and control procedures that are staples of effective management in government and the private sector alike. The FBI's Carnivore system for spying on e-mail, for example, desperately needs procedures to preserve audit trails and ensure the accountability of agents who have access to it.

Finally, nuggets or even piles of telling information are useless unless our agencies have the capability to make sense of them. It is now well known that before September 11 the FBI and the Central Intelligence Agency had important clues to the plot in hand, but as one FBI agent put it, "We didn't know what we knew." Since a large part of what we lack is not raw data but the ability to separate significant intelligence from so-called noise, pulling more information into government files will not help and may aggravate the difficulty. Even before 9/11, Treasury officials complained to Congress that the staggering volume of reports they received (more than one million every month) was interfering with enforcement. Absent a substantial infusion of resources (which the Bush administration has not yet provided), powerful new surveillance tools can give us only a false sense of comfort.

NEW FBI GUIDELINES

In May 2002, headlines featured for days the startling news that during the summer of 2001, before the terrorist attacks, agents in Minneapolis and Phoenix had urged investigations of Zacharias Moussaoui and the flight schools, only to be stifled by FBI headquarters—an enormous blunder. In response, on May 30, 2002, Attorney General Ashcroft called a press conference to denounce "bureaucratic restrictions" that were preventing FBI agents from doing their jobs.

The rules he had in mind grew out of extensive FBI abuses in the 1950s and 1960s. Free to pursue random tips and their own hunches, FBI agents of that era intimidated dissidents, damaged the reputations of many who were not, and produced thousands of thick dossiers on public figures and private citizens. Agents spent years monitoring political groups of all stripes, from the Socialist Workers Party to the Conservative American Christian Action Council. They maintained files on student clubs, civil rights groups, antiwar groups, and other social movements. By 1975, FBI headquarters held more than a half million domestic intelligence files.

Such sprawling dragnets are as inefficient as they are abusive, and rules to rein them in, adopted in 1976 under President Gerald Ford, were carried forward by every president since. Nonetheless, Attorney General Ashcroft ridiculed these guidelines as absurdly restrictive. He said, incorrectly, that the rules barred FBI agents from surfing the Internet and even from observing activities in public places. He announced that he was solving this problem by allowing FBI agents to operate with much less supervision.

The civil liberties community responded with furious criticism. But far from hurting the attorney general's popularity, the criticism reinforced his intended message: that law enforcement had been tied down by defendants' rights. The failure to pursue the flight school leads was in effect blamed on the American Civil Liberties Union, and the Justice Department presented itself as taking firm corrective action.

What actually occurred was rather different. One part of the rules the attorney general relaxed governs investigations of "general crimes"—gambling, theft, and other offenses not related to terrorism. The other rules he relaxed govern investigations of domestic terrorist groups. Unnoticed in the brouhaha, the rules that govern international terrorism cases—the ones that apply to al Qaeda—were not affected by the changes at all.

Behind the screen of this public relations maneuver, damage was inflicted in several directions. Public frustration with central oversight was understandable under the circumstances, but none of the previous guidelines, even the more restrictive domestic regimes, impeded the kinds of investigative steps the Minneapolis and Phoenix agents had urged. What the field offices needed was better supervision, not less of it. Yet Ashcroft's actions obscured responsibility for FBI missteps, and instead of censure, the FBI was rewarded with greater discretion. As in the case of the PATRIOT Act, fear of terrorism offered an occasion for the bait-and-switch: the guideline revisions are irrelevant to the concerns about al Qaeda that preoccupy the American public, yet they leave us with a large risk to civil liberties and large losses to effective management of the FBI.

DETENTION OF FOREIGN NATIONALS

In the months following September 11, federal agents arrested approximately twelve hundred foreign nationals. Hundreds were held for months before being cleared and released; others (the precise number is unknown) remain in detention, ostensibly to await deportation. Courts are still sorting out the many issues posed by these actions.

The length of these detentions and the absence of any judicial finding on the need for it are one of the primary concerns. Preventive detention is not unknown in American law, and the extraordinary uncertainties in the days after September 11 presented a virtually unique public safety emergency. Nonetheless, even making ample allowance for the pressure of circumstances, the outer boundaries of executive power in emergency situations were easily reached and exceeded in these roundups.

The most glaring of the problems posed is that the executive branch assumed the power to decide unilaterally who would be detained and for how long. Supreme Court decisions make clear that for preventive confinement to satisfy due process, measures like these be strictly confined to limited time periods, with adequate safeguards against the arbitrary exercise of executive power. At a minimum, there must be provision for prompt independent review of relevant evidence in an adversary hearing, and the judge must find a substantial government need, reasonably related to the nature and duration of the detention.

The 9/11 detentions of foreign nationals are sharply at odds with these norms. Without statutory authority—and in apparent violation of the extended seven-day period for precharge detention that the PATRIOT Act allows in terrorism cases—the Immigration and Naturalization Service held some of these suspects for months without affording hearings and without charging any violation of criminal or administrative law. Even after review by semi-independent administrative judges, immigration law violators who would normally be excused or deported were held, and are still being held, for preventive and investigative purposes without any independent review of the grounds for suspicion or the relation of government need to the individual hardship created. Aside from the relocation of Japanese Americans during World War II, the 9/11 detentions appear to be unprecedented in terms of the unilateral, unreviewable executive branch powers on which they rest.

Equally troubling is the extraordinary secrecy surrounding these sweeps. The government has refused to release the names of any of the detainees, and when they are charged and afforded immigration hearings, all hearings are closed to the press and even to their own families.

The government's justifications for secrecy are revealing. Secrecy, Attorney General Ashcroft stated, is necessary to protect the privacy of detainees. Since many of the detainees desperately wanted their names made public (so that aid organizations and lawyers could contact them), and since the Justice Department could have provided secrecy to detainees who requested it, the privacy claim was painfully disingenuous. In litigation, Justice Department lawyers added the argument that releasing the names of terrorists would give their cohorts clues about the progress of the investigation. This "road map" argument, though harder to dismiss outright, is still embarrassingly thin. Because all detainees have the right to make phone calls, and because gag orders have not been imposed on their family members or on their lawyers, the true terrorists among them can easily find ways to signal their confederates.

The shallow character of these arguments led the US Court of Appeals for the Sixth Circuit to rule unanimously in August 2002 that the government's secrecy policy violates the First Amendment. The court accepted that secrecy might occasionally be warranted, when case-specific reasons for it were accepted by a judge. The crucial point was to provide an independent check on the supposed necessity and ensure that a closed-door policy did not become a cloak for government incompetence or abuse of power.

In October 2002, however, the US Court of Appeals for the Third Circuit, in a 2–1 decision, reached the opposite conclusion, relying on the government's assertion that openness could damage national security. But as Judge Anthony Scirica (a Reagan appointee) noted in his dissent, the issue was not whether deportation hearings should be closed; at issue was only the question of who should make that determination. Closure of all proceedings, regardless of circumstances, was clearly unnecessary, he stressed, because a simple alternative to protect national security was available: judges could determine national security needs on a case-by-case basis, in a closed proceeding if necessary, just as they do when national security matters arise in a formal criminal trial. In determining the need for secrecy, moreover, judges would of course give great weight to the national security interest and would extend great deference to executive branch expertise.

Secrecy across the board, without any obligation to present case-specific reasons for it to a court, has less to do with the war on terrorism than with the administration's consistent efforts, firmly in place before 9/11, to insulate executive action from public scrutiny. The cumulative effect of these efforts is an unprecedented degree of power—an attempt simultaneously to cut off the right to counsel, judicial review, and even any ability of the press to report what happens to individuals arrested on our own soil. As Judge Damon Keith wrote in the Sixth Circuit decision striking down the blanket secrecy order:

> The Executive Branch seeks to uproot people's lives, outside the public eye, and behind a closed door. Democracies die behind closed doors. The First Amendment, through a free press, protects the people's right to know that their government acts fairly, lawfully, and accurately in deportation proceedings. . . . The Framers of the First Amendment "did not trust any government to separate the true from the false for us." They protected the people against secret government.

NOTE

1. The court did, however, accept amicus curiae briefs supporting the FISA courts decision from the American Civil Liberties Union and other groups.

8.

FREEDOM AND SECURITY AFTER SEPTEMBER 11

Viet D. Dinh

An oft-repeated refrain since the September 11 terrorist attacks is that Americans must now choose between a robust national defense and their vital civil liberties. Security versus freedom: the underlying assumption is that the two can coexist only uneasily in times of national crisis. The loss of certain freedoms, so goes the prevailing wisdom, is the price that must be paid for additional security. Some are eager to make that exchange, while others consider the price too dear. Both sides, however, seem to agree that freedom and security are competing virtues, and that the expansion of one necessarily entails the contraction of the other.

This is not a new dichotomy. In 1759, Benjamin Franklin reminded his fellow colonists that "they that can give up essential liberty to obtain a little temporary safety deserve neither liberty nor safety."[1] For Franklin, liberty is the supreme good, and a people capable of surrendering its freedoms in exchange for security is not fit for self-governance, or even "safety." A century later, Abraham Lincoln appeared before Congress to justify his unilateral decision

Reprinted from the *Harvard Journal of Law and Public Policy* (Spring 2002). Copyright © 2002 by the Harvard Society for Law and Public Policy, Inc. Used with permission.

to suspend the writ of habeas corpus. "[A]re all the laws, but one," the president asked, "to go unexecuted, and the government itself go to pieces, lest that one be violated?"[2] For Lincoln, the Great Emancipator, liberty was an obstacle to the government's proper functioning and, worse, a threat to the government's very existence.

The dichotomy between freedom and security is not new, but it is false. For security and freedom are not rivals in the universe of possible goods; rather, they are interrelated, mutually reinforcing goods. Security is the very precondition of freedom. Edmund Burke teaches that civil liberties cannot exist unless a state exists to vindicate them: "[t]he only liberty I mean is a liberty connected with order; that not only exists along with order and virtue, but which cannot exist at all without them."[3] In the same way that an individual's moral right to property would be meaningless unless the government establishes courts of law in which those rights can be declared and enforced, so too Americans' civil liberties would be a nullity unless they are protected from those who seek to destroy our way of life.

If much post–September 11 commentary mistakenly casts security as a rival to freedom, it also exhibits an unduly narrow understanding of freedom itself. "Freedom" does not refer simply to the absence of governmental restraint; it also refers, at a more fundamental level, to the absence of fear. Terrorists do not measure success with a body count. Their objective is to spread fear among all Americans, preventing our nation from playing an active part on the world's stage and our citizens from living their lives in the manner to which they are accustomed. Without confidence in the safety of their persons and the security of their nation, Americans will not be able to go about doing those ordinary things that make America an extraordinary nation.

As the Department of Justice prosecutes the war on terror, we have committed to protect Americans not just against unwarranted governmental intrusion, but also against the incapacitating fear that terrorists seek to engender. To ensure the safety of our citizens and the security of our nation, the department has fundamentally redefined our mission. The enemy we confront is a multinational network of evil that is fanatically committed to the slaughter of innocents. Unlike enemies that we have faced in past wars, this one operates cravenly, in disguise. It may operate through so-called sleeper cells, sending terrorist agents into potential target areas, where they may assume outwardly normal identities, waiting months, sometimes years, before springing into action to carry out or assist terrorist attacks.[4] And unlike garden-variety criminals the department has investigated and prosecuted in the past, terrorists are willing to give up their own lives to take the lives of thousands of innocent citizens. We cannot afford to wait for them to execute their plans; the death toll is too high, the consequences too great. We must neutralize terrorists *before* they strike.

To respond to this threat of terrorism, the department has pursued an aggressive and systematic campaign that utilizes all available information, all authorized investigative techniques, and all legal authorities at our disposal. The overriding goal is to prevent and disrupt terrorist activity by questioning, investigating, and arresting those who violate the law and threaten our national security. In doing so, we take care to discharge fully our responsibility to uphold the laws and Constitution of the United States. All investigative techniques we employ are legally permissible under applicable constitutional, statutory, and regulatory standards. As the president and the attorney general repeatedly have stated, we will not permit, and we have not permitted, our values to fall victim to the terrorist attacks of September 11.

The Department of Justice has taken a number of concrete steps to advance the goal of incapacitating terrorists before they are able to claim another innocent American life. First, the department has detained a number of persons on immigration or federal criminal charges. Second, in cooperation with our colleagues in state and local law enforcement, the department's Anti-Terrorism Task Forces have conducted voluntary interviews of individuals who may have information relating to our investigation. Third, the Bureau of Prisons has promulgated a regulation that permits the monitoring of communications between a limited class of detainees and their lawyers, after providing notice to the detainees. And fourth, the president has exercised his congressionally delegated authority to establish military commissions, which would try noncitizen terrorists for offenses against the laws of war.

With respect to detentions, the department has taken several hundred persons into custody in connection with our investigation of the September 11 attacks. Every one of these detentions is consistent with established constitutional and statutory authority. Each of the detainees has been charged with a violation of either immigration law or criminal law, or is the subject of a material witness warrant issued by a court. The aim of the strategy is to reduce the risk of terrorist attacks on American soil, and the department's detention policy already may have paid dividends. These detentions may have incapacitated an al Qaeda sleeper cell that was planning to strike a target in Washington, DC—perhaps the Capitol building—soon after September 11.[5]

The detainees enjoy a variety of rights, both procedural and substantive. Each of them has the right of access to counsel. In the criminal cases and in the case of material witnesses, the person has the right to a lawyer at government expense if he cannot afford one. Persons detained on immigration violations also have a right of access to counsel, and the Immigration and Naturalization Service provides each person with information about available pro bono representation. Every person detained has access to telephones, which they may use to contact their family members or attorneys, during normal waking hours.

Once taken into INS custody, aliens are given a copy of the "Detainee Handbook," which details their rights and responsibilities, including their living conditions, clothing, visitation, and access to legal materials. In addition, every alien is given a comprehensive medical assessment, including dental and mental health screenings. Aliens are informed of their right to communicate with their nation's consular or diplomatic officers, and, for some countries, the INS will notify those officials that one of their nationals has been arrested or detained. Finally, immigration judges preside over legal proceedings involving aliens, and aliens have the right to appeal any adverse decision, first to the Board of Immigration Appeals, and then to the federal courts.

Second, the Department of Justice has conducted voluntary interviews of individuals who may have information relating to terrorist activity. On November 9, the attorney general directed all United States Attorneys and members of the joint federal and state Anti-Terrorism Task Forces, or "ATTFs," to meet with certain noncitizens in their jurisdictions. That same day, the deputy attorney general issued a memorandum outlining the procedures and questions to be asked during those interviews. The names of approximately five thousand individuals that were sent to the ATTFs as part of this effort are those who we believe may have information that is helpful to the investigation or to disrupting ongoing terrorist activity. The names were compiled using commonsense criteria that take into account the manner, according to our intelligence sources, in which al Qaeda traditionally has operated. Thus, for example, the list includes individuals who entered the United States with a passport from a foreign country in which al Qaeda has operated or recruited; who entered the United States after January 1, 2000; and who are males between the ages of eighteen and thirty-three.

The president and attorney general continually have emphasized that our war on terrorism will be fought not just by our soldiers abroad, but also by civilians here at home. The department instituted a program that would enable our nation's guests to play a part in this campaign. Noncitizens are being asked, on a purely voluntary basis, to come forward with useful and reliable information about persons who have committed, or who are about to commit, terrorist attacks. Those who do so will qualify for the Responsible Cooperators Program. They may receive S visas or deferred action status that would allow them to remain in the United States for a period of time. Aliens who are granted S visas may later apply to become permanent residents and, ultimately, American citizens. The Responsible Cooperators Program enables us to extend America's promise of freedom to those who help us protect that promise.

Third, the Bureau of Prisons on October 31 promulgated a regulation permitting the monitoring of attorney-client communications in very limited circumstances. Since 1996, BOP regulations have subjected a very small group of the most dangerous federal detainees to "special administrative measures," if the attorney general determines that unrestricted communication with these detainees could result in death or serious bodily harm to others. Those measures include placing a detainee in administrative detention, limiting or monitoring his correspondence and telephone calls, restricting his opportunity to receive visitors, and limiting his access to members of the news media.[6] The preexisting regulations cut off all channels of communication through which detainees could plan or foment acts of terrorism, except one: communications through their attorneys. The new regulation closes this loophole. It permits the monitoring of attorney-client communications for these detainees only if the attorney general, after having invoked the existing special administrative measures authority, makes the additional finding that reasonable suspicion exists to believe that a particular detainee may use communications with attorneys to further or facilitate acts of terrorism.[7] Currently, only 12 of the approximately 158,000 inmates in federal custody would be eligible for monitoring.

The department has taken steps to protect the attorney-client privilege and the detainees' Sixth Amendment right to the effective assistance of counsel. As an initial matter, not all communications between a lawyer and his client are protected by the attorney-client privilege; statements that are designed to facilitate crimes, including acts of terrorism, are not privileged. The "crime/fraud exception" applies even if the attorney is not aware that he is being used to facilitate crime,[8] and even if the attorney takes no action to assist the client.[9]

Moreover, the monitoring regulation includes a number of procedural safeguards to protect privileged communications.[10] First and foremost, the attorney and client would be given written advance notification that their communication will be monitored pursuant to the regulation. Second, the regulation erects a "firewall" between the team monitoring the communications and the outside world, including persons involved with any ongoing prosecution of the client. Third, absent imminent violence or terrorism, the government would have to obtain court approval before any information from monitored communications is used for any purpose, including for investigative purposes. And fourth, no privileged information would be retained by the monitoring team; only information that is not privileged may be retained.

Finally, the president has authorized military commissions to try members of al Qaeda and other noncitizen terrorists for violations of the laws of war. Trying terrorists before military commissions offers a number of practical advantages over ordinary civilian trials. First, commissions enable the government to protect classified and other sensitive national security information that would have to be disclosed publicly before an Article III court. Second, ordinary criminal trials would subject court personnel, jurors, and other civilians to the threat of terrorist reprisals; the military is better suited to coping with these dangers. And third, military commissions can operate with more flexible rules of evidence, which would allow the introduction of all relevant evidence regardless of whether, for example, it has been properly authenticated.

The Supreme Court has unanimously upheld the constitutionality of military commissions,[11] and since its founding our nation has used them to try war criminals, as have our international allies. During World War II, President Roosevelt ordered eight Nazi saboteurs tried by military commission. After the Civil War, a commission was used to try Confederate sympathizers who conspired to assassinate President Lincoln. And during the Revolutionary War, General Washington convened a military commission to try British Major Andre as a spy. Moreover, the president's authority to convene military commissions is confirmed by Article 21 of the Uniform Code of Military Justice.[12] In 1942, the Supreme Court interpreted identical language, then appearing in the Articles of War, as recognizing the president's power to try war crimes before military commissions.[13] And America and her allies made liberal use of military commissions after World War II to try war criminals both in the European and Pacific theaters.[14]

After September 11, Americans in their own ways have sought answers to the seemingly unfathomable question: why? Because Americans are somehow different from and better than the people of the world? I do not think so. We *are* the people of the world. We are not, as individuals, different from those who would rain terror upon us. But there is something special that defines us as Americans —the benefits and responsibilities of living in this nation. America gives to people who come to her shores the freedom to achieve extraordinary things. Our uniqueness lies in our ability as ordinary people to do extraordinary ordinary things as Americans. It was this foundation of freedom that was under attack.

America's tradition of freedom thus is not an obstacle to be over-come in our campaign to rid the world of individuals capable of the evil we saw on September 11. It is, rather, an integral objective of our campaign to defend and preserve the security of our nation and the safety of our citizens. Indeed, as the images of liberated Afghan men shaving their beards and freed Afghan women shedding their burquas eloquently testify, freedom is itself a weapon in our war on terror. Just as we unleash our armed forces abroad, and empower our law enforcement officers here at home, America's campaign against terrorism will extend freedom for our citizens, as well as for the people of the world.

NOTES

1. Benjamin Franklin, "Historical Review of Pennsylvania (1759)," in *The Oxford Dictionary of Political Quotations*, ed. Anthony Jay (Oxford: Oxford University Press, 1996), p. 141.

2. Abraham Lincoln, "Message to Congress in Special Session (July 4, 1861)," in *The Collected Works of Abraham Lincoln*, vol. 4, ed. Roy P. Basler (New Brunswick, N.J.: Rutgers University Press, 1953–1955), pp. 421, 430.

3. Edmund Burke, "Speech at His Arrival at Bristol before the Election in That City (1774)," in *Slouching Towards Gomorrah: Modern Liberalism and American Decline*, ed. Robert H. Bork (New York: Regan Books, 1996), p. 64.

4. Karen DeYoung, "'Sleeper Cells' of Al-Qaeda Are Next Target," *Washington Post*, December 3, 2001, sec. A1.

5. See Jeffrey Bartholet, "Al-Qaeda Runs for the Hills," *Newsweek*, December 17, 2001, pp. 21, 23.

6. Department of Justice, Bureau of Prisons, "National Security; Prevention of Acts of Violence and Terrorism," *Federal Register*, 28 C.F.R. Part 500 (2001).

7. Ibid., Part 501.3(d) (2001).

8. See *United States v. Soudan*, 812 F.2d 920, 927 (5th Cir. 1986).

9. See *In re Grand Jury Proceedings*, 87 F.3d 377, 382 (9th Cir. 1996).

10. Department of Justice, Bureau of Prisons, "National Security; Prevention of Acts of Violence and Terrorism," Part 501.3(d)(1), (2), (3) (2001).

11. See *In re Yamashita*, 327 US 1 (1946); *Ex parte Quirin*, 317 US 1 (1942).

12. See *Uniform Code of Military Justice, U.S. Code*, vol. 10, sec. 821.

13. See *Ex parte Quirin*, 317 US 27, 29 (1942).

14. See, generally, Department of the Army, *International Law*, pamphlet 27-161-2, vol. 2 (1962): 235; Philip R. Piccigallo, *The Japanese on Trial: Allied War Crimes Operations in the East, 1945–1951* (Austin: University of Texas Press, 1979).

9.

FEAR AS INSTITUTION

9/11 AND SURVEILLANCE TRIUMPHANT

Christian Parenti

Experience should teach us to be most on our guard to protect liberty when the Government's purposes are beneficent. Men born to freedom are naturally alert to repel invasion of their liberty by evil-minded rulers. The greatest dangers to liberty lurk in insidious encroachment by men of zeal, well meaning but without understanding.

—Supreme Court Justice Louis Brandeis,
Olmstead v. United States (1928)

There are reminders to all Americans that they need to watch what they say, watch what they do. . . .

—Ari Fleischer, White House spokesman, 2001
This comment was later removed from the official transcript.

U ltimately, 9/11 did not create a technical or legal rupture in the developing infrastructure of everyday superintendence. It did, however, radically accelerate momentum toward the soft cage of a surveillance society, just as it gave the culture of fear a rejuvenating jolt. In many ways the frightening thing about the postattack crackdown has been how much of everyday life was prefabricated to fit neatly into a new and larger project of intensified state observation and repression. In this we see again that the problem with routine surveillance is not that any single instance is so abhorrent, especially when viewed in isolation, but rather that the cumulative overall effect of such measures is corrosive of popular democratic rights and traditions.

PATRIOTS GALORE

As the smoke of the attacks cleared, there emerged in Congress a hastily discussed yet massive schedule of domestic repression: the Uniting and Strengthening America by Providing Appropriate Tools Required to Intercept and Obstruct Terrorism (USA PATRIOT) Act. This hyperbolically named legislation introduced a sweeping arsenal of new federal powers. Put simply, the PATRIOT Act liberalized use of the federal government's four main tools of surveillance: wiretaps, search warrants, subpoenas, and pen/trap orders (which allow investigators to log and map all the telephone numbers called by a suspect). It was the attorney general's ultimate wish list. But in other ways it was just a mopping-up operation that legalized already existing and ongoing, yet illegal, forms of investigation.

Proof of this point came almost exactly a year after the attacks when several major papers ran the story of an internal FBI memo from 2000 that detailed the bureau's routine and widespread violations of privacy laws. Among the memo's many revelations: field agents were improperly tapping and recording phones, illegally videotaping suspects, and, without warrants, intercepting and analyzing e-mails with the data-mining software application formerly known as Carnivore. Furthermore, the memo rooted these transgressions in the pathological permissiveness of the 1978 Foreign Intelligence Surveillance Act (FISA). Under this law agents were permitted easy access to warrants if they could show that there was a substantial "foreign intelligence" angle to their work; the warrants would be granted by a special FISA court. It turned out that the leeway of FISA was being used as cover for otherwise illegal investigations.

Despite the exposé of FBI lawlessness, Ashcroft's PATRIOT Act had as one of its key features a further reduction in FISA's already low standard of proof. Now, even in cases that are entirely criminal in nature, agents can get automatic "administrative" FISA warrants (as opposed to real warrants from potentially hostile judges). As long as the agents assert that there is some foreign intelligence angle to the cases, they receive search warrants on demand. In 2000 alone the docile, highly secretive FISA bench approved 1,012 warrants.[1] And since 9/11 FBI demands for FISA warrants have become so insistent that even the secret FISA court has publicly admonished the FBI for misrepresenting facts on more than seventy-five occasions. This, from a court that civil libertarians ridiculed as an FBI rubberstamp and that approved *all but one of* the warrant requests put before it in the previous *twenty-four years.*[2]

The key distinction to keep in mind about FISA is that the standard of proof in criminal cases is supposed to be much higher than for intelligence cases, the assumption being that criminal cases can lead to prosecution and imprisonment of citizens and thus must be conducted in a restrained and fair fashion. Foreign intelligence, on the other hand, is merely about collecting information on a foreign power; domestic prosecution is not its goal. Since there is less risk of wrongful conviction from foreign intelligence investigations, requests for search warrants in such cases are held to a lower standard of proof.

The PATRIOT Act also allows federal investigators to "shop" for judges nationally when seeking warrants. Instead of being forced to possibly face a liberal judge, agents can now pick the judge of their choice from whichever circuit court they please and that warrant can be used in any part of the country. The raft of new laws also allows for nationwide roving wiretaps. In the past the feds were supposed to get a warrant for each telephone line they tapped. Now one easy warrant allows them to tap all the phones that a single subject might use. Such a warrant could thus cover a person's home phone, work phone, and cell phone, as well as the lines of their friends, family, work associates, and social acquaintances.[3]

Other PATRIOT Act provisions expand the government's automatic access to information stored and generated by Internet service providers. This is done by retooling the parameters of what are called pen registration tap-and-trace warrants. Traditionally such administrative warrants were granted when cops wanted to generate a simple list of all the numbers that had been called from and that had called a particular phone. Because it was deemed that no "content" was revealed by such a list, the standard of proof for a tap-and-trace warrant was very low; agents had only to "certify" or assert that they had a good reason for needing the information—in other words, they didn't have to prove probable cause. After the PATRIOT Act, the same low standard holds true for gleaning information about Web surfing and e-mailing. But Web addresses and e-mail subject lines, unlike simple phone numbers, all contain revealing content.[4] If you visit the Web site of a radical environmental group, this fact will likely be clear from the Web address alone.

Gone too are the firewalls that once prevented the various intelligence agencies from sharing information. Crucially the PATRIOT Act creates a new massively expanded definition of what a terrorist is. Now anyone who breaks the law so as to impact policy or change public opinion and does so in a way that might endanger human life (including their own) can be investigated and prosecuted as a terrorist.[5] An analysis of the USA PATRIOT Act could go on for many pages. The point for our purposes is that it liberalizes the legal environment in which federal cops will be gathering and processing the routine informational detritus of the digital age.

TOTAL INFORMATION AWARENESS: THE LOGICAL NEXT STEP

The most explicit and dramatic connection between government spying and the infrastructure of everyday surveillance was the Total Information Awareness (TIA) project of the Pentagon's Defense

Advanced Research Projects Agency (DARPA). Begun in January 2002 and defunded in March 2003, DARPA's Information Awareness Office stated that it would "imagine, develop, apply, integrate, demonstrate, and transition information technologies, components, and prototype closed-loop information systems that will counter asymmetric threats by achieving total information awareness that is useful for preemption, national security warning, and national security decision making."[6]

Much like the Transportation Security Agency's airline-oriented CAPPS II, the TIA office was working on a plan to pull together all the disparate records of everyday life. From the digital trails of credit cards, electronic tolls, banking transactions, health records, and library use it sought to create one "virtual, grand database" that could be data-mined for interesting and incriminating patterns.[7] The program was also tasked with inventing "new algorithms for mining, combining, and refining" this information.[8] Connected to this was another DARPA program called Human ID that would mathematically map biometric information from video cameras and other image sources and then use this to track images of people across and through different databases. This would allow the government to identify people with just a photo and to automatically track people as they travel in public space. A rather perturbed-sounding *Fortune* magazine described DARPA's efforts this way: "Every telephone call you make, every credit card transaction, all your e-mail and instant messages, all your medical records, your magazine subscriptions, your police record, driver's license records, gun purchases, travel records, banking records—all would be fed into a hopper and sifted by the TIA spy software."[9]

This complaint from the *Washington Post* was typical: "The potential for abuse is enormous."[10] One could add that the system was abusive by its very nature, that its intended function was to destroy privacy and subordinate the population, above and beyond any "mistakes" that might be made. Heading up this project was the politically radioactive retired rear admiral John Poindexter, who was infamously convicted on five felony counts of lying to Congress and destroying official documents during the Iran/Contra Affair (he was later acquitted on technicalities).[11]

Another important and developing part of the same general project was the administration's "National Strategy to Secure Cyberspace"—essentially an attempt (still in the planning stages) to centralize the World Wide Web. Currently the purview of the president's Critical Infrastructure Protection Board, this cyber enclosure would require all Internet service providers to help build a centralized system for tracking and filtering online traffic. One data-industry specialist compared the system to the FBI's Internet surveillance and data-mining program called Carnivore, but added that "it's ten times worse."[12] Eventually the TIA office of DARPA had its funding cut, thanks to popular outcry against the project. But many of these functions continue in modified form under other names.

FRIEND/ENEMY KULTURKAMPF

Perhaps the most revealing surveillance idea from the Bush team was the failed Terrorism Information and Prevention System (TIPS) program, which sought to turn one in every twenty-four Americans into a snitch. The idea was to recruit meter readers, UPS drivers, and letter carriers to report on "suspicious activities" they witnessed while inside homes. Floated as a serious proposal by Attorney General John Ashcroft in the summer of 2002, TIPS was quickly ripped to pieces by everyone from the mainstream press to the post office, delivery firms, and utility companies it was to rely on. By late fall TIPS had died in its crib. But the program is an important political artifact because of the twisted fundamentals it reveals.

On Planet Ashcroft, society appears as a hub-and-spoke system where citizens mistrust each other, share no popular solidarity, and place all trust in unlimited state and corporate power. Furthermore, this system plays out along the lines of race. Recall Eunice Stone, at best a malicious busy-body, at worst a stone-cold bigot, who called in the Florida police when she overheard three Middle Eastern–looking medical students at a restaurant talking about dates in September. Mrs. Stone insisted they were joking about imminent terrorist attacks. After a huge paramilitary police bust that shut down

Alligator Alley, the "terrorists" turned out to be totally innocent, rather square and apolitical medical students who had been talking about how they could return their rental car to Kansas and still get to their residencies in Georgia on time.[13]

This willingness to snitch on anyone who looks remotely Arab is also reflected in polls. A *Newsweek* survey conducted immediately in the wake of 9/11 found that 32 percent of Americans favored putting Arabs under "special surveillance" like that used against Japanese Americans during World War II.[14] A *San Jose Mercury News* poll had 66 percent of respondents favoring "heightened surveillance of Middle Eastern immigrants."[15]

GET THE IMMIGRANTS, AGAIN

So how do such sentiments translate into policy? Jump back to the autumn of 2002, when men from an ever-growing list of countries are required to report for "special registration" requiring them to be photographed, fingerprinted, and interviewed. In Southern California, *la migra* detains hundreds of law-abiding immigrants, many of whom have only minor technical problems with their paperwork. In Los Angeles the mass arrests are so numerous that officials run out of plastic handcuffs and start shipping the estimated four hundred to nine hundred detainees out to more permanent holding facilities.[16] Fear and outrage grip the Arab, Persian, and South Asian communities; soon hundreds of law-abiding Pakistani immigrants are rushing to the Canadian border seeking political asylum.

"I feel sorrow for this society," says a Mr. Pirazdeh, an Iranian political refugee held in an immigration detention facility in San Pedro. "I still believe this society and this country is based on freedom." Pirazdeh was on the verge of getting his residency papers when he was jailed and threatened with deportation.[17] It was all part of ramping up the cumbersome machinery of the new National Security Entry-Exit Registration System, a futuristic version of the methods first used on the Chinese that will now allow the Department of Homeland Security to better monitor all foreign visitors and immigrants.[18]

To begin with, the new immigration program required all residents from Iran, Iraq, Libya, Sudan, and Syria who are not permanent residents or naturalized citizens to register their fingerprints and photos with the local immigration authorities. Next to be called in were all male visa holders over the age of sixteen from thirteen other countries, including Afghanistan, Eritrea, Lebanon, North Korea, and Yemen. Foreign students are also to be tracked with a new and totalizing vigor, thanks to the Student and Exchange Visitor Information System (SEVIS). As the State Department explained, in the newspeak of compassionate xenophobia, "The new system is designed to better maintain accurate records of aliens inside the nation, at the same time it supports a policy of openness toward people from other nations." The DHS will attempt to maintain "updated information on approximately one million nonimmigrant foreign students and exchange visitors" every year.

Thanks to the Internet, universities and colleges will be compelled to do most of the bureaucratic policing and update the feds electronically as necessary. In their new role as the eyes and ears of homeland security overkill, educational institutions will be required to report if a foreign student fails to enroll, drops out, has poor grades, changes his or her address or name or field of study. Such data will be electronically transmitted to the immigration cops at the DHS and to the Department of State. "When a student falls out of status, INS will be informed and able to take appropriate action." The goal of all this is more data mining, enabling "the INS to better identify trends and patterns to assist in planning and analyzing risks."[19] Ultimately such security strategies amount to hunting fleas with a sledgehammer. Terrorists are captured when their networks are infiltrated, not when whole populations are harassed.

While the immigration officials were getting SEVIS up and running, the FBI was shaking down schools for voluntary information transfers. According to the law, universities are free to give limited personal student information to law enforcement agencies without a court order. Department of Education guidelines allow all of the following to be handed over to law enforcement: name, address, e-mail address, telephone number, field of study, the weight and height of athletes, and the date and place of birth. However, investigators still need a subpoena to get student ID numbers, Social Security numbers, or information on a student's ethnicity, race, citizenship, and gender.[20]

IN THE SERVICE OF ORDER

Here again the central question arises: what harm is caused by the proliferation of everyday surveillance? How will carrying a smart-card ID through an environment of swipe scanners, meters, cameras, sensors, and databanks hurt us? Is it just that a few innocent people, like the immigrants discussed above, will be pushed around? That's bad, but is there even more at stake?

Justice Louis Brandeis framed the issue of surveillance in terms of individual quality of life. Recall his famous dissenting opinion in *Olmstead* on the use of police wiretaps, in which he vaunted "man's spiritual nature . . . his feelings" and "his intellect . . ." and saw the Constitution as protecting "Americans in their beliefs, their thoughts, their emotions and their sensations."[21]

Brandeis offers a definition and defense of privacy as eloquent as any before or since, but are these purely individual, experiential parameters enough? What about the political life of the collective? And what about the dangerous implications of privacy? Is not the case for privacy also an argument for lawlessness? Are we protecting the "privacy" to run red lights, steal, abuse children, or kill with airplanes? Put differently, what does one have to fear from total surveillance as long as one obeys all laws? Indeed, total surveillance and total accountability plus total obedience add up to business as usual for the "good citizen."

Already we see signs of this type of ultratrusting, superobedient postmodern subject emerging from within the regime of routine observation and regulation. The *Christian Science Monitor* reports:

Polls show that kids have been the least surprised by new security measures since they're the most used to having ID cards examined, luggage searched, and jokes screened by authorities. Today's kids trust and confide in authorities, set up Web cams in their rooms, and keep in constant electronic contact with parents and friends. For better or worse, privacy isn't a big issue among teens, and challenges to civil liberties are less of a worry than to older people.[22]

In other words, the structure of feeling is being transformed by increasingly ubiquitous surveillance. Liberty and autonomy are being replaced by obedience and trust in authority.

Underlying this question of obedience is the implicit assumption that state, corporate, and parental powers are infallible. Thus the heart of the matter emerges: are the rules and laws of this society all rational, benevolent, and just? If they are not, and if many of them serve to reproduce racism, stupidity, exploitation, environmental devastation, and general brutality, then should we not resist them?

CIVIL LIBERTIES AND RESISTANCE

Perhaps a view from the past might help reframe the issue. Milton Mayer, once a well-known essayist, described a similar escalation of surveillance, rules, and obedience in the gathering storm of German fascism. He interviewed a German philologist who described the process in terms that might sound familiar:

What happened was the gradual habituation of the people, little by little, to be governed by surprise, to receiving decisions deliberated in secret; to believe that the situation was so complicated that the government had to act on information which the people could not understand, or so dangerous that, even if people could understand it, it could not be released because of national security. . . . This separation of government from the people, this widening of the gap, took place so gradually and insensibly, each step disguised (perhaps not even intentionally) as a temporary emergency measure or associated with true patriotic allegiance or with real social purposes. And all the crises and reforms (real reforms too) so occupied the people that they did not see the slow motion underneath, of the whole process of government growing remoter and remoter. . . . Each step was so small, so inconsequential, so well explained or, on occasion, "regretted." That, unless one were to detach from the whole process from the beginning, unless one understood what the whole thing was in principle, what all these "little measures" that no "patriotic German" could resist must some day lead to, one no more saw it developing from day to day than a farmer in his field sees the corn growing.

Believe me this is true. Each act, each occasion is worse than the last, but only a little worse. You wait for the next and the next. You wait for one shocking occasion, thinking that others, when such a shock comes, will join you in resisting somehow. . . . Suddenly it all comes down, all at once. You see what you are, what you have done, or, more accurately, what you haven't done (for that was all that was required of most of us: that we did nothing). . . . You remember everything now, and your heart breaks. Too late. You are compromised beyond repair.[23]

Now, consider again the question of civil liberties: what *are* they for? As far back as the early Greek philosophers we can find notions of "natural law" that transcend the legality of any given state. We find the recurring idea that the law is not the sum total of morality and that at times there must be transgressions against legal norms. Sophocles, for example, has Antigone explain why she willfully disobeyed the king's orders: "Nor deemed I that thy decrees were of such force, that a mortal could override the unwritten and unfailing statutes of heaven. For their life is not of today or yesterday, but for all time, and no man knows when they were first put forth."[24]

Connected to this is the idea that the state's power over individuals may be simultaneously necessary and dangerous. Thus John Locke's argument for legislative government and against the divine right of kings made a similar case for limitations on state power and what is essentially the right to commit illegalities. To his critics who saw dissolving government as a sin Locke answered:

But if they, who say it lays a foundation for rebellion, mean that it may occasion civil wars, or intestine broils, to tell the people they are absolved from obedience when illegal attempts are made upon their liberties or properties, and may oppose the unlawful violence

of those who were their magistrates, when they invade their properties contrary to the trust put in them; and that therefore this doctrine is not to be allowed, being so destructive to the peace of the
world: they may as well say, upon the same ground, that honest
men may not oppose robbers or pirates, because this may occasion
disorder or bloodshed. . . . The end of government is the good of
mankind; and which is best for mankind, that the people should
be always exposed to the boundless will of tyranny, or that the
rulers should be sometimes liable to be opposed, when they grow
exorbitant in the use of their power, and employ it for the destruction, and not the preservation of the properties of their people?[25]

Admittedly, Locke preferred orderly legislative change to open
contest and rebellion, but the philosophical door to illegality is
open. The ultimate capstone in this tradition of recognizing an
implicit right to illegality is of course the US Declaration of Independence.[26] The key passage, once again:

We hold these truths to be self-evident, that all men are created
equal, that they are endowed by their Creator with certain unalien-
able rights, that among these are life, liberty and the pursuit of
happiness. That to secure these rights, governments are instituted
among men, deriving their just powers from the consent of the
governed. That whenever any form of government becomes
destructive to these ends, it is the right of the people to alter or to
abolish it, and to institute new government, laying its foundation
on such principles and organizing its powers in such form, as to
them shall seem most likely to effect their safety and happiness.
Prudence, indeed, will dictate that governments long established
should not be changed for light and transient causes; and accordingly all experience hath shown that mankind are more disposed
to suffer, while evils are sufferable, than to right themselves by
abolishing the forms to which they are accustomed. But when a
long train of abuses and usurpations, pursuing invariably the same
object evinces a design to reduce them under absolute despotism,
it is their right, it is their duty, to throw off such government, and
to provide new guards for their future security.

The message here is nothing less than an in-your-face proclamation of state fallibility and an assertion of the people's right to commit illegalities. It is from this recognition in part that the Bill of Rights, the first ten amendments to the Constitution, emerges with its potentially meaningful containment of state power. We are given protection against "unreasonable search and seizure" and "security in our personal effects" precisely because the state and the social hierarchies served by the law are neither infallible nor the perfection of morality. Read together with the Declaration of Independence, the Bill of Rights and the civil liberties it enshrines begin to reveal themselves not just as protection for the innocent who might be wronged by the excess of the law, but also as an ambiguous protection for types of political guilt. There is in the tradition of natural law a space for rebellion.

It is no coincidence then that the women who met at Seneca Falls in 1848 to declare their "natural rights" and their implicit right to commit illegal acts first quoted verbatim the Declaration of Independence before then setting forth the following challenge to existing law:

> Resolved, That such laws as conflict, in any way with the true and substantial happiness of woman, are contrary to the great precept of nature and of no validity, for his is "superior in obligation to any other."
>
> Resolved, That all laws which prevent woman from occupying such a station in society as her conscience shall dictate, or which place her in a position inferior to that of man, are contrary to the great precept of nature, and therefore of no force or authority.[27]

The same subtextual recognition of the right to commit illegalities compelled Henry David Thoreau to write *Resistance to Civil Government*. That book's most libertine lines also recapitulate the essences of the declaration:

> All men recognize the right of revolution; that is, the right to refuse allegiance to, and to resist, the government, when its tyranny or its inefficiency are great and unendurable. . . . Unjust laws exist: shall

we be content to obey them, or shall we endeavor to amend them, and obey them until we have succeeded, or shall we transgress them at once?[28]

Mahatma Gandhi and Martin Luther King Jr. both invoked the same obedience to higher laws in defending their disobedience vis-à-vis specific laws. In that light one might ask: would the civil rights movement have been as effective if the world of the 1950s and early 1960s had been as wired with surveillance gear as today's America? If J. Edgar Hoover had something like Total Information Awareness, would his agents have used it, as they did all the other means available to them, to harass civil rights activists, reds, poor peoples' organizations, unionists, and peaceniks? Most certainly.

Much of the history of social progress—from winning the eight-hour workday to women's suffrage to desegregation—was achieved in large part because citizens organized political movements that involved illegal forms of protests. Privacy and civil liberties were essential tools in all these cases. Illegal protests created a nuisance value that served the less powerful as a disposable political resource. The logic was always simple: Agree to a civilized work regime and the strikes and sabotage will stop. Let the ladies vote and they'll stop getting arrested. Desegregate public facilities, and the siege of sit-ins, boycotts, and blockades will stop. Or today: Stop raping old-growth forests and the rugged tree sitters will come down out of their redwoods. At times when government is truly "remote" and unresponsive, disruptive and sometimes illegal protest is the only resource people have.

Similarly, the right to illegality is revealed in the fact that often the only way to get a constitutional test of a law is to violate the statute in question. Viewed from this angle the specter of a totally transparent society in which obedience and self-policing are the ideal is a threat to the basic preconditions of oppositional politics and social progress.

What would it take to wind back the "thousand things" that make up the soft cage? Clearly there must be prohibitions against ever-expanding surveillance, but only popular pressure will cause the state to build new firewalls of privacy. Only sustained protest will compel regulators to tell corporations, police, schools, hospitals, and other institutions that there are limits. As a society, we want to say: Here you may not go. Here you may not record. Here you may not track and identify people. Here you may not trade and analyze information and build dossiers. There are risks in social anonymity, but the risks of omniscient and omnipotent state and corporate power are far worse.

NOTES

1. Ted Bridis, "FBI Memo Details Surveillance Lapses in Terror, Spy Cases," Associated Press, October 10, 2002; "One Year Later," *Nation*, September 23, 2002.

2. Dan Eggen, "FBI Misused Secret Wiretaps, According to Memo," *Washington Post*, October 10, 2002.

3. "USA PATRIOT Act Boosts Government Powers While Cutting Back on Traditional Checks and Balances," ACLU Legislative Analysis on USA PATRIOT Act, November 1, 2001; "USA PATRIOT Act—An Analysis by the ACLU," January 12, 2002; "Civil Liberties after 9/11: The ACLU Defends Freedom," September 20, 2002.

4. See Electronic Frontier Foundation, http://www.eff.org/Privacy/ Surveillance/Terrorism_militias/20011031_ eff_usa_patriot_analysis.html.

5. Ibid.

6. See Defense Advanced Research Projects Agency, http://www.darpa .mil/iao.

7. Jeffery Rosen, "Total Information Awareness," in "The Year in Ideas," *New York Times Magazine*, December 15, 2002.

8. The real total for TIA funding comes from Electronic Privacy Information Center (EPIC), http://www.epic.org/events/tia_briefing. In many ways TIA is the worst-case scenario, the end result of proliferating digital everyday surveillance. When I began this book, the attacks of 9/11 had not yet happened, TIA did not exist, and my argument called on readers to *imagine* the digitalized informational landscape that could be centrally monitored with a something like TIA. Much has changed since then, and one need not try and imagine anything since the critical imagination has once again been overtaken by the implementation of actual policies.

9. Peter Lewis, "At Last," *Fortune*, December 30, 2002; William Safire, "You Are a Suspect," *New York Times*, November 14, 2002; William New, "Back to the Future," *National Journal*, June 14, 2002; William New, "The Poindexter Plan," *National Journal*, September 7, 2002. For one of the earliest mentions, see Dr. Tony Tether, "Statement by Director, Defense Advanced Research Projects Agency," Submitted to the Subcommittee on Emerging Threats and Capabilities, Committee on Armed Services, United States Senate, *Hearings on Fiscal 2003 Defense Request: Combating Terrorism* (April 10, 2002).

10. "Total Information Awareness," *Washington Post*, November 16, 2002.

11. For discussion of this point, see Safire, "You Are a Suspect"; Matthew Engel, "This Perfect System," *Guardian* (London), November 19, 2002.

12. John Markoff and John Swartz, "Bush Administration to Propose System for Wide Monitoring of Internet," *New York Times*, December 20, 2002.

13. Christine Chinlund, "Getting the Rest of the Story," *Boston Globe*, September 23, 2002; Clarence Page, "The Failings of Arab Profiling," *Chicago Tribune*, September 22, 2002; *Democracy Now*, September 24, 2002, http://www.webactive.com/pacifica/demnow/dn20020924.html.

14. Daniel Levitas, "The Radical Right after 9/11," *Nation*, July 22, 2002.

15. John Giuffo and Joshua Lipton, "Reverberations," *Columbia Journalism Review*, January 1, 2002.

16. *Chicago Tribune*, December 20, 2002.

17. Henry Weinstein and Greg Krikorian, "Caught between Dueling Policies," *Los Angeles Times*, December 21, 2002.

18. *Los Angeles Daily News*, December 19, 2002.

19. State Department press releases and documents, Federal Information & News Dispatch, Inc., December 13, 2002. According to this press release, "SEVIS implements section 641 of the Illegal Immigration Reform and Immigrant Responsibilities Act (IIRIRA) of 1996. IIRIRA requires the INS to collect current information on an ongoing basis from schools and exchange programs relating to nonimmigrant foreign students and exchange visitors during the course of their stay in the United States. In addition, the USA PATRIOT Act amended section 641 to require full implementation of SEVIS prior to January 1, 2003. In addition, the Enhanced Border Security and Visa Entry Reform Act of 2002 adds to and clarifies the

requirement to collect information, as well as requires an educational institution to report any failure of an alien to enroll no later than thirty days after registration deadline."

20. Ann Davis, "Some Colleges Balk at FBI Request for Data on Foreigners," *Wall Street Journal*, November 25, 2002.

21. *Olmstead v. United States*, 277 US 438 (1928).

22. Neil Howe and William Strauss, "Through Prism of Tragedy, Generations Are Defined," *Christian Science Monitor*, September 23, 2002.

23. Milton Mayer, *They Thought They Were Free: The Germans, 1933–1945* (Chicago: University of Chicago Press, 1955), pp. 166–72.

24. Sophocles, cited in Charles Grove Haines, *The Revival of Natural Law Concepts: A Study of the Establishment and of the Interpretation of Limits on Legislatures with Special Reference to the Development of Certain Phases of American Constitutional Law* (Cambridge: Harvard University Press, 1930), p. 5.

25. John Locke, *Second Treatise on Government* (1690, http://www.constitution.org/jl/2ndtreat.htm).

26. Among its fans were Ho Chi Minh and Fidel Castro.

27. Elizabeth Cady Stanton, "The Seneca Falls Declaration, Adopted in Convention, 1848," http://www.constitution.org/woll/seneca.htm.

28. Henry David Thoreau, *On the Duty of Civil Disobedience* [1849, original title: *Resistance to Civil Government*], http://www.constitution.org/civ/civildis.htm.

PART 3.

RACIAL PROFILING

10.

KOREMATSU V. UNITED STATES

US Supreme Court

Decided December 18, 1944.

Mr. Justice Black delivered the opinion of the Court.

The petitioner, an American citizen of Japanese descent, was convicted in a federal district court for remaining in San Leandro, California, a "Military Area," contrary to Civilian Exclusion Order No. 34 of the Commanding General of the Western Command, US Army, which directed that after May 9, 1942, all persons of Japanese ancestry should be excluded from that area. No question was raised as to petitioner's loyalty to the United States. The Circuit Court of Appeals affirmed, and the importance of the constitutional question involved caused us to grant certiorari.

It should be noted, to begin with, that all legal restrictions which curtail the civil rights of a single racial group are immediately suspect. That is not to say that all such restrictions are unconstitutional. It is to say that courts must subject them to the most rigid scrutiny. Pressing public necessity may sometimes justify the existence of such restrictions; racial antagonism never can.

In the instant case prosecution of the petitioner was begun by information charging violation of an Act of Congress, of March 21, 1942, which provides that ". . . whoever shall enter, remain in, leave, or commit any act in any military area or military zone prescribed, under the authority of an Executive order of the President, by the Secretary of War, or by any military commander designated by the Secretary of War, contrary to the restrictions applicable to any such area or zone or contrary to the order of the Secretary of War or any such military commander, shall, if it appears that he knew or should have known of the existence and extent of the restrictions or order and that his act was in violation thereof, be guilty of a misdemeanor and upon conviction shall be liable to a fine of not to exceed $5,000 or to imprisonment for not more than one year, or both, for each offense."

Exclusion Order No. 34, which the petitioner knowingly and admittedly violated, was one of a number of military orders and proclamations, all of which were substantially based upon Executive Order No. 9066. That order, issued after we were at war with Japan, declared that "the successful prosecution of the war requires every possible protection against espionage and against sabotage to national defense material, national defense premises, and national defense utilities. . . ."

One of the series of orders and proclamations, a curfew order, which like the exclusion order here was promulgated pursuant to Executive Order 9066, subjected all persons of Japanese ancestry in prescribed West Coast military areas to remain in their residences from 8 PM to 6 AM. As is the case with the exclusion order here, that prior curfew order was designed as a "protection against espionage and against sabotage." In *Kiyoshi Hirabayashi v. United States*, we sustained a conviction obtained for violation of the curfew order. The *Hirabayashi* conviction and this one thus rest on the same 1942 Congressional Act and the same basic executive and military orders, all of which orders were aimed at the twin dangers of espionage and sabotage.

The 1942 Act was attacked in the *Hirabayashi* case as an unconstitutional delegation of power; it was contended that the curfew order and other orders on which it rested were beyond the war powers of the Congress, the military authorities and of the President, as Commander in Chief of the Army; and finally that to apply the curfew order against none but citizens of Japanese ancestry amounted to a constitutionally prohibited discrimination solely on account of race. To these questions, we gave the serious consideration which their importance justified. We upheld the curfew order as an exercise of the power of the government to take steps necessary to prevent espionage and sabotage in an area threatened by Japanese attack.

In the light of the principles we announced in the *Hirabayashi* case, we are unable to conclude that it was beyond the war power of Congress and the Executive to exclude those of Japanese ancestry from the West Coast war area at the time they did. True, exclusion from the area in which one's home is located is a far greater deprivation than constant confinement to the home from 8 PM to 6 AM. Nothing short of apprehension by the proper military authorities of the gravest imminent danger to the public safety can constitutionally justify either. But exclusion from a threatened area, no less than curfew, has a definite and close relationship to the prevention of espionage and sabotage. The military authorities, charged with the primary responsibility of defending our shores, concluded that curfew provided inadequate protection and ordered exclusion. They did so, as pointed out in our *Hirabayashi* opinion, in accordance with Congressional authority to the military to say who should, and who should not, remain in the threatened areas.

In this case the petitioner challenges the assumptions upon which we rested our conclusions in the *Hirabayashi* case. He also urges that by May 1942, when Order No. 34 was promulgated, all danger of Japanese invasion of the West Coast had disappeared. After careful consideration of these contentions we are compelled to reject them.

Here, as in the *Hirabayashi* case, ". . . we cannot reject as unfounded the judgment of the military authorities and of Congress that there were disloyal members of that population, whose number and strength could not be precisely and quickly ascertained. We cannot say that the war-making branches of the Government did not have ground for believing that in a critical hour such persons could not readily be isolated and separately dealt with, and constituted a menace to the national defense and safety, which demanded that prompt and adequate measures be taken to guard against it."

Like curfew, exclusion of those of Japanese origin was deemed necessary because of the presence of an unascertained number of disloyal members of the group, most of whom we have no doubt were loyal to this country. It was because we could not reject the finding of the military authorities that it was impossible to bring about an immediate segregation of the disloyal from the loyal that we sustained the validity of the curfew order as applying to the whole group. In the instant case, temporary exclusion of the entire group was rested by the military on the same ground. The judgment that exclusion of the whole group was for the same reason a military imperative answers the contention that the exclusion was in the nature of group punishment based on antagonism to those of Japanese origin. That there were members of the group who retained loyalties to Japan has been confirmed by investigations made subsequent to the exclusion. Approximately five thousand American citizens of Japanese ancestry refused to swear unqualified allegiance to the United States and to renounce allegiance to the Japanese Emperor, and several thousand evacuees requested repatriation to Japan.

We uphold the exclusion order as of the time it was made and when the petitioner violated it. In doing so, we are not unmindful of the hardships imposed by it upon a large group of American citizens. But hardships are part of war, and war is an aggregation of hardships. All citizens alike, both in and out of uniform, feel the impact of war in greater or lesser measure. Citizenship has its responsibilities as well as its privileges, and in time of war the burden is always heavier. Compulsory exclusion of large groups of citizens from their homes, except under circumstances of direst emergency and peril, is inconsistent with our basic governmental institutions. But when under conditions of modern warfare our shores are threatened by hostile forces, the power to protect must be commensurate with the threatened danger. . . .

On May 9, the effective date of the exclusion order, the military authorities had already determined that the evacuation should be effected by assembling together and placing under guard all those of

Japanese ancestry, at central points, designated as "assembly centers," in order "to insure the orderly evacuation and resettlement of Japanese voluntarily migrating from military area No. 1 to restrict and regulate such migration." And on May 19, 1942, eleven days before the time petitioner was charged with unlawfully remaining in the area, Civilian Restrictive Order No. 1, provided for detention of those of Japanese ancestry in assembly or relocation centers. It is now argued that the validity of the exclusion order cannot be considered apart from the orders requiring him, after departure from the area, to report and to remain in an assembly or relocation center. The contention is that we must treat these separate orders as one and inseparable; that, for this reason, if detention in the assembly or relocation center would have illegally deprived the petitioner of his liberty, the exclusion order and his conviction under it cannot stand.

We are thus being asked to pass at this time upon the whole subsequent detention program in both assembly and relocation centers, although the only issues framed at the trial related to petitioner's remaining in the prohibited area in violation of the exclusion order. Had petitioner here left the prohibited area and gone to an assembly center we cannot say either as a matter of fact or law, that his presence in that center would have resulted in his detention in a relocation center. Some who did report to the assembly center were not sent to relocation centers but were released upon condition that they remain outside the prohibited zone until the military orders were modified or lifted. This illustrates that they pose different problems and may be governed by different principles. The lawfulness of one does not necessarily determine the lawfulness of the others. This is made clear when we analyze the requirements of the separate provisions of the separate orders. These separate requirements were that those of Japanese ancestry (1) depart from the area; (2) report to and temporarily remain in an assembly center; (3) go under military control to a relocation center there to remain for an indeterminate period until released conditionally or unconditionally by the military authorities. Each of these requirements, it will be noted, imposed distinct duties in connection with the separate steps in a complete evacuation program. Had Congress directly incorporated into one Act the language of these separate orders, and provided sanctions for their violations, disobedience of any one would have constituted a separate offense. There is no reason why violations of these orders, insofar as they were promulgated pursuant to congressional enactment, should not be treated as separate offenses. . . .

Since the petitioner has not been convicted of failing to report or to remain in an assembly or relocation center, we cannot in this case determine the validity of those separate provisions of the order. It is sufficient here for us to pass upon the order which petitioner violated. To do more would be to go beyond the issues raised, and to decide momentous questions not contained within the framework of the pleadings or the evidence in this case. It will be time enough to decide the serious constitutional issues which petitioner seeks to raise when an assembly or relocation order is applied or is certain to be applied to him, and we have its terms before us.

Some of the members of the Court are of the view that evacuation and detention in an Assembly Center were inseparable. After May 3, 1942, the date of Exclusion Order No. 34, Korematsu was under compulsion to leave the area not as he would choose but via an Assembly Center. The Assembly Center was conceived as a part of the machinery for group evacuation. The power to exclude includes the power to do it by force if necessary. And any forcible measure must necessarily entail some degree of detention or restraint whatever method of removal is selected. But whichever view is taken, it results in holding that the order under which petitioner was convicted was valid.

It is said that we are dealing here with the case of imprisonment of a citizen in a concentration camp solely because of his ancestry, without evidence or inquiry concerning his loyalty and good disposition toward the United States. Our task would be simple, our duty clear, were this a case involving the imprisonment of a loyal citizen in a concentration camp because of racial prejudice. Regardless of the true nature of the assembly and relocation centers—and we deem it unjustifiable to call them concentration camps with all the ugly connotations that term implies—we are dealing specifically with nothing but an exclusion order. To cast this case into outlines of racial prejudice, without reference to the real military dangers which were presented, merely confuses the issue. Korematsu was not excluded from the Military Area because of hostility to him or his race. He was excluded because we are at war with the Japanese Empire, because the properly constituted military authorities feared an invasion of our West Coast and felt constrained to take proper security measures, because they decided that the military urgency of the situation demanded that all citizens of Japanese ancestry be segregated from the West Coast temporarily, and finally, because Congress, reposing its confidence in this time of war in our military leaders—as inevitably it must—determined that they should have the power to do just this. There was evidence of disloyalty on the part of some, the military authorities considered that the need for action was great, and time was short. We cannot—by availing ourselves of the calm perspective of hindsight—now say that at that time these actions were unjustified.

Affirmed.

Mr. Justice Jackson, dissenting.

Korematsu was born on our soil, of parents born in Japan. The Constitution makes him a citizen of the United States by nativity and a citizen of California by residence. No claim is made that he is not loyal to this country. There is no suggestion that apart from the matter involved here he is not law-abiding and well disposed. Korematsu, however, has been convicted of an act not commonly a crime. It consists merely of being present in the state whereof he is a citizen, near the place where he was born, and where all his life he has lived.

Even more unusual is the series of military orders which made this conduct a crime. They forbid such a one to remain, and they also forbid him to leave. They were so drawn that the only way Korematsu could avoid violation was to give himself up to the military authority. This meant submission to custody, examination, and transportation out of the territory, to be followed by indeterminate confinement in detention camps.

A citizen's presence in the locality, however, was made a crime only if his parents were of Japanese birth. Had Korematsu been one of four—the others being, say, a German alien enemy, an Italian alien enemy, and a citizen of American-born ancestors, convicted of treason but out on parole—only Korematsu's presence would have violated the order. The difference between their innocence and his crime would result, not from anything he did, said, or thought, different than they, but only in that he was born of different racial stock.

Now, if any fundamental assumption underlies our system, it is that guilt is personal and not inheritable. Even if all of one's antecedents had been convicted of treason, the Constitution forbids its penalties to be visited upon him, for it provides that "no Attainder of Treason shall work Corruption of Blood, or Forfeiture except during the Life of the Person attained." But here is an attempt to make an otherwise innocent act a crime merely because this prisoner is the son of parents as to whom he had no choice, and belongs to a race from which there is no way to resign. If Congress in peacetime legislation should enact such a criminal law, I should suppose this Court would refuse to enforce it.

But the "law" which this prisoner is convicted of disregarding is not found in an act of Congress, but in a military order. Neither the Act of Congress nor the Executive Order of the President, nor both together, would afford a basis for this conviction. It rests on the orders of General DeWitt. And it is said that if the military commander had reasonable military grounds for promulgating the orders, they are constitutional and become law, and the Court is required to enforce them. There are several reasons why I cannot subscribe to this doctrine.

It would be impracticable and dangerous idealism to expect or insist that each specific military command in an area of probable operations will conform to conventional tests of constitutionality. When an area is so beset that it must be put under military control at all, the paramount consideration is that its measures be successful, rather than legal. The armed services must protect a society, not merely its Constitution. The very essence of the military job is to marshal physical force, to remove every obstacle to its effectiveness, to give it every strategic advantage. Defense measures will not, and often should not, be held within the limits that bind civil authority in peace. . . .

But if we cannot confine military expedients by the Constitution, neither would I distort the Constitution to approve all that the military may deem expedient. This is what the Court appears to be doing, whether consciously or not. I cannot say, from any evidence before me, that the orders of General DeWitt were not reasonably expedient military precautions, nor could I say that they were. But even if they were permissible military procedures, I deny that it follows that they are constitutional. If, as the Court holds, it does follow, then we may as well say that any military order will be constitutional and have done with it.

The limitation under which courts always will labor in examining the necessity for a military order are illustrated by this case. How does the Court know that these orders have a reasonable basis in necessity? No evidence whatever on that subject has been taken by this or any other court. There is sharp controversy as to the credibility of the DeWitt report. So the Court, having no real evidence before it, has no choice but to accept General DeWitt's own unsworn, self-serving statement, untested by any cross-examination, that what he did was reasonable. And thus it will always be when courts try to look into the reasonableness of a military order.

In the very nature of things military decisions are not susceptible of intelligent judicial appraisal. They do not pretend to rest on evidence, but are made on information that often would not be admissible and on assumptions that could not be proved. Information in support of an order could not be disclosed to courts without danger that it would reach the enemy. Neither can courts act on communications made in confidence. Hence courts can never have any real alternative to accepting the mere declaration of the authority that issued the order that it was reasonably necessary from a military viewpoint.

Much is said of the danger to liberty from the Army program for deporting and detaining these citizens of Japanese extraction. But a judicial construction of the due process clause that will sustain this order is a far more subtle blow to liberty than the promulgation of the order itself. A military order, however unconstitutional, is not apt to last longer than the military emergency. Even during that period a succeeding commander may revoke it all. But once a judicial opinion rationalizes such an order to show that it conforms to the Constitution, or rather rationalizes the Constitution to show that the Constitution sanctions such an order, the Court for all time has validated the principle of racial discrimination in criminal procedure and of transplanting American citizens. The principle then lies about like a loaded weapon ready for the hand of any authority that can bring forward a plausible claim of an urgent need. Every repetition imbeds that principle more deeply in our law and thinking and expands it to new purposes. All who observe the work of courts are familiar with what Judge Cardozo described as "the tendency of a principle to expand itself to the limit of its logic." A military commander may overstep the bounds of constitutionality, and it is an incident. But if we review and approve, that passing incident becomes the doctrine of the Constitution. There it has a generative power of its own, and all that it creates will be in its own image. Nothing better illustrates this danger than does the Court's opinion in this case. . . .

I should hold that a civil court cannot be made to enforce an order which violates constitutional limitations even if it is a reasonable exercise of military authority. The courts can exercise only the judicial power, can apply only law, and must abide by the Constitution, or they cease to be civil courts and become instruments of military policy.

Of course the existence of a military power resting on force, so vagrant, so centralized, so necessarily heedless of the individual, is an inherent threat to liberty. But I would not lead people to rely on this Court for a review that seems to me wholly delusive. The military reasonableness of these orders can only be determined by military superiors. If the people ever let command of the war power fall into irresponsible and unscrupulous hands, the courts wield no power equal to its restraint. The chief restraint upon those who command the physical forces of the country, in the future as in the past, must be their responsibility to the political judgments of their contemporaries and to the moral judgments of history.

My duties as a justice as I see them do not require me to make a military judgment as to whether General DeWitt's evacuation and detention program was a reasonable military necessity. I do not suggest that the courts should have attempted to interfere with the Army in carrying out its task. But I do not think they may be asked to execute a military expedient that has no place in law under the Constitution. I would reverse the judgment and discharge the prisoner.

11.

PROFILING IN THE WAKE OF SEPTEMBER 11

THE PRECEDENT OF THE JAPANESE AMERICAN INTERNMENT

Frank H. Wu

The internment of Japanese Americans during World War II is the obvious precedent for the treatment of Arab Americans and Muslim Americans in the aftermath of the September 11, 2001, terrorist attacks. Whether the example should be followed or avoided and what it means generally, however, remains a subject of controversy. The ambivalence is not surprising, because judgments about the internment have vacillated between strong approval and equally strong disapproval. Advocates for the internment during World War II invoked national security and opponents of it in a more recent era appeal to civil rights, but the dialogue over it has rarely proceeded beyond the superficial level. The internment has been the most studied aspect of Asian American history, but it deserves greater consideration by all citizens who care about the proper course of conduct during the present crisis.

At the time, virtually everyone in public life supported the mass incarceration of approximately 120,000 men, women, elderly, and children, some two-thirds of them native-born US citizens. There were no criminal charges brought against them, no trials before juries, and no findings of guilt before almost all persons of Japanese descent on the West Coast were ordered, in many cases on only a few days' notice, into camps built in desolate swamp and desert areas. Allowed to take only what they could carry in what was euphemistically termed an "evacuation," they remained behind barbed wire, under the watch of armed soldiers in guard towers.

President Franklin Delano Roosevelt signed the executive order authorizing the internment to proceed. Congress subsequently passed a public law ratifying his action with no deliberation. The Supreme Court took four cases in which it effectively allowed the internment without ever directly passing on the constitutionality of the indefinite detention of persons based on racial suspicion. Future chief justice Earl Warren, then a California politician, favored the plans. Erudite newspaper columnist Walter Lippmann did so as well. . . .

Even the national ACLU refused to challenge the internment, because it backed President Roosevelt on other policies. Its California chapters broke away, taking on that responsibility. . . . Only a few individuals and organizations, such as the pacifist Society of Friends (Quakers), sided with Japanese Americans.

The internment can be readily critiqued in retrospect because the racial prejudice was open. After all, this was still the "Jim Crow" era. . . .

At heart, the internment was the association of Japanese Americans with the Japanese empire. Although the shock, anger, and fear generated by the devastating strike on Pearl Harbor was perhaps natural, the displacement of those volatile emotions on Japanese Americans, who made up less than 1 percent of the population of California, the state in which they were concentrated, depended on assumptions about ancestry. What Japan had done was blamed on Japanese Americans. After the day of infamy, they became officially "enemy aliens" in the eyes of other Americans. Citizenship ceased to matter. The justification of the internment as employing ethnicity, rather than race, as the dispositive issue is unpersuasive. The category of "Japanese" was at the time less an ethnicity than a race. Ethnicity only became a common term as a euphemism for race; and in any event ethnicity is only slightly less crude but no less immutable than race, for both are rooted in the idea of "blood" determining identity.

There were spectacular allegations made at the time—all of them eventually proven to be unfounded—that Japanese Americans had planted their crops in Hawaii to point toward targets to be bombed; that Japanese Americans had used amateur radio signals to direct Japanese ships; and that pilots on the Zero fighter planes wore sweatshirts from United States high schools. Others said that Japanese Americans blocked the roads to prevent rescue vehicles from passing and that they were lacing their produce with poison before sending it to the markets. Japanese Americans were rumored to have formed a "fifth column" that would enable Japanese troops to invade triumphantly. (The term "fifth column" comes from the Spanish Civil War. Asked, as they marched toward Madrid, which of their four columns would take the city, the Nationalists said it would be the fifth column of sympathizers already inside the city.)

Remarkably, in the period of officially sanctioned racial prejudice that preceded *Brown v. Board of Education* (1954), Justice Hugo Black, who authored the majority opinion in the *Korematsu* decision, made it appear as if racial animus would be improper in government action. In the best known of the Supreme Court cases on the internment, Justice Black wrote that "our task would be simple, our duty clear, were this a case involving the imprisonment of a loyal citizen in a concentration camp because of racial prejudice."

As often happens, even though race had been politically relevant, it was rendered legally irrelevant. Justice Black dismissed the accusation that any such bias was involved in the internment. He stated, "Korematsu was not excluded from the Military Area because of hostility to him or his race." Rather, "he was excluded because we are at war with the Japanese Empire" and there was "evidence of disloyalty on the part of some."

Thus, Justice Black's opinion has an unsettling gap in it. There is nothing that connects Korematsu to Japan or others who may have been disloyal. Justice Black, a former member of the Ku Klux Klan who downplayed his affiliation with the group as a political obligation, tried to preempt objections to his reasoning with the caveat: "To cast this case into outlines of racial prejudice, without reference to the real military dangers which were presented, merely confuses the issue."

Justice Black's disclaimer notwithstanding, the nexus between Korematsu and Japan, or Korematsu and other individuals, is crucial but missing. It is Korematsu's heritage. Other than that, Korematsu has no more linkage to Japan than any other Californian and he was not shown to be personally disloyal. . . .

Strangely, the internment cases appear to have evaded the most basic question. That question is whether it is constitutional to order the mass incarceration of persons as to whom no individual showing of guilt has been made, ostensibly because of national security, though also with the use of racial classifications. The internment proceeded in stages, however, and not all at once. The Court was able to take up cases that addressed the preliminary phases, delaying addressing the camps themselves until the government had ordered their closure. . . .

In the *Korematsu* case, it is astonishing that the court states: "It will be time enough to decide the serious constitutional issues which petitioner seeks to raise when an assembly or relocation order is applied or is certain to be applied to him, and we have its terms before us." The Court's decision allowed the internment, but did not approve of it. The Court actually was adamant that it was not passing upon "the whole subsequent detention program in both assembly and relocation centers." . . .

This less than forthright reasoning of the legal cases matched the politics of the internment. As numerous commentators have pointed out, the intelligence community had already concluded that the Japanese American threat, such as it was, had been adequately contained. The naval intelligence officer who had the Japan portfolio even wrote an anonymous magazine article cautioning that the risks from Japanese Americans were being dramatically overstated.

Legal historian Peter Irons has amply documented Justice Department apprehensions that military claims about Japanese Americans were exaggerated or even false. The lawyers who wished to alert the Supreme Court to the factual flaws infecting the basis for the internment were overruled by their superiors at the last minute.[1]

The inconsistencies of the internment become apparent if the territory of Hawaii is considered. If the internment was warranted, it should have been instituted in Hawaii with greatest priority because Pearl Harbor had occurred there and it sat within the theater of operations. Although such a possibility was briefly considered, it was quickly dismissed. Locking up Japanese Americans in Hawaii would have meant that a third of the population, and the bulk of the workforce on the plantations that were the mainstay of the islands' economy, would be removed. The need for workers and the profits they produced trumped racial hatred. The military, as well, was not interested in the task of rounding up and shipping out thousands of civilians.

Likewise, the impression that the internment concerned only foreign nationals, who manifestly do not enjoy the same rights as citizens, is belied by the handling of German immigrants and Italian immigrants. Unlike Japanese immigrants, who could not have become citizens due to the racial bar, their German and Italian counterparts were not sent to internment camps as a group (though the former had faced extensive discrimination during the Great War). . . . German Americans and Italian Americans were deemed to be dangerous only in extreme individual instances and internment was thought to be impractical. . . .

Almost a half century later, when compensation for the internees was being debated, a few members of Congress insisted that Japanese Americans should not be paid until Japan made amends to United States prisoners of war. They still equated Japanese Americans with Japan.

By and large, though, the contemporary conception of the internment has been negative. Our national memory until recently has been radically different from the outlook of the World War II era. After a lengthy period when most Americans forgot about the internment and even many Japanese Americans felt shame over their fate and strove to overcome its effects, a consensus gradually developed that it had been a mistake.

Presidents of both political parties, beginning with Gerald Ford, apologized for it. Ford also rescinded Roosevelt's Executive Order 9066. According to the nonpartisan independent government commission that convened hearings and undertook a thorough investigation some forty years later, the internment had been motivated by wartime hysteria, racial prejudice, and failure of political leadership—not military necessity. Its report, representative of later opinion, persuaded Congress in 1988 to pass legislation paying reparations in the amount of $20,000 to each surviving individual who had been confined in the camps. Even the convictions of the three men who litigated the propriety of the internment to the highest court in the land—Fred Korematsu, Gordon Hirabayashi, and Min Yasui—were vacated on obscure writs of coram nobis. The vacating of the convictions in individual cases has not diminished the strength of the Supreme Court precedent.

The events of September 11, 2001, have prompted further reconsideration. Politicians, pundits, and a majority of the population have embraced diversity at least on the surface. Other than a few ideologues, who foresee an ultimate "clash of civilizations," and a handful of extremists, nobody has described the war on terrorism as a war against all Arabs or all Muslims. Regardless of partisan affiliation, most leaders have taken pains to disavow such notions.

All the same, respected voices are being raised for racial profiling, and the rhetoric of welcoming all races and religions may not match the reality of law enforcement. Syndicated columnist Stuart Taylor Jr., among others, has argued that at airport checkpoints, individuals who are Arab- or Muslim-appearing should be subjected to more intensive searches.

It turns out, once again, to be easy enough to surrender the civil rights of somebody else. Oddly, few have bothered to explain how or why racial profiling would be effective. The tension between national security and civil liberties is taken for granted. Yet the national security side of the equation is speculative and rests on the familiar warning that if this war is lost there will be no rights or liberties for anybody at all. Even those who embraced color blindness, primarily in attacks on racial remedies, have given up their beliefs. Whatever the pros and cons of racial profiling, color blindness and racial profiling are inherently incompatible.

Some opinion polls even suggest that African Americans, long victims of racial profiling in domestic criminal prosecutions and despite their protests about the "driving while black" problem, are just as willing as everyone else to adopt racial profiling of Arab Americans and Muslim Americans as potential terrorists. Bush administration transportation secretary Norman Mineta has been assailed for his refusal to direct the racial profiling of Arab Americans and Muslim Americans at airport checkpoints. The cabinet member has even been mocked for recalling his own experience as a Japanese American, interned as a child of eight.

The condemnation of the internment may lead to the condoning of milder measures in the classical fallacy of false alternatives. Anything short of an internment is compared to the internment, as if to say it could be worse and so there is no cause for complaint. To be fair, racial profiling can be carried out in a much milder form than internment camps. To be precise, the current secret detentions are best likened to the apprehension of hundreds of Japanese Americans, German Americans, and Italian Americans and the curfews and other measures that preceded the internment itself.

In that context, the conclusion that the internment was wrong is not enough. The reasons it was wrong must be articulated again. As lawyers well know, the rationale may be as important as the result by itself in comprehending the meaning of legal authority. What is constitutional is not necessarily advisable. Technically, for all the contempt directed at the Supreme Court's internment cases, it is worth noting that the decisions have never been repudiated and actually have been followed consistently. Indeed, Chief Justice William H. Rehnquist penned a book a few years ago intimating that if a similar matter were to come before the Court again he would not expect it do otherwise.[2]

Imagining the counterfactual hypothetical of a Supreme Court that struck down the internment, then, also entails supplying an intellectual foundation. There are multiple possibilities. They lead to different outcomes in today's circumstances. If the internment was wrong because racial classifications are to be regarded as immoral or unconstitutional as an absolute rule, then there is no distinction to be made between Japanese Americans on the one hand and Arab Americans or Muslim Americans on the other hand. The form of the argument does not vary by specific groups.

If the internment was wrong because the particular racial generalization was in the aggregate false, then it may well be possible and appropriate to distinguish between the Japanese Americans and Arab Americans or Muslim Americans. The premise is that the conduct of Japanese Americans on the whole does not predict the conduct of Arab Americans or Muslim Americans on the whole.

There are more possibilities. If the internment was wrong because of the lack of any semblance of due process, then even the German Americans and Italian Americans in isolated cases had their rights violated. Individual Arabs and Muslims who are aliens may be entitled to more due process than equal protection.

If the internment was wrong because it yields other social costs that were not properly weighted in a utilitarian calculus, then all such factors should be taken into account. The incentives created by racial profiling for its subjects may be considerable. Some Arab Americans and Muslim Americans, like anyone else, might be more eager to cooperate with patriotic efforts if they did not have the sense that war was being waged on a racial or religious ground. Even the suggestion that people should tolerate modest impositions is galling, because it is only some persons, already marginalized, who are imposed upon. What looks like a light touch to observers can feel like an awfully heavy hand to those who feel it. . . .

Whatever the Court's resolution of the cases that are already arising, the internment offers lessons. Consider the argument that all of the hijackers involved in the World Trade Center and Pentagon suicide bombings were Arab or Muslim men, and, therefore, it is common sense to subject all Arab and Muslim men to extra security measures at airports because the likelihood is greater that they will be terrorists. Paralleling the contention that some Japanese Americans were surely traitors and it was impossible to verify who exactly among them, this line of thinking accepts without any skepticism that what is superficially reasonable is automatically right. It permits low probabilities to prevail over civil liberties.

The argument relies on the logical fallacy of illicit conversion. That most X are Y or, even, all X are Y, does not mean that most Y are X: all men are human beings, but not all human beings are men. The error lies in believing that if a large number or all the terrorists are Arab or Muslim, that all Arabs or Muslims—and even those who resemble Arabs and Muslims—are terrorists or should be treated as if they were.

The trouble is not solely academic. Most Arab Americans are not Muslim; most Muslims in the United States are South Asian or African American; and the post–September 11 backlash of violence has revealed our collective carelessness in assaulting Indian Sikhs— neither Arab nor Muslim but persons who look like they might be Arab or Muslim because of skin color, accents, and dress.

The casual characterization of the current detainees in various contexts as "immigrants" also groups together many categories whose constitutional and statutory rights are not at all identical. It may include naturalized citizens or native-born citizens who have been raised outside the United States; it certainly encompasses lawful permanent residents, along with nonimmigrants who have overstayed or violated their visas, and entrants without inspection ("illegal aliens"). The prisoners who were Taliban fighters, held by the military at Guantanamo Bay, are not the same as the internees, though: the former are combatants for an enemy (even if not a government), but the latter were civilians of the United States itself.

Critics of racial profiling have two independent arguments available to them. One argument is the direct rebuttal of the factual claim. It may well be that the respective probabilities that a random older, white, Protestant American woman and the probability that a younger, Arab Muslim immigrant male are wrongdoers are not the same. But even were there a thousand sleeper agents of Arab descent or Muslim faith ready to rise up in arms against democracy they would constitute far less than a fraction of one-tenth of 1 percent of the Arab and Muslim populations of the United States. It is worth disputing whether the disparity in the chances are great enough to offset the tremendous cost to not just Arab Americans and Muslims but all of us if we relinquish our principle of individualism and presumption of innocence. Another argument is a more robust moral claim. It is the conviction that even were it rational in an accounting of costs and benefits to eliminate civil rights for a "discrete and insular" minority group, it would not be right to do so.

Whatever we decide to do to respond to the risks following September 11, 2001, we must regard the internment cases seriously again. In the most practical sense, every litigator—challenging or defending practices that are alleged to be both necessary for national security but infringements on civil rights—and every court will have to opt for one of the readings of the internment cases suggested above. The choices we make will set new precedent, which will extend into many other areas. It will reshape our shared understanding of who can become a citizen, what it means to be a citizen, of the rights and responsibilities that define such status.

It is true, even if it became a cliché instantly, that our nation was changed profoundly on September 11, 2001, and will never be the same again. It also is true, even if less noticed, that our nation is as it was, a diverse democracy, and those twin values of diversity and democracy are enduring ideals that are worth fighting for. The bumper sticker slogan and sound bite "United We Stand" has become popular. If it is to be a reality, more than a bumper sticker slogan and sound bite, we all must stand up and speak out, each of us standing alongside, by, and for somebody else who does not look like us.

NOTES

1. Peter Irons, *Justice at War: The Story of the Japanese American Internment Cases* (Oxford: Oxford University Press, 1983).

2. William H. Rehnquist, *All the Laws but One: Civil Liberties in Wartime* (New York: Alfred A. Knopf, 1998).

12.

THE SKIES WON'T BE SAFE UNTIL WE USE COMMONSENSE PROFILING

Stuart Taylor Jr.

T he government's effort to upgrade airport security over the past six months has been massive and expensive: federalizing airport security forces; confiscating toenail clippers; frisking randomly chosen grandmothers, members of Congress, former CIA directors, and decorated military officers; stationing National Guard troops in airports; putting sky marshals on planes. Has it been effective?

Not effective enough. The main reason is that civil libertarians, Arab American activists, editorial writers, and most of polite society have virtuously eschewed the one measure—profiling based in part on national origin—that holds out the best hope of thwarting any skillful al Qaeda terrorists who may try to smuggle bombs aboard airliners. More important, Transportation Secretary Norman Mineta has done the same in his public statements as of this writing, such as his assertion in a television interview aired on December 2 that seventy-year-old white women should get the same scrutiny as young Muslim men.

Mineta is said to be considering the radical step of injecting some common sense into the profiling rules, if he has not done so already. (The detailed rules are secret.) . . . But there has been no hint that he will depart from his previous suggestions (mirroring the rules he inherited from the Clinton administration) that security screeners may pay no attention at all, ever, to the outwardly apparent traits—skin color, facial features, speech patterns, accents, names—that correlate with Middle Eastern origins. If that remains the rule, a passenger who looks and sounds just like Mohamed Atta, and who has, say, a Florida driver's license, will apparently not be targeted for individual searching unless he is too dense to avoid the various suspicious behaviors that trigger the profiling system. Those behaviors—paying cash, holding a one-way ticket, acting furtive, arriving recently from Pakistan, and the like—are not all that hard to avoid.

It's easy to understand the reluctance of Mineta and others to target passengers for individual searches based solely on how they look and sound. History gives us ample reasons to fear the slippery slope to which such profiling could lead. But the next Mohamed Atta may give us no other clue that would trigger an individual search. It's an agonizing dilemma.

I fear that a policy of ignoring apparent national origin and ethnicity may court disaster. And the social taboo against any approach that could be characterized (unfairly) as racial profiling has muzzled honest discussion of profiling, in the media and among politicians. Fewer than 10 percent of all checked bags go through any kind of bomb-detection machine, because we now have fewer than two hundred of the more than twenty-two hundred high-tech, minivan-sized bomb-detection machines that it would take to screen all bags. Only a small fraction of passengers and bags can be searched by hand without intolerable delays. The stopgap bag-matching system instituted earlier this year does not match bags to passengers on connecting flights and would have no effect on suicidal terrorists.

In short, as the *New York Times* reports, the "soothing veneer of security . . . may be far thinner than many passengers imagine," and "no real progress has been made on bomb detection." What the *Times* won't tell you, lest it break the taboo, is that we might be able to make flying far safer almost overnight by using profiles that take account not only of suspicious behaviors, gender, and age, but also of the outwardly apparent traits shared by most militant Muslims from those regions where al Qaeda finds most of its recruits—the very traits that the government's published rules tell security screeners to ignore. A well-designed profile that included such traits would properly be called "national-origin profiling," not "racial profiling." The main difference is that millions of Americans of Middle Eastern ethnicity would not fit the profile, because their speech patterns and travel documents would clearly indicate that they are long-standing residents of this country.

To be sure, a profile that takes account of apparent national origin (as well as one that does not) might miss a John Walker Lindh or a Timothy McVeigh. No profile is foolproof. But that doesn't justify being foolish. A well-designed profiling system would have singled out all nineteen of the September 11 hijackers for special attention. And even though box cutters were not then prohibited on planes, security screeners might have wondered why groups of four and five Middle Eastern men were all carrying such potential weapons onto airliners the same morning.

The odds that any Middle Eastern passenger is a terrorist are, of course, tiny. But if you make the plausible assumptions that al Qaeda terrorists are at least one hundred times as likely to be from the Middle East as to be native-born Americans, and that fewer than 5 percent of all passengers on domestic flights are Middle Eastern men, it would follow that a randomly chosen Middle Eastern male passenger is roughly two thousand times as likely to be an al Qaeda terrorist as a randomly chosen native-born American. It is crazy to ignore such odds.

While the politically correct approach to profiling still seems to be an article of faith in many quarters, some liberals (along with many conservatives) are talking sense. One is Rep. Barney Frank (D-MA), perhaps the smartest civil libertarian in Congress. During a March 6 debate at Georgetown University Law Center, Frank forthrightly asserted that airline security profiles should take account of national origin. He cautioned that a well-designed profile would also include "a bunch of factors" that may warrant suspicion; that "if only . . . young men from the Middle East were being profiled, it would be a problem"; and that the ideal system would be to search all passengers and their luggage thoroughly for bombs and other weapons. But Frank also stressed: "I do think that at this point, [national] origin would be part of it. . . . In certain countries, people are angrier at us than elsewhere."

Frank distinguished such airport profiling from the discredited police practice of "pulling over some black kid because he's driving," to search for drugs, which he called "a terrible intrusion." In airport screening, Frank said, the stakes are much higher—with many lives at risk if a bomb or weapon slips through—and the "incremental" intrusion on those profiled is minimal. "If no harm is being done, and you're not being in any way disadvantaged, I am reluctant to think that there's any great problem," he said.

The vacuousness of the arguments that have been made against politically incorrect profiling is typified by a recent *Newsweek* column by Anna Quindlen asserting that the case for "selective screening" based on ethnicity "collapsed amid reports that nine of the September 11 hijackers were indeed specially screened." That's about 180 degrees off. Those nine were apparently chosen based on their reservation-buying patterns, not ethnicity or national origin. And the screening appears to have been limited largely to searching checked bags: Arab American activists and civil libertarians had prevailed on the government, not only to bar any profiling based on ethnicity, religion, or national origin in its Computer-Assisted Passenger Prescreening System, but also to avoid intrusive searches of the persons or carry-on bags of even those passengers who did fit the CAPPS profile.

Similar lobbying also succeeded in denying security screeners any access to law enforcement databases. That may help explain why the two hijackers who were on the CIA-FBI "watch list" of suspected terrorists were nonetheless able to board airliners with such ease on September 11. The new profiling system will include sharing of such intelligence. Good. But most al Qaeda terrorists—including seventeen of the September 11 hijackers—appear in no intelligence database.

"The most offensive profiles are those that are based on characteristics a person cannot change," including "race, religion, national origin, [and] gender," Katie Corrigan of the American Civil Liberties Union said in congressional testimony on February 27. But offensive or no, the only profiles likely to be effective against a well-trained terrorist are those triggered by traits that he cannot change or easily conceal. Corrigan added that profiling is a cheap, imperfect alternative to expensive security devices. She's right. But those security devices are not and will not be in place for many months, perhaps years. For now, intelligent profiling is indispensable.

The blessed absence of terrorist attacks on airliners since September 11 (excepting would-be shoe-bomber Richard Reid) appears to be fostering the complacent assumption that our security system works. The assumption is dubious. The politically correct approach to profiling amounts to a bet that al Qaeda is no longer interested in airline terrorism. The bet is irrational.

13.

RACIAL PROFILING REVISITED

"JUST COMMON SENSE" IN THE FIGHT AGAINST TERROR?

David A. Harris

W e have all heard, many times, that the events of September 11 "changed everything." Many political issues that had stood front and center in the national debate before that day abruptly assumed back-burner status; others disappeared altogether.

Racial profiling—an issue of broad national concern before September 11—did not become less important nor did it disappear. Instead, it was recast and dramatically changed. Before September 11, polling data had shown that almost 60 percent of Americans—not just African Americans and Latinos, but all Americans—understood what racial profiling was, thought it was an unfair and unwise law enforcement tactic, and wanted it eliminated. After September 11, that same percentage, including those minority citizens most often subjected to past profiling, said that they thought some racial or ethnic profiling in the context of airport searches was acceptable and even necessary as long as the group profiled consisted of Arabs, Muslims, and other Middle Easterners.

From "Racial Profiling Revisited: 'Just Common Sense' in the Fight against Terror?" *Criminal Justice* (Summer 2002). Copyright © 2002 by the American Bar Association; David A. Harris. Reprinted by permssion.

This is not particularly hard to understand. After all, the nineteen suicide hijackers who attacked the World Trade Center and the Pentagon on September 11 were all young Arab Muslims from the Middle East. And the group claiming responsibility for the attacks, al Qaeda, draws its legitimacy from an interpretation of Islam that cites the wrongs done to Muslims in the Middle East by nonbelievers. Therefore, most people say it simply makes sense to focus our law enforcement energies on Arab and Middle Eastern men; like it or not, they are the people who constitute the real threat to us, and no amount of political correctness will change that.

But just because it is easy to understand this reasoning does not mean it is correct. No matter how intuitively obvious it may seem, the use of racial and ethnic profiling, even in today's circumstances, is a huge mistake that jeopardizes the strength of our antiterrorism initiatives. When we look at what we have learned about racial profiling on highways and city streets over the last few years, we see there is good reason to avoid using this tool to fight al Qaeda—to refuse to take the easy, quick-fix path of racial profiling.

In times of great national fear and real threat, it is tempting to say that we must do everything we can to make ourselves safe, even if that means sacrificing individual liberties we normally seek to preserve. But we should not restructure our society and the principles that make it great without asking whether these changes would, in fact, make us any safer.

WHAT WE KNEW BEFORE SEPTEMBER 11

Before September 11, a national consensus had emerged about racial profiling: it is a biased and unfair police practice that Americans wanted eliminated. This consensus resulted, in no small part, from the data released in the mid-1990s that substantiated, for the first time, the stories told by African Americans and Latinos of being stopped, searched, and treated like suspects by the police. The data proved to a majority of Americans that these were not just stories or excuses used by criminals trying to escape wrongdoing, but manifestations of a real phenomenon, something we could observe and measure.

For example, in data submitted by the Maryland State Police to a federal court, African Americans comprised more than 70 percent of all drivers stopped and searched, even though they represented just 17 percent of all drivers on the road. To be sure, not every police department, and not every police officer, used racial or ethnic profiling. But it was common enough that most minority men and women, of all ages, professions, and classes, had either experienced it firsthand, or had close relatives or friends who had.

The availability of these data brought about an important shift in the public debate. Fewer defenders of the police denied the existence of racial profiling. Rather, they insisted that such profiling was not racist; it was just commonsense crime fighting. Defenders of profiling argued that because African Americans and Latinos were disproportionately represented among those arrested and imprisoned, smart police officers focused their enforcement efforts on these racial and ethnic groups. The fact that this resulted in disproportionate numbers of stops, searches, and arrests of African Americans and Latinos was, according to a spokesman for the Maryland State Police, simply "the unfortunate by-product of sound police policy."

In order to advance the debate, researchers and scholars needed to confront the assumption head-on. Did racial profiling, in fact, make for better and more productive law enforcement? It was already clear that racial profiling existed, given the data from the mid-1990s. Many Americans were already aware of the high social costs of profiling: the distrust of police, cynicism about the courts and the law, an unwillingness to believe police officers testifying as witnesses in court. These factors were often dismissed as just the costs of fighting crime and drugs, since it was assumed that profiling did, indeed, fight crime. Thus the importance of testing the assumption. Did racial profiling really help police officers find the bad guys more often?

Data that became available in the late 1990s made such testing possible for the first time. These data, from police departments of all kinds from all over the country, allowed the study of "hit rates"—the success rates for police stops and searches using racial profiling as opposed to those stops and searches using traditional, nonracial criteria that focus simply on observation of suspicious behavior. Hit rates indicate the rate at which police find what they seek—drugs, guns, people with arrest warrants, and the like—when they execute a stop and search. In these studies, stops and searches of Caucasians were not counted as profiling because they were based not on race, but on observed behavior that appeared suspicious. Stops and searches of African Americans and Latinos, on the other hand, may have been based on some suspicious behavior, but were driven, overwhelmingly, by race or ethnic appearance. This is why, in all of these studies, African Americans and Latinos were stopped in numbers greatly disproportionate to their presence on the highways, roads, or city sidewalks. With these data broken down by racial categories for each of the police departments studied, I was able to make an apples-to-apples, side-by-side comparison of police behavior within particular police departments, both with and without the variable of race or ethnicity.

The results of these hit-rate studies were striking, all the more so for their consistency across many different jurisdictions and law enforcement agencies. The data on hit rates show that targeting by law enforcement using racial or ethnic appearance does not, in fact, improve policing. It actually makes policing worse—less successful, less productive, less likely to find guns, drugs, and bad guys. Contrary to what the proponents of profiling might expect, hit rates were not higher using racial profiling. In fact, hit rates for race-based stops were lower—significantly lower—than the hit rates for traditional, nonprofile-based policing. That is, when police used racial and ethnic profiling to target black and brown populations as suspicious, the results they got were uniformly poorer than the results they got when they stopped whites simply on the basis of suspicious behavior. Racial profiling, then, doesn't improve policing; it pulls it down, delivering less bang for the law enforcement buck. Even if we ignore the high social costs—distrust of all government, including police and the legal system; exacerbation of existing problems such as residential segregation and employment discrimination; and destruction of valuable law enforcement initiatives such as community policing—racial profiling as a means to crime reduction simply does not deliver.

A LITTLE HISTORY

The use of race or ethnic appearance as a proxy to tell police officers who the likely criminals might be did not begin recently. Some trace profiling back all the way to the slave patrols, which were empowered to stop and demand an explanation from any black person unaccompanied by a white person, as well as to search blacks' dwellings for contraband, such as books. But it was in the 1980s that certain segments of law enforcement certainly honed the tactic to perfection. Racial profiling was not an accident, and it was not the result of a few bad apples in policing. It was the predictable outcome of a number of decisions by the US Supreme Court that allowed police to use traffic enforcement as a convenient and universally available means to make end runs around the requirements of the Fourth Amendment. And it was the federal government, through the Drug Enforcement Administration, that deliberately made use of these opportunities.

As far back as 1973, the US Supreme Court confronted the possibility that police officers might use arrests, traffic stops, and other traditional enforcement mechanisms as pretexts to do what would otherwise be forbidden by the Fourth Amendment in the absence of probable cause or a warrant or both. In *Robinson v. United States* (1973) the Supreme Court allowed police to perform a full search incident to a traffic arrest, despite the lack of any reason to fear the presence of weapons or the destruction of evidence, the two traditional rationales for searches incident to a valid arrest. The real intentions of the police officer in making the arrest, that is, whether the arrest might be nothing but an excuse for a search or seizure for which there was no supporting evidence at all, did not matter. All that was important, the Court said, was that there was valid probable cause for the arrest.

Robinson set the stage for a series of decisions through the 1970s, 1980s, and 1990s that increased police discretion and the ability to use stops and searches as pretexts to do what would otherwise be impermissible under the Fourth Amendment. . . .

As a result, racial profiling became a national topic of conversation in the mid- and late 1990s not simply because of occasional overzealous law enforcement. On the contrary, profiling was an entirely predictable outcome of US Supreme Court decisions that broadened police power and discretion to make traffic and pedestrian stops and searches to the point that this discretion was for all practical purposes unlimited. That police took advantage of the authority these decisions gave them is understandable. Indeed, it would have been surprising if they had not. . . .

Yet the inhospitability of the courts to opponents of racial profiling is, perhaps surprisingly, where the story grows more encouraging. Lack of success in using judicial routes to create change has forced opponents of profiling to find other avenues: the use and mobilization of public opinion and concerted pushes for legislative measures. These efforts have met with surprising success. By the beginning of 2002, fifteen state legislatures had enacted some kind of law concerning racial profiling. These laws ranged from simple requirements that police departments collect data on some or all of their traffic stops to laws that require new antiprofiling policies, training, and other initiatives, in addition to data collection. Besides these new laws, hundreds of police departments have, on their own and without any state law requirement, begun to collect data to track their traffic and other stops and searches, and have revised their policies. In a way, this is far more important than state legislative action. It shows that these police departments have recognized the fact that it is in their own interest to face the issue of profiling head-on and to forthrightly collect information on police practices, regardless of what it may or may not show. . . .

WHAT ABOUT NOW?

Since September 11, of course, much has changed in our national discussion of policing strategy, not least the shift in focus from anticrime to antiterrorism. Given all that we now know—a lethal attack upon thousands of innocent civilians by al Qaeda, a Muslim organization in which the weapons of mass destruction were airplanes hijacked and flown by nineteen Muslim Arab men from the Middle East—how is it possible to ignore the fact that being Arab or Muslim means that one is more likely to be involved in terrorism? Doesn't it just make sense to use a racial or ethnic profile that singles out Arabs, Muslims, and other Middle Easterners for greater attention, including more frequent stops and searches? Isn't anyone suggesting tactics to the contrary simply suffering from blindness of political correctness? Syndicated columnist Kathleen Parker has given voice to this way of thinking. "When a police officer apprehends and searches an African American only because he's black, assuming no other mitigating factors, that's unjustified racial profiling. When an airport security guard searches a male of Middle Eastern extraction following a historical terrorist attack by males of Middle Eastern extraction, that's common sense." Parker wrote that "a terrorist attack of such enormous proportions, followed by a declaration of war, makes racial profiling a temporary necessity that no patriotic American should protest."[1]

To a large extent, that is the way things have gone. In the wake of the attacks of September 11, Arabs and other Middle Easterners were removed from planes. Others were repeatedly searched and questioned. More serious, the US Department of Justice detained hundreds of Arabs and Muslims—not one of whom has been linked to the September 11 attacks. The department also undertook the "voluntary" questioning of five thousand, and then another three thousand, young Arab men who were, according to the US attorney general, not suspects, in the hope of learning something, anything, that might help. (Law enforcement professionals reacted by quietly refusing to take part in the questioning and commenting that this tactic differed markedly from established methods for conducting antiterrorism investigations.) The government has also announced an "absconder initiative" in which it will focus its deportation efforts on six thousand men from Middle Eastern nations who have violated their visas—despite the fact that they make up only the tiniest fraction of all the hundreds of thousands of violators.

These actions may seem intuitively correct, but it is not at all clear that they are, in fact, the right way to proceed. If we look at what has happened in the past with racial profiling, we will see that there are real reasons to hesitate to take the profiling path now. In fact, using racial or ethnic profiles to protect ourselves against al Qaeda operatives will likely have an effect opposite of what we desire. Our antiterrorism cause will be set back, not advanced.

First, think of what we might call the gold standard of traditional policing: the observation of suspicious behavior. Veteran police officers know there is no substitute for this. It's not what people look like that tells the savvy officer who is suspicious; it's what people do that matters. Using a racial or ethnic profile to decide whom to regard as suspicious cuts directly against this experience-based principle. Some people do look different than the majority, of course, and we know that those in the majority often tend to see people who are different as threatening or suspicious. The net result is that those who look different, especially in some skin-deep way that we equate with danger, come under immediate suspicion without any suspicious behavior; our law enforcement agents shift their attention from what counts—how people behave—to what doesn't: what they look like. We could not make a bigger mistake than to take our eyes so completely off the ball.

A second point is related to the first. If we use racial and ethnic profiles, instead of behavioral clues, to decide which people we think should be treated as suspects, we will greatly enlarge our suspect pool. This is true whether our profiles are based only on race or ethnicity (a very unlikely event) or if race or ethnicity is just one characteristic among many in a multifactor profile. This means that our enforcement resources will be spread thinner than they would if they were part of an effort focused on suspicious behavior. This is not a trivial consequence. On the contrary, our enforcement resources will be stretched to address many more individuals, and, therefore, they will be that much less effective. This points to one of profiling's inherent flaws: it is always overinclusive. Judging whether individuals are suspicious based on their racial or ethnic characteristics means that many people who would not otherwise draw the attention of law enforcement get swept into the dragnet. Of course, this is exactly what happened to African Americans and Latinos profiled during the war on drugs. It wasn't just the drug dealer on the corner, but the minister, the doctor, and the businessman who were stopped, searched, and treated like suspects. Many more minorities were stopped because of their color than would have been the case had police simply looked for suspicious behavior. In the antiterrorism context, not even the FBI has unlimited manpower. Even with the aid of state and local antiterrorism task forces, little can hold us back more completely than increasing the enforcement burden beyond what focusing on behavior would call for.

If focusing on suspicious behavior is the gold standard in policing, an accompanying principle is the importance of collecting and using information and intelligence. If we are to avoid attacks in the future by al Qaeda operatives based on our own soil, we need to do much better in the intelligence arena than we did before September 11. And that, of course, means we will have to get information from those likely to know the Arab, Muslim, and Middle Eastern men we might suspect. This information is going to have to come not from the population at large, but from the Middle Eastern communities themselves; there is simply no avoiding this. It stands to reason, then, that what we need most right now are good, solid relations with the Arab and Muslim communities in the United States. Profiling that focuses on Arab and Muslim heritage will effectively communicate to these very same communities that we regard all of their members not as our partners in law enforcement and terror prevention, but just the opposite: as potential terrorists. When every young Arab or Muslim man is effectively labeled a potential terrorist, when many are detained indefinitely on petty immigration violations, and even those who have come forward to help have been rewarded with incarceration, it is not hard to imagine the result: alienation and anger toward the authorities at a time when we can least afford it.

The interesting thing about the "common sense" of profiling Middle Easterners is how roundly and quickly many law enforcement professionals rejected it. Attorney General John Ashcroft's directive ordering the "voluntary" questioning of five thousand Middle Eastern men was met by skepticism in a number of major police departments. Command staff quickly recognized the damage that this questioning would do to their long-term efforts to build crime-fighting partnerships with their Middle Eastern communities. Some departments quietly refused to take part or were happy to leave the task to FBI agents; a few police officials publicly rejected the Department of Justice's requests that they take part. Eight former FBI officials, including the former chief of both the FBI and the CIA, William H. Webster, went on record with [their] doubts about the law enforcement value of these tactics; one former official called the wholesale questioning "the Perry Mason School of Law Enforcement."[2] Little wonder, then, that senior US intelligence officials circulated a memorandum early in the fall that warned about the dangers of profiling. This memorandum, first reported in the *Boston Globe*, urged law enforcement and intelligence agents to balk at racial profiling. Profiling would fail, the memorandum said; the only way to catch terrorists was the observation of suspicious behavior.[3] Too bad that this warning never seems to have penetrated to the senior levels of the Department of Justice leadership.

Despite all of this, many continue to argue that it doesn't make sense to screen anyone at airports besides young Arab and Middle Eastern men. After all, why waste time and resources stopping or searching anyone else when we already know exactly who the "real" suspicious people are? This argument shows a serious misunderstanding of the nature of what we are up against in al Qaeda. The most important thing for us to realize about this organization is that beyond its vicious and murderous elements, it has also shown itself to be intelligent, patient, and thoroughly adaptable. These are the qualities that make it a formidable enemy. The attack on the World Trade Center on September 11 was not the first but the second assault on this landmark. When the first attack in 1993 failed to accomplish their goal, the terrorists pulled back and spent eight years devising an entirely new method of attack—planned to the smallest detail and then practiced so that it could be carried out almost perfectly. Despite our important military successes in Afghanistan, this set of qualities remains very much alive in the al Qaeda structure. In the aftermath of September 11, we began to harden cockpit doors, to check carry-on bags for even the smallest potential weapons, and to profile Middle Eastern men. Al Qaeda's answer was Richard Reid—a non-Arab, non–Middle Easterner from England; a British citizen with a valid British passport and a bomb in his shoe. Clearly, they knew what we were looking for, and they did not repeat what they had done in the past.

Those who insist that it is a waste of time to look at any non-Arab, who want all Arabs carefully screened and searched despite the lack of any suspicious behavior, seem to have missed this point entirely. Terrorists generally, and al Qaeda specifically, will always look for new weaknesses to use as their point of attack. Just such a weakness became glaringly obvious in mid-January 2002 when the government announced that it could not meet the deadline for having all bags aboard airliners electronically screened for explosives. Instead, the authorities said, they would use a group of other stopgap measures such as partial bag matching. It is much more likely that the next attack on an airplane will come not in the form of a suicide hijacking, but through efforts to bring an explosive aboard a plane—either in the checked baggage of an al Qaeda suicide soldier who boards the plane and avoids detection through bag matching, or in the luggage of an innocent passenger. Who can forget the foiled terrorist attempt some years ago to bomb a plane by putting explosives in the luggage of the terrorist's unsuspecting pregnant girlfriend? And, as some federal law enforcement officials have already said, the next face of a terrorist we will see is unlikely to be a Middle Easterner; instead, we may see someone from Asia, Malaysia, the Philippines, or even a European country. Thus, random searches and searches of non-Arabs are, in fact, extremely important security tactics. Without them, we create a weak point that begs to be exploited by our enemies.

Those who insist on the "commonsense" approach of focusing

on Middle Eastern men would, of course, have us ignore all of this. They want a fast-food solution—something convenient and comforting for "us" that only inconveniences "them." But there is little reason to think that type of profiling will see any greater success than profiling for drugs and other crimes did. If we go down that failed path, we will likely reap the same kind of reward: poor results and the alienation of our citizens from the police at a time when we most need cooperation between the two.

Ironically, if we keep ourselves focused on traditional methods of police procedures—surveillance of suspicious behavior and the collection and effective use of intelligence—we do not have to fail. We can do a better job of policing, even as we do right by our fellow citizens.

NOTES

1. Kathleen Parker, "All Is Fair in This War Except for Insensitivity," *Chicago Tribune*, September 26, 2001, p. 19.

2. Jim McGee, "Ex-FBI Officials Criticize Tactics on Terrorism," *Washington Post*, November 28, 2001.

3. Bill Dedman, "Airport Security: Memo Warns against Use of Profiling as Defense," *Boston Globe*, October 12, 2001.

14.

GUIDANCE REGARDING THE USE OF RACE BY FEDERAL LAW ENFORCEMENT AGENCIES

US Department of Justice, Civil Rights Division
June 2003

INTRODUCTION AND EXECUTIVE SUMMARY

In his February 27, 2001, address to a joint session of Congress, President George W. Bush declared that racial profiling is "wrong and we will end it in America." He directed the attorney general to review the use by federal law enforcement authorities of race as a factor in conducting stops, searches, and other law enforcement investigative procedures. The attorney general, in turn, instructed the Civil Rights Division to develop guidance for federal officials to ensure an end to racial profiling in law enforcement.

"Racial profiling" at its core concerns the invidious use of race or ethnicity as a criterion in conducting stops, searches, and other law enforcement investigative procedures. It is premised on the erroneous assumption that any particular individual of one race or ethnicity is more likely to engage in misconduct than any particular individual of another race or ethnicity.

Racial profiling in law enforcement is not merely wrong, but also ineffective. Race-based assumptions in law enforcement perpetuate negative racial stereotypes that are harmful to our rich and diverse democracy, and materially impair our efforts to maintain a fair and just society.

The use of race as the basis for law enforcement decision making clearly has a terrible cost, both to the individuals who suffer invidious discrimination and to the nation, whose goal of "liberty and justice for all" recedes with every act of such discrimination. For this reason, this guidance in many cases imposes more restrictions on the consideration of race and ethnicity in federal law enforcement than the Constitution requires. This guidance prohibits racial profiling in law enforcement practices without hindering the important work of our nation's public safety officials, particularly the intensified antiterrorism efforts precipitated by the events of September 11, 2001. . . .

I. GUIDANCE FOR FEDERAL OFFICIALS ENGAGED IN LAW ENFORCEMENT ACTIVITIES

A. *Routine or Spontaneous Activities in Domestic Law Enforcement*

In making routine or spontaneous law enforcement decisions, such as ordinary traffic stops, federal law enforcement officers may not use race or ethnicity to any degree, except that officers may rely on race and ethnicity in a specific suspect description. This prohibition applies even where the use of race or ethnicity might otherwise be lawful.

- *Example:* While parked by the side of the George Washington Parkway, a Park Police officer notices that nearly all vehicles on the road are exceeding the posted speed limit. Although each such vehicle is committing an infraction that would legally justify a stop, the officer may not use race or ethnicity as a factor in deciding which motorists to pull over. Likewise, the officer may not use race or ethnicity in deciding which detained motorists to ask to consent to a search of their vehicles.

Some have argued that overall discrepancies in certain crime rates among racial groups could justify using race as a factor in general traffic enforcement activities and would produce a greater number of arrests for nontraffic offenses (e.g., narcotics trafficking). We emphatically reject this view. The president has made clear his concern that racial profiling is morally wrong and inconsistent with our core values and principles of fairness and justice. Even if there were overall statistical evidence of differential rates of commission of certain offenses among particular races, the affirmative use of such generalized notions by federal law enforcement officers in routine, spontaneous law enforcement activities is tantamount to stereotyping. It casts a pall of suspicion over every member of cetain racial and ethnic groups without regard to the specific circumstances of a particular investigation or crime, and it offends the dignity of the individual improperly targeted. Whatever the motivation, it is patently unacceptable and thus prohibited under this guidance for federal law enforcement officers to act on the belief that race or ethnicity signals a higher risk of criminality. This is the core of "racial profiling" and it must not occur. The situation is different when an officer has specific information, based on trustworthy sources, to "be on the lookout" for specific individuals identified at least in part by race or ethnicity. In such circumstances, the officer is not acting based on a generalized assumption about persons of different races; rather, the officer is helping locate specific individuals previously identified as involved in crime.

- *Example:* While parked by the side of the George Washington Parkway, a Park Police officer receives an "All Points Bulletin" to be on the lookout for a fleeing bank robbery suspect, a man of a particular race and particular hair color in his thirties driving a blue automobile. The officer may use this description, including the race of the particular suspect, in deciding which speeding motorists to pull over.

B. *Law Enforcement Activities Related to Specific Investigations*

> In conducting activities in connection with a specific investigation, federal law enforcement officers may consider race and ethnicity only to the extent that there is trustworthy information, relevant to the locality or time frame, that links persons of a particular race or ethnicity to an identified criminal incident, scheme, or organization. This standard applies even where the use of race or ethnicity might otherwise be lawful.

As noted above, there are circumstances in which law enforcement activities relating to particular identified criminal incidents, schemes, or enterprises may involve consideration of personal identifying characteristics of potential suspects, including age, sex, ethnicity, or race. Common sense dictates that when a victim describes the assailant as being of a particular race, authorities may properly limit their search for suspects to persons of that race. Similarly, in conducting an ongoing investigation into a specific criminal organization whose membership has been identified as being overwhelmingly of one ethnicity, law enforcement should not be expected to disregard such facts in pursuing investigative leads into the organization's activities.

Reliance upon generalized stereotypes is absolutely forbidden. Rather, use of race or ethnicity is permitted only when the officer is pursuing a specific lead concerning the identifying characteristics of persons involved in an identified criminal activity. The rationale underlying this concept carefully limits its reach. In order to qualify as a legitimate investigative lead, the following must be true:

- The information must be relevant to the locality or time frame of the criminal activity;
- The information must be trustworthy;
- The information concerning identifying characteristics must be tied to a particular criminal incident, a particular criminal scheme, or a particular criminal organization.

The following policy statements more fully explain these principles.

1. Authorities May Never Rely on Generalized Stereotypes, but May Rely Only on Specific Race- or Ethnicity-Based Information

This standard categorically bars the use of generalized assumptions based on race.

- *Example:* In the course of investigating an auto theft in a federal park, law enforcement authorities could not properly choose to target individuals of a particular race as suspects, based on a generalized assumption that those individuals are more likely to commit crimes.

This bar extends to the use of race-neutral pretexts as an excuse to target minorities. Federal law enforcement may not use such pretexts. This prohibition extends to the use of other, facially race-neutral factors as a proxy for overtly targeting persons of a certain race or ethnicity. This concern arises most frequently when aggressive law enforcement efforts are focused on "high crime areas." The issue is ultimately one of motivation and evidence; certain seemingly race-based efforts, if properly supported by reliable, empirical data, are in fact race-neutral.

- *Example:* In connection with a new initiative to increase drug arrests, local authorities begin aggressively enforcing speeding, traffic, and other public area laws in a neighborhood predominantly occupied by people of a single race. The choice of neighborhood was not based on the number of 911 calls, number of arrests, or other pertinent reporting data specific to that area, but only on the general assumption that more drug-related crime occurs in that neighborhood because of its racial composition. This effort would be improper because it is based on generalized stereotypes.

By contrast, where authorities are investigating a crime and have received specific information that the suspect is of a certain race (e.g., direct observations by the victim or other witnesses), authorities may reasonably use that information, even if it is the only descriptive information available. In such an instance, it is the victim or other witness making the racial classification, and federal authorities may use reliable incident-specific identifying information to apprehend criminal suspects. Agencies and departments, however, must use caution in the rare instance in which a suspect's race is the only available information. Although the use of that information may not be unconstitutional, broad targeting of discrete racial or ethnic groups always raises serious fairness concerns.

- *Example:* The victim of an assault at a local university describes her assailant as a young male of a particular race with a cut on his right hand. The investigation focuses on whether any students at the university fit the victim's description. Here investigators are properly relying on a description given by the victim, part of which included the assailant's race. Although the ensuing investigation affects students of a particular race, that investigation is not undertaken with a discriminatory purpose. Thus use of race as a factor in the investigation, in this instance, is permissible.

2. The Information Must Be Relevant to the Locality or Time Frame

Any information concerning the race of persons who may be involved in specific criminal activities must be locally or temporally relevant.

- *Example:* The DEA issues an intelligence report that indicates that a drug ring whose members are known to be predominantly of a particular race or ethnicity is trafficking drugs in Charleston, South Carolina. An agent operating in Los Angeles reads this intelligence report. In the absence of information establishing that this intelligence is also applicable in Southern California, the agent may not use ethnicity as a factor in making local law enforcement decisions about individuals who are of the particular race or ethnicity that is predominant in the Charleston drug ring.

3. The Information Must Be Trustworthy

Where the information concerning potential criminal activity is unreliable or is too generalized and unspecific, use of racial descriptions is prohibited.

- *Example:* ATF special agents receive an uncorroborated anonymous tip that a male of a particular race will purchase an illegal firearm at a Greyhound bus terminal in a racially diverse northern Philadelphia neighborhood. Although agents surveilling the location are free to monitor the movements of whomever they choose, the agents are prohibited from using the tip information, without more, to target any males of that race in the bus terminal. . . . The information is neither sufficiently reliable nor sufficiently specific.

4. Race- or Ethnicity-Based Information Must Always Be Specific to Particular Suspects or Incidents, or Ongoing Criminal Activities, Schemes, or Enterprises

These standards contemplate the appropriate use of both "suspect-specific" and "incident-specific" information. As noted above, where a crime has occurred and authorities have eyewitness accounts including the race, ethnicity, or other distinguishing characteristics of the perpetrator, that information may be used. Federal authorities may also use reliable, locally relevant information linking persons of a certain race or ethnicity to a particular incident, unlawful scheme, or ongoing criminal enterprise—even absent a description of any particular individual suspect. In certain cases, the circumstances surrounding an incident or ongoing criminal activity will point strongly to a perpetrator of a certain race, even though authorities lack an eyewitness account.

- *Example:* The FBI is investigating the murder of a known gang member and has information that the shooter is a member of a rival gang. The FBI knows that the members of the rival gang are exclusively members of a certain ethnicity. This information, however, is not suspect-specific because there is no description of the particular assailant. But because authorities have reliable, locally relevant information linking a rival group with a distinctive ethnic character to the murder, federal law enforcement officers could properly consider ethnicity in conjunction with other appropriate factors in the course of conducting their investigation. Agents could properly decide to focus on persons dressed in a manner consistent with gang activity, but ignore persons dressed in that manner who do not appear to be members of that particular ethnicity.

It is critical, however, that there be reliable information that ties persons of a particular description to a specific criminal incident, ongoing criminal activity, or particular criminal organization. Otherwise, any use of race runs the risk of descending into reliance upon prohibited generalized stereotypes.

- *Example:* While investigating a car theft ring that dismantles cars and ships the parts for sale in other states, the FBI is informed by local authorities that it is common knowledge locally that most car thefts in that area are committed by individuals of a particular race. In this example, although the source (local police) is trustworthy, and the information potentially verifiable with reference to arrest statistics, there is no particular incident—or scheme-specific information linking individuals of that race to the particular interstate ring the FBI is investigating. Thus, without more, agents could not use ethnicity as a factor in making law enforcement decisions in this investigation.

II. GUIDANCE FOR FEDERAL OFFICIALS ENGAGED IN LAW ENFORCEMENT ACTIVITIES INVOLVING THREATS TO NATIONAL SECURITY OR THE INTEGRITY OF THE NATION'S BORDERS

> In investigating or preventing threats to national security or other catastrophic events (including the performance of duties related to air transportation security), or in enforcing laws protecting the integrity of the nation's borders, federal law enforcement officers may not consider race or ethnicity except to the extent permitted by the Constitution and laws of the United States.

Since the terrorist attacks on September 11, 2001, the president has emphasized that federal law enforcement personnel must use every legitimate tool to prevent future attacks, protect our nation's borders, and deter those who would cause devastating harm to our nation and its people through the use of biological or chemical weapons, other weapons of mass destruction, suicide hijackings, or any other means. . . .

The Constitution prohibits consideration of race or ethnicity in law enforcement decisions in all but the most exceptional instances. Given the incalculably high stakes involved in such investigations, however, federal law enforcement officers who are protecting national security or preventing catastrophic events (as well as airport security screeners) may consider race, ethnicity, and other relevant factors to the extent permitted by our laws and the Constitution. Similarly, because enforcement of the laws protecting the nation's borders may necessarily involve a consideration of a person's alienage in certain circumstances, the use of race or ethnicity in such circumstances is properly governed by existing statutory and constitutional standards. This policy will honor the rule of law and promote vigorous protection of our national security.

As the Supreme Court has stated, all racial classifications by a governmental actor are subject to the "strictest judicial scrutiny." *Adarand Constructors, Inc. v. Peña* (1995). The application of strict scrutiny is of necessity a fact-intensive process. Thus, the legality of particular, race-sensitive actions taken by federal law enforcement officials in the context of national security and border integrity will depend to a large extent on the circumstances at hand. In absolutely no event, however, may federal officials assert a national security or border integrity rationale as a mere pretext for invidious discrimination. Indeed, the very purpose of the strict scrutiny test is to "smoke out" illegitimate use of race, and law enforcement strategies not actually premised on bona fide national security or border integrity interests therefore will not stand.

In sum, constitutional provisions limiting government action on the basis of race are wide ranging and provide substantial protections at every step of the investigative and judicial process. Accordingly, and as illustrated below, when addressing matters of national security, border integrity, or the possible catastrophic loss of life, existing legal and constitutional standards are an appropriate guide for federal law enforcement officers.

- *Example:* The FBI receives reliable information that persons affiliated with a foreign ethnic insurgent group intend to use suicide bombers to assassinate that country's president and his entire entourage during an official visit to the United States. Federal law enforcement may appropriately focus investigative attention on identifying members of that ethnic insurgent group who may be present and active in the United States and who, based on other available information, might conceivably be involved in planning some such attack during the state visit.
- *Example:* US intelligence sources report that terrorists from a particular ethnic group are planning to use commercial jetliners as weapons by hijacking them at an airport in California during the next week. Before allowing men of that ethnic group to board commercial airplanes in California airports during the next week, Transportation Security Administration personnel, and other federal and state authorities, may subject them to heightened scrutiny.

Because terrorist organizations might aim to engage in unexpected acts of catastrophic violence in any available part of the country (indeed, in multiple places simultaneously, if possible), there can be no expectation that the information must be specific to a particular locale or even to a particular identified scheme.

Of course, as in the example below, reliance solely upon generalized stereotypes is forbidden.

- *Example:* At the security entrance to a federal courthouse, a man who appears to be of a particular ethnicity properly submits his briefcase for x-ray screening and passes through the metal detector. The inspection of the briefcase reveals nothing amiss, the man does not activate the metal detector, and there is nothing suspicious about his activities or appearance. In the absence of any threat warning, the federal security screener may not order the man to undergo a further inspection solely because he appears to be of a particular ethnicity.

PART 4.

INTERROGATING SUSPECTS AND TORTURE

15.

SHOULD THE TICKING BOMB TERRORIST BE TORTURED?

A CASE STUDY IN HOW A DEMOCRACY SHOULD MAKE TRAGIC CHOICES

Alan M. Dershowitz

Authorizing torture is a bad and dangerous idea that can easily be made to sound plausible. There is a subtle fallacy embedded in the traditional "ticking bomb" argument for torture to save lives.
　　　　—Philip Heymann, former deputy attorney general

In my nearly forty years of teaching at Harvard Law School I have always challenged my students with hypothetical and real-life problems requiring them to choose among evils. The students invariably try to resist these tragic choices by stretching their ingenuity to come up with alternative—and less tragic—options. The

From *Why Terrorism Works: Understanding the Threat, Responding to the Challenge* (New Haven: Yale University Press, 2002). Copyright © 2002 by Alan M. Dershowitz. Used by permission.

classic hypothetical case involves the train engineer whose brakes become inoperative. There is no way he can stop his speeding vehicle of death. Either he can do nothing, in which case he will plow into a busload of schoolchildren, or he can swerve onto another track, where he sees a drunk lying on the rails. (Neither decision will endanger him or his passengers.) There is no third choice. What should he do? . . .

Students love to debate positive choices: good, better, best. They don't mind moderately negative choices: bad, worse, worst. They hate tragic choices: unthinkable versus inconceivable. . . .

HOW THE CURRENT TORTURE DEBATE BEGAN

Before September 11, 2001, no one thought the issue of torture would ever reemerge as a topic of serious debate in this country. Yet shortly after that watershed event, FBI agents began to leak stories suggesting that they might have to resort to torture to get some detainees, who were suspected of complicity in al Qaeda terrorism, to provide information necessary to prevent a recurrence. An FBI source told the press that because "we are known for humanitarian treatment" of arrestees, we have been unable to get any terrorist suspects to divulge information about possible future plans. "We're into this thing for thirty-five days and nobody is talking," he said in obvious frustration. "Basically we're stuck." A senior FBI aide warned that "it could get to the spot where we could go to pressure, . . . where *we won't have a choice*, and we are probably getting there."[1] But in a democracy there is *always* a choice. . . .

Constitutional democracies are, of course, constrained in the choices they may lawfully make. The Fifth Amendment prohibits compelled self-incrimination, which means that statements elicited by means of torture may not be introduced into evidence against the defendant who has been tortured.[2] But if a suspect is given immunity and then tortured into providing information about a future terrorist act, his privilege against self-incrimination has not been violated.[3] . . . The only constitutional barriers would be the "due process" clauses of the Fifth and Fourteenth Amendments, which are quite general and sufficiently flexible to permit an argument that the only process "due" a terrorist suspected of refusing to disclose information necessary to prevent a terrorist attack is the requirement of probable cause and some degree of judicial supervision.[4] . . .

There are legal steps we could take, if we chose to resort to torture, that would make it possible for us to use this technique for eliciting information in dire circumstances. Neither the presence nor the absence of legal constraints answers the fundamental moral question: should we? This is a choice that almost no one wants to have to make. Torture has been off the agenda of civilized discourse for so many centuries that it is a subject reserved largely for historians rather than contemporary moralists (though it remains a staple of abstract philosophers debating the virtues and vices of absolutism). I have been criticized for even discussing the issue, on the ground that academic discussion confers legitimacy on a practice that deserves none. I have also been criticized for raising a red herring, since it is "well known" that torture does not work—it produces many false confessions and useless misinformation, because a person will say anything to stop being tortured.[5]

This argument is reminiscent of the ones my students make in desperately seeking to avoid the choice of evils by driving the hypothetical railroad train off the track. The tragic reality is that torture sometimes works, much though many people wish it did not. There are numerous instances in which torture has produced self-proving, truthful information that was necessary to prevent harm to civilians. The *Washington Post* has recounted a case from 1995 in which Philippine authorities tortured a terrorist into disclosing information that may have foiled plots to assassinate the pope and to crash eleven commercial airliners carrying approximately four thousand passengers into the Pacific Ocean, as well as a plan to fly a private Cessna filled with explosives into CIA headquarters. For sixty-seven days, intelligence agents beat the suspect "with a chair and a long piece of wood [breaking most of his ribs], forced water into his mouth, and crushed lighted cigarettes into his private parts"—a procedure that the Philippine intelligence service calls "tactical interrogation." After successfully employing this procedure they turned him over to American authorities, along with the lifesaving information they had beaten out of him.[6]

It is impossible to avoid the difficult moral dilemma of choosing among evils by denying the empirical reality that torture *sometimes* works, even if it does not always work.[7] No technique of crime prevention always works. . . .

It is precisely because torture sometimes does work and can sometimes prevent major disasters that it still exists in many parts of the world and has been totally eliminated from none. . . . As we began to come to grips with the horrible evils of mass murder by terrorists, it became inevitable that torture would return to the agenda, and it has. The recent capture of a high-ranking al Qaeda operative, possibly with information about terrorist "sleeper cells" and future targets, has raised the question of how to compel him to disclose this important information. We must be prepared to think about the alternatives in a rational manner. We cannot evade our responsibility by pretending that torture is not being used or by having others use it for our benefit. . . .

HOW I BEGAN THINKING ABOUT TORTURE

In the late 1980s I traveled to Israel to conduct some research and teach a class at Hebrew University on civil liberties during times of crisis. In the course of my research I learned that the Israeli security services were employing what they euphemistically called "moderate physical pressure" on suspected terrorists to obtain information deemed necessary to prevent future terrorist attacks. . . . In most cases the suspect would be placed in a dark room with a smelly sack over his head. Loud, unpleasant music or other noise would blare from speakers. The suspect would be seated in an extremely uncomfortable position and then shaken vigorously until he disclosed the information. . . .

In my classes and public lectures in Israel, I strongly condemned these methods as a violation of core civil liberties and human rights.

The response that people gave, across the political spectrum from civil libertarians to law-and-order advocates, was essentially the same: but what about the "ticking bomb" case?

The ticking bomb case refers to a scenario that has been discussed by many philosophers, including Michael Walzer, Jean-Paul Sartre, and Jeremy Bentham. Walzer described such a hypothetical case in an article titled "Political Action: The Problem of Dirty Hands." In this case, a decent leader of a nation plagued with terrorism is asked "to authorize the torture of a captured rebel leader who knows or probably knows the location of a number of bombs hidden in apartment buildings across the city, set to go off within the next twenty-four hours. He orders the man tortured, convinced that he must do so for the sake of the people who might otherwise die in the explosions—even though he believes that torture is wrong, indeed abominable, not just sometimes, but always."[8]

In Israel, the use of torture to prevent terrorism was not hypothetical; it was very real and recurring. I soon discovered that virtually no one was willing to take the "purist" position against torture in the ticking bomb case: namely, that the ticking bomb must be permitted to explode and kill dozens of civilians, even if this disaster could be prevented by subjecting the captured terrorist to nonlethal torture and forcing him to disclose its location. I realized that the extraordinarily rare situation of the hypothetical ticking bomb terrorist was serving as a moral, intellectual, and legal justification for a pervasive *system* of coercive interrogation, which, though not the paradigm of torture, certainly bordered on it. It was then that I decided to challenge this system by directly confronting the ticking bomb case. I presented the following challenge to my Israeli audience: If the reason you permit nonlethal torture is based on the ticking bomb case, why not limit it exclusively to that compelling but rare situation? Moreover, if you believe that nonlethal torture is justifiable in the ticking bomb case, why not require advance judicial approval—a "torture warrant"? That was the origin of a controversial proposal that has received much attention, largely critical, from the media. Its goal was, and remains, to reduce the use of torture to the smallest amount and degree possible, while creating public accountability for its rare use. I saw it not as a compromise with civil liberties but rather as an effort to maximize civil liberties in the face of a realistic likelihood that torture would, in fact, take place below the radar screen of accountability. . . .

THE CASE FOR TORTURING THE TICKING BOMB TERRORIST

The arguments in favor of using torture as a last resort to prevent a ticking bomb from exploding and killing many people are both simple and simpleminded. Bentham constructed a compelling hypothetical case to support his utilitarian argument against an absolute prohibition on torture:

> Suppose an occasion were to arise, in which a suspicion is entertained, as strong as that which would be received as a sufficient ground for arrest and commitment as for felony—a suspicion that at this very time a considerable number of individuals are actually suffering, by illegal violence inflictions equal in intensity to those which if inflicted by the hand of justice, would universally be spoken of under the name of torture. For the purpose of rescuing from torture these hundred innocents, should any scruple be made of applying equal or superior torture, to extract the requisite information from the mouth of one criminal, who having it in his power to make known the place where at this time the enormity was practising or about to be practised, should refuse to do so? To say nothing of wisdom, could any pretence be made so much as to the praise of blind and vulgar humanity, by the man who to save one criminal, should determine to abandon one hundred innocent persons to the same fate?[9]

If the torture of one guilty person would be justified to prevent the torture of a hundred innocent persons, it would seem to follow—certainly to Bentham—that it would also be justified to prevent the murder of thousands of innocent civilians in the ticking bomb case. Consider two hypothetical situations that are not, unfortunately, beyond the realm of possibility. In fact, they are both extrapolations on actual situations we have faced.

Several weeks before September 11, 2001, the Immigration and Naturalization Service detained Zacarias Moussaoui after flight instructors reported suspicious statements he had made while taking flying lessons and paying for them with large amounts of cash.[10] The government decided not to seek a warrant to search his computer. Now imagine that they had, and that they discovered he was part of a plan to destroy large occupied buildings, but without any further details. They interrogated him, gave him immunity from prosecution, and offered him large cash rewards and a new identity. He refused to talk. They then threatened him, tried to trick him, and employed every lawful technique available. He still refused. They even injected him with sodium pentothal and other truth serums, but to no avail. The attack now appeared to be imminent, but the FBI still had no idea what the target was or what means would be used to attack it. We could not simply evacuate all buildings indefinitely. An FBI agent proposes the use of nonlethal torture—say, a sterilized needle inserted under the fingernails to produce unbearable pain without any threat to health or life, or the method used in the film *Marathon Man*, a dental drill through an unanesthetized tooth.

The simple cost-benefit analysis for employing such nonlethal torture seems overwhelming: it is surely better to inflict nonlethal pain on one guilty terrorist who is illegally withholding information needed to prevent an act of terrorism than to permit a large number of innocent victims to die.[11] Pain is a lesser and more remediable harm than death; and the lives of a thousand innocent people should be valued more than the bodily integrity of one guilty person.

If the variation on the Moussaoui case is not sufficiently compelling to make this point, we can always raise the stakes. Several weeks after September 11, our government received reports that a ten-kiloton nuclear weapon may have been stolen from Russia and was on its way to New York City, where it would be detonated and kill hundreds of thousands of people. The reliability of the source, code-named Dragonfire, was uncertain, but assume for purposes of this hypothetical extension of the actual case that the source was a captured terrorist—like the one tortured by the Philippine authorities—who knew precisely how and where the weapon was being brought into New York and was to be detonated. Again, everything short of torture is tried, but to no avail. It is not absolutely certain torture will work, but it is our last, best hope for preventing a cataclysmic nuclear devastation in a city too large to evacuate in time. Should nonlethal torture be tried? Bentham would certainly have said yes.

The strongest argument against any resort to torture, even in the ticking bomb case, also derives from Bentham's utilitarian calculus. Experience has shown that if torture, which has been deemed illegitimate by the civilized world for more than a century, were now to be legitimated—even for limited use in one extraordinary type of situation—such legitimation would constitute an important symbolic setback in the worldwide campaign against human rights abuses. Inevitably, the legitimation of torture by the world's leading democracy would provide a welcome justification for its more widespread use in other parts of the world. Two Bentham scholars, W. L. Twining and P. E. Twining, have argued that torture is unacceptable even if it is restricted to an extremely limited category of cases:

> There is at least one good practical reason for drawing a distinction between justifying an isolated act of torture in an extreme emergency of the kind postulated above and justifying the *institutionalisation* of torture as a regular practice. The circumstances are so extreme in which most of us would be prepared to justify resort to torture, if at all, the conditions we would impose would be so stringent, the practical problems of devising and enforcing adequate safeguards so difficult and the risks of abuse so great that it would be unwise and dangerous to entrust any government, however enlightened, with such a power. Even an out-and-out utilitarian can support an absolute prohibition against institutionalised torture on the ground that no government in the world can be trusted not to abuse the power and to satisfy in practice the conditions he would impose.[12]

Bentham's own justification was based on *case* or *act* utilitarianism—a demonstration that in a *particular case*, the benefits that would flow from the limited use of torture would outweigh its costs. The argument against any use of torture would derive from rule utilitarianism—which considers the implications of establishing a precedent that would inevitably be extended beyond its limited case utilitarian justification to other possible evils of lesser magnitude. Even terrorism itself could be justified by a case utilitarian approach. Surely one could come up with a singular situation in which the targeting of a small number of civilians could be thought necessary to save thousands of other civilians—blowing up a German kindergarten by the relatives of inmates in a Nazi death camp, for example, and threatening to repeat the targeting of German children unless the death camps were shut down.

The reason this kind of single-case utilitarian justification is simpleminded is that it has no inherent limiting principle. If nonlethal torture of one person is justified to prevent the killing of many important people, then what if it were necessary to use lethal torture—or at least torture that posed a substantial risk of death? What if it were necessary to torture the suspect's mother or children to get him to divulge the information? What if it took threatening to kill his family, his friends, his entire village?[13] Under a simpleminded quantitative case utilitarianism, anything goes as long as the number of people tortured or killed does not exceed the number that would be saved. This is morality by numbers, unless there are other constraints on what we can properly do. These other constraints can come from rule utilitarianisms or other principles of morality, such as the prohibition against deliberately punishing the innocent. Unless we are prepared to impose some limits on the use of torture or other barbaric tactics that might be of some use in preventing terrorism, we risk hurtling down a slippery slope into the abyss of amorality and ultimately tyranny. . . .

It does not necessarily follow from this understandable fear of the slippery slope that we can never consider the use of nonlethal infliction of pain, if its use were to be limited by acceptable principles of morality. After all, imprisoning a witness who refuses to testify after being given immunity is designed to be punitive—that is painful. Such imprisonment can, on occasion, produce more pain and greater risk of death than nonlethal torture. Yet we continue to threaten and use the pain of imprisonment to loosen the tongues of reluctant witnesses.[14]

It is commonplace for police and prosecutors to threaten recalcitrant suspects with prison rape. As one prosecutor put it: "You're going to be the boyfriend of a very bad man." The slippery slope is an argument of caution, not a debate stopper, since virtually every compromise with an absolutist approach to rights carries the risk of slipping further. An appropriate response to the slippery slope is to build in a principled break. For example, if nonlethal torture were legally limited to convicted terrorists who had knowledge of future massive terrorist acts, were given immunity, and still refused to provide the information, there might still be objections to the use of torture, but they would have to go beyond the slippery slope argument.[15]

The case utilitarian argument for torturing a ticking bomb terrorist is bolstered by an argument from analogy—an a fortiori argument. What moral principle could justify the death penalty for past individual murders and at the same time condemn nonlethal torture to prevent future mass murders? Bentham posed this rhetorical question as support for his argument. The death penalty is, of course, reserved for convicted murderers. But again, what if torture was limited to convicted terrorists who refused to divulge information about future terrorism? Consider as well the analogy to the use of deadly force against suspects fleeing from arrest for dangerous felonies of which they have not yet been convicted. Or military retaliations that produce the predictable and inevitable collateral killing of some innocent civilians. The case against torture, if made by a Quaker who opposes the death penalty, war, self-defense, and the use of lethal force against fleeing felons, is understandable. But for anyone who justifies killing on the basis of a cost-benefit analysis, the case against the use of nonlethal torture to save multiple lives is more difficult to make. In the end, absolute opposition to torture—even nonlethal torture in the ticking bomb case—may rest more on historical and aesthetic considerations than on moral or logical ones.

In debating the issue of torture, the first question I am often asked is, "Do you want to take us back to the Middle Ages?" The association between any form of torture and gruesome death is powerful in the minds of most people knowledgeable of the history of its abuses. This understandable association makes it difficult for many people to think about nonlethal torture as a technique for *saving* lives.

The second question I am asked is, "What kind of torture do you have in mind?" When I respond by describing the sterilized needle being shoved under the fingernails, the reaction is visceral and often visible—a shudder coupled with a facial gesture of disgust. Discussions of the death penalty on the other hand can be conducted without these kinds of reactions, especially now that we literally put the condemned prisoner "to sleep" by laying him out on a gurney and injecting a lethal substance into his body. There is no breaking of the neck, burning of the brain, bursting of internal organs, or gasping for breath that used to accompany hanging, electrocution, shooting, and gassing. The executioner has been replaced by a paramedical technician, as the aesthetics of death have become more acceptable. All this tends to cover up the reality that death is forever while nonlethal pain is temporary. In our modern age death is underrated, while pain is overrated.

I observed a similar phenomenon several years ago during the debate over corporal punishment that was generated by the decision of a court in Singapore to sentence a young American to medically supervised lashing with a cane. Americans who support the death penalty and who express little concern about inner-city prison conditions were outraged by the specter of a few welts on the buttocks of an American. It was an utterly irrational display of hypocrisy and double standards. Given a choice between a medically administrated whipping and one month in a typical state lockup or prison, any rational and knowledgeable person would choose the lash. No one dies of welts or pain, but many inmates are raped, beaten, knifed, and otherwise mutilated and tortured in American prisons. The difference is that we don't see—and we don't want to see—what goes on behind their high walls. Nor do we want to think about it. Raising the issue of torture makes Americans think about a brutalizing and unaesthetic phenomenon that has been out of our consciousness for many years.[16]

THE THREE—OR FOUR—WAYS

The debate over the use of torture goes back many years, with Bentham supporting it in a limited category of cases, Kant opposing it as part of his categorical imperative against improperly using people as means for achieving noble ends, and Voltaire's views on the matter being "hopelessly confused."[17] The modern resort to terrorism has renewed the debate over how a rights-based society should respond to the prospect of using nonlethal torture in the ticking bomb situation. In the late 1980s the Israeli government appointed a commission headed by a retired Supreme Court justice to look into precisely that situation. The commission concluded that there are "three ways for solving this grave dilemma between the vital need to preserve the very existence of the state and its citizens, and maintain its character as a law-abiding state." The first is to allow the security services to continue to fight terrorism in "a twilight zone which is outside the realm of law." The second is "the way of the hypocrites: they declare that they abide by the rule of law, but turn a blind eye to what goes on beneath the surface." And the third, "the truthful road of the rule of law," is that the "law itself must insure a proper framework for the activity" of the security services in seeking to prevent terrorist acts.[18]

There is of course a fourth road: namely, to forgo any use of torture and simply allow the preventable terrorist act to occur.[19] After the Supreme Court of Israel outlawed the use of physical pressure, the Israeli security services claimed that, as a result of the Supreme Court's decision, at least one preventable act of terrorism had been allowed to take place, one that killed several people when a bus was bombed.[20] Whether this claim is true, false, or somewhere in between is difficult to assess.[21] But it is clear that if the preventable act of terrorism was of the magnitude of the attacks of September 11, there would be a great outcry in any democracy that had deliberately refused to take available preventive action, even if it required the use of torture. During numerous public appearances since September 11, 2001, I have asked audiences for a show of hands as to how many would support the use of nonlethal torture in a ticking bomb case. Virtually every hand is raised. The few that remain down go up when I ask how many believe that torture would actually be used in such a case.

Law enforcement personnel give similar responses. This can be seen in reports of physical abuse directed against some suspects that have been detained following September 11, reports that have been taken quite seriously by at least one federal judge.[22] It is confirmed by the willingness of US law enforcement officials to facilitate the torture of terrorist suspects by repressive regimes allied with our intelligence agencies. As one former CIA operative with thirty years of experience reported: "A lot of people are saying we need someone at the agency who can pull fingernails out. Others are saying, 'Let others use interrogation methods that we don't use.' The only question then is, do you want to have CIA people in the room?" The real issue, therefore, is not whether some torture would or would not be used in the ticking bomb case—it would. The question is whether it would be done openly, pursuant to a previously established legal procedure, or whether it would be done secretly, in violation of existing law.[23]

Several important values are pitted against each other in this conflict. The first is the safety and security of a nation's citizens. Under the ticking bomb scenario this value may require the use of torture, if that is the only way to prevent the bomb from exploding and killing large numbers of civilians. The second value is the preservation of civil liberties and human rights. This value requires that we not accept torture as a legitimate part of our legal system. In my debates with two prominent civil libertarians, Floyd Abrams and Harvey Silverglate, both have acknowledged that they would want nonlethal torture to be used if it could prevent thousands of deaths, but they did not want torture to be officially recognized by our legal system. As Abrams put it: "In a democracy sometimes it is necessary to do things off the books and below the radar screen." Former presidential candidate Alan Keyes took the position that although torture might be *necessary* in a given situation it could never be *right*. He suggested that a president *should* authorize the torturing of a ticking bomb terrorist, but that this act should not be legitimated by the courts or incorporated into our legal system. He argued that wrongful and indeed unlawful acts might sometimes be necessary to preserve the nation, but that no aura of legitimacy should be placed on these actions by judicial imprimatur.

This understandable approach is in conflict with the third important value: namely, open accountability and visibility in a democracy. "Off-the-book actions below the radar screen" are antithetical to the theory and practice of democracy. . . .

In a democracy governed by the rule of law, we should never want our soldiers or our president to take any action that we deem wrong or illegal. A good test of whether an action should or should not be done is whether we are prepared to have it disclosed—perhaps not immediately, but certainly after some time has passed. No legal system operating under the rule of law should ever tolerate an "off-the-books" approach to necessity. Even the defense of necessity must be justified lawfully. The road to tyranny has always been paved with claims of necessity made by those responsible for the security of a nation. Our system of checks and balances requires that all presidential actions, like all legislative or military actions, be consistent with governing law. If it is necessary to torture in the ticking bomb case, then our governing laws must accommodate this practice. If we refuse to change our law to accommodate any particular action, then our government should not take that action.[24]

Only in a democracy committed to civil liberties would a triangular conflict of this kind exist. Totalitarian and authoritarian regimes experience no such conflict, because they subscribe to neither the civil libertarian nor the democratic values that come in conflict with the value of security. The hard question is: which value is to be preferred when an inevitable clash occurs? One or more of these values must inevitably be compromised in making the tragic choice presented by the ticking bomb case. If we do not torture, we compromise the security and safety of our citizens. If we tolerate torture, but keep it off the books and below the radar screen, we compromise principles of democratic accountability. If we create a legal structure for limiting and controlling torture, we compromise our principled opposition to torture in all circumstances and create a potentially dangerous and expandable situation.

. . . As Bentham put it more than two centuries ago: "Government throughout is but a choice of evils." In a democracy, such choices must be made, whenever possible, with openness and democratic accountability, and subject to the rule of law.[25]

. . . On a purely rational basis, it is far worse to shoot a fleeing felon in the back and kill him, yet every civilized society authorizes shooting such a suspect who poses dangers of committing violent crimes against the police or others. In the United States we execute convicted murderers, despite compelling evidence of the unfairness and ineffectiveness of capital punishment. Yet many of us recoil at the prospect of shoving a sterilized needle under the finger of a suspect who is refusing to divulge information that might prevent multiple deaths. Despite the irrationality of these distinctions, they are understandable, especially in light of the sordid history of torture.

We associate torture with the Inquisition, the Gestapo, the Stalinist purges, and the Argentine colonels responsible for the "dirty war." We recall it as a prelude to death, an integral part of a regime of gratuitous pain leading to a painful demise. We find it difficult to imagine a benign use of nonlethal torture to save lives.

Yet there was a time in the history of Anglo-Saxon law when torture was used to save life, rather than to take it, and when the limited administration of nonlethal torture was supervised by judges, including some who are well remembered in history.[26] This fascinating story has been recounted by Prof. John Langbein of Yale Law School, and it is worth summarizing here because it helps inform the debate over whether, if torture would in fact be used in a ticking bomb case, it would be worse to make it part of the legal system, or worse to have it done off the books and below the radar screen.

In his book on legalized torture during the sixteenth and seventeenth centuries, *Torture and the Law of Proof*, Langbein demonstrates the trade-off between torture and other important values. Torture was employed for several purposes. First, it was used to secure the evidence necessary to obtain a guilty verdict under the rigorous criteria for conviction required at the time—either the testimony of two eyewitnesses or the confession of the accused himself. Circumstantial evidence, no matter how compelling, would not do. As

Langbein concludes, "No society will long tolerate a legal system in which there is no prospect in convicting unrepentant persons who commit clandestine crimes. Something had to be done to extend the system to those cases. The two-eyewitness rule was hard to compromise or evade, but the confession invited 'subterfuge.'" The subterfuge that was adopted permitted the use of torture to obtain confessions from suspects against whom there was compelling circumstantial evidence of guilt. The circumstantial evidence, alone, could not be used to convict, but it was used to obtain a torture warrant. That torture warrant was in turn used to obtain a confession, which then had to be independently corroborated—at least in most cases (witchcraft and other such cases were exempted from the requirement of corroboration).[27]

Torture was also used against persons already convicted of capital crimes, such as high treason, who were thought to have information necessary to prevent attacks on the state.

Langbein studied eighty-one torture warrants, issued between 1540 and 1640, and found that in many of them, especially in "the higher cases of treasons, torture is used for discovery, and not for evidence." Torture was "used to protect the state" and "mostly that meant preventive torture to identify and forestall plots and plotters." It was only when the legal system loosened its requirement of proof (or introduced the "black box" of the jury system) and when perceived threats against the state diminished that torture was no longer deemed necessary to convict guilty defendants against whom there had previously been insufficient evidence, or to secure preventive information.[28] . . .

Every society has insisted on the incapacitation of dangerous criminals regardless of strictures in the formal legal rules. Some use torture, others use informal sanctions, while yet others create the black box of a jury, which need not explain its commonsense verdicts. Similarly, every society insists that, if there are steps that can be taken to prevent effective acts of terrorism, these steps should be taken, even if they require some compromise with other important principles.

In deciding whether the ticking bomb terrorist should be tortured, one important question is whether there would be less torture if it were done as part of the legal system, as it was in sixteenth- and seventeenth-century England, or off the books, as it is in many countries today. The Langbein study does not definitively answer this question, but it does provide some suggestive insights. The English system of torture was more visible and thus more subject to public accountability, and it is likely that torture was employed less frequently in England than in France. . . . In England "no law enforcement officer . . . acquired the power to use torture without special warrant." Moreover, when torture warrants were abolished, "the English experiment with torture left no traces." Because it was under centralized control, it was easier to abolish than it was in France, where it persisted for many years.[29]

It is always difficult to extrapolate from history, but it seems logical that a formal, visible, accountable, and centralized system is somewhat easier to control than an ad hoc, off-the-books, and under-the-radar-screen nonsystem. I believe, though I certainly cannot prove, that a formal requirement of a judicial warrant as a prerequisite to nonlethal torture would decrease the amount of physical violence directed against suspects. At the most obvious level, a double check is always more protective than a single check. In every instance in which a warrant is requested, a field officer has already decided that torture is justified and, in the absence of a warrant requirement, would simply proceed with the torture. Requiring that decision to be approved by a judicial officer will result in fewer instances of torture even if the judge rarely turns down a request. Moreover, I believe that most judges would require compelling evidence before they would authorize so extraordinary a departure from our constitutional norms, and law enforcement officials would be reluctant to seek a warrant unless they had compelling evidence that the suspect had information needed to prevent an imminent terrorist attack. A record would be kept of every warrant granted, and although it is certainly possible that some individual agents might torture without a warrant, they would have no excuse, since a warrant procedure would be available. They could not claim "necessity," because the decision as to whether the torture is indeed necessary has been taken out of their hands and placed in the hands of a judge. In addition, even if torture were deemed totally illegal without any exception, it would still occur, though the public would be less aware of its existence.

I also believe that the rights of the suspect would be better protected with a warrant requirement. He would be granted immunity, told that he was now compelled to testify, threatened with imprisonment if he refused to do so, and given the option of providing the requested information. Only if he refused to do what he was legally compelled to do—provide necessary information, which could not incriminate him because of the immunity—would he be threatened with torture. Knowing that such a threat was authorized by the law, he might well provide the information.[30] . . .

Let me cite two examples to demonstrate why I think there would be less torture with a warrant requirement than without one. Recall the case of the alleged national security wiretap placed on the phones of Martin Luther King by the Kennedy administration in the early 1960s. This was in the days when the attorney general could authorize a national security wiretap without a warrant. Today no judge would issue a warrant in a case as flimsy as that one. When Zacarias Moussaoui was detained after raising suspicions while trying to learn how to fly an airplane, the government did not even seek a national security wiretap because its lawyers believed that a judge would not have granted one. If Moussaoui's computer could have been searched without a warrant, it almost certainly would have been.

. . . Although torture is very different from a search, the policies underlying the warrant requirement are relevant to the question whether there is likely to be more torture or less if the decision is left entirely to field officers, or if a judicial officer has to approve a request for a torture warrant. As Abraham Maslow once observed, to a man with a hammer, everything looks like a nail. If the man with the hammer must get judicial approval before he can use it, he will probably use it less often and more carefully.

There are other, somewhat more subtle, considerations that should be factored into any decision regarding torture. There are some who see silence as a virtue when it comes to the choice among such horrible evils as torture and terrorism. It is far better, they argue, not to discuss or write about issues of this sort, lest they become legitimated. And legitimation is an appropriate concern. Justice Jackson, in his opinion in one of the cases concerning the detention of Japanese Americans during World War II, made the following relevant observation:

> Much is said of the danger to liberty from the Army program for deporting and detaining these citizens of Japanese extraction. But a judicial construction of the due process clause that will sustain this order is a far more subtle blow to liberty than the promulgation of the order itself. A military order, however unconstitutional, is not apt to last longer than the military emergency. Even during that period a succeeding commander may revoke it all. But once a judicial opinion rationalizes such an order to show that it conforms to the Constitution, or rather rationalizes the Constitution to show that the Constitution sanctions such an order, the Court for all time has validated the principle of racial discrimination in criminal procedure and of transplanting American citizens. The principle then lies about like a loaded weapon ready for the hand of any authority that can bring forward a plausible claim of an urgent need. Every repetition imbeds that principle more deeply in our law and thinking and expands it to new purposes. All who observe the work of courts are familiar with what Judge Cardozo described as "the tendency of a principle to expand itself to the limit of its logic." A military commander may overstep the bounds of constitutionality, and it is an incident. But if we review and approve, that passing incident becomes the doctrine of the Constitution. There it has a generative power of its own, and all that it creates will be in its own image.[31]

A similar argument can be made regarding torture: if an agent tortures, that is "an incident," but if the courts authorize it, it becomes a precedent. There is, however, an important difference between the detention of Japanese American citizens and torture. The detentions were done openly and with presidential accountability; torture would be done secretly, with official deniability. Tolerating an off-the-book system of secret torture can also establish a dangerous precedent. . . .

Whatever option our nation eventually adopts—no torture even to prevent massive terrorism, no torture except with a warrant authorizing nonlethal torture, or no "officially" approved torture but its selective use beneath the radar screen—the choice is ours to make in a democracy. We do have a choice, and we should make it— before local FBI agents make it for us on the basis of a false assumption that we do not really "have a choice." . . .

NOTES

1. Walter Pincus, "Silence of 4 Terror Probe Suspects Poses a Dilemma for FBI," *Washington Post*, October 21, 2001. (Emphasis added.)

2. But see the case of *Leon v. Wainwright*, 734 F.2d 770 (11th Cir. 1984), holding that a *subsequent* statement made by a man who had been *previously* tortured into revealing the whereabouts of a kidnap victim could be introduced into evidence.

3. *Kastigar v. United States*, 406 US 441 (1972).

4. See *Leon v. Wainwright*. I have written previously on how the due process clauses could allow torture in certain circumstances. The following analysis is from Alan M. Dershowitz, "Is There a Torturous Road to Justice?" *Los Angeles Times*, November 8, 2001.

> The constitutional answer to this question may surprise people who are not familiar with the current Supreme Court interpreta- tion of the 5th Amendment privilege against self-incrimination, which does not prohibit *any* interrogation techniques including the use of truth serum or even torture. The privilege only prohibits the *introduction into evidence of the fruits* of such techniques in a criminal trial against the person on whom the techniques were used. Thus, if a confession were elicited from a suspect by the use of truth serum or torture, that confession—and its fruits—could not be used against the suspect. But it could be used against *another* suspect, or against *that* suspect in a noncriminal case, such as a deportation hearing.
>
> If a suspect is given "use immunity"—a judicial decree

announcing in advance that nothing the defendant says (or its fruits) can be used against him in a criminal case—he can be *compelled* to answer all proper questions. The question then becomes what sorts of pressures can constitutionally be used to implement that compulsion. We know that he can be imprisoned until he talks. But what if imprisonment is insufficient to compel him to do what he has a legal obligation to do? Can other techniques of compulsion be attempted?

Let's start with truth serum. What right would be violated if an immunized suspect who refused to comply with his legal obligations to answer questions truthfully were compelled to submit to an injection which made him do so? Not his privilege against self-incrimination, since he has no such privilege now that he has been given immunity. What about his right of bodily integrity? The involuntariness of the injection itself does not pose a constitutional barrier. No less a civil libertarian than Justice William J. Brennan rendered a decision that permitted an allegedly drunken driver to be involuntarily injected in order to remove blood for testing. Certainly there can be no constitutional distinction between an injection that *removes* a liquid and one that *injects* a liquid. What about the nature of the substance injected? If it is relatively benign and creates no significant health risk, the only issue would be that it compels the recipient to do something he doesn't want to do. But he has a legal obligation to do precisely what the serum compels him to do: answer all questions truthfully.

What if the truth serum doesn't work? Could the judge issue a "torture warrant," authorizing the FBI to employ specified forms of nonlethal physical pressure in order to compel the immunized suspect to talk? Here we run into another provision of the Constitution—the "due process" clause, which may include a general "shock the conscience" test. And torture in general certainly shocks the conscience of most civilized nations. But what if it were limited to the rare "ticking bomb" case—the situation in which a captured terrorist who knows of an imminent large-scale threat but refuses to disclose it?

5. William F. Buckley, among others, points to the case of the person who was tortured by Philippine authorities and confessed to having taken part in the Oklahoma City bombing, but of course no one believed him.

Compare this to the account described in the next paragraph of the tortured suspect whose information may have prevented a serious act of terrorism.

6. Matthem Brzezinski, "Bust and Boom: Six Years before the September 11 Attacks, Philippine Police Took Down an al Qaeda Cell That Had Been Plotting, among Other Things, to Fly Explosives-Laden Planes into the Pentagon—and Possibly Some Skyscrapers," *Washington Post*, December 30, 2001. See also Alexander Cockburn, "The Wide World of Torture," *Nation*, November 26, 2001; Doug Struck et al., "Bin Laden Followers Reach across the Globe," *Washington Post*, September 23, 2001.

7. There can be no doubt that torture sometimes works. Jordan apparently broke the most notorious terrorist of the 1980s, Abu Nidal, by threatening his mother. Philippine police reportedly helped crack the 1993 World Trade Center bombings by torturing a suspect. Steve Chapman, "No Tortured Dilemma," *Washington Times*, November 5, 2001. It is, of course, possible that judicially supervised torture will work less effectively than unsupervised torture, since the torturee will know that there are limits to the torture being inflicted. At this point in time, any empirical resolution of this issue seems speculative.

8. Michael Walzer, "Political Action: The Problem of Dirty Hands," *Philosophy and Public Affairs* 2, no. 2 (Winter 1973).

9. Quoted in W. L. Twining and P. E. Twining, "Bentham on Torture," *Northern Ireland Legal Quarterly* (Autumn 1973): 347. Bentham's hypothetical question does not distinguish between torture inflicted by private persons and by governments.

10. David Johnston and Philip Shenon, "F.B.I. Curbed Scrutiny of Man Now a Suspect in the Attacks," *New York Times*, October 6, 2001.

11. It is illegal to withhold relevant information from a grand jury after receiving immunity. See *Kastigar v. United States*, 406 US 441 (1972).

12. Twining and Twining, "Bentham on Torture," pp. 348–49. The argument for the limited use of torture in the ticking bomb case falls into a category of argument known as "argument from the extreme case," which is a useful heuristic to counter arguments for absolute principles.

13. To demonstrate that this is not just in the realm of the hypothetical: "The former CIA officer said he also suggested the agency begin targeting close relatives of known terrorists and use them to obtain intelligence. 'You get their mothers and their brothers and their sisters under your complete control, and then you make that known to the target,' he said. 'You imply or you directly threaten [that] his family is going to pay the price if he makes the wrong decision.'" Bob Drogin and Greg Miller, "Spy Agencies Facing Questions of Tactics," *Los Angeles Times*, October 28, 2001.

14. One of my clients, who refused to testify against the mafia, was threatened by the government that if he persisted in his refusal the government would "leak" false information that he was cooperating, thus exposing him to mob retaliation.

15. *United States v. Cobb*, 1 S.C.R. 587 (2001).

16. On conditions in American prisons, see Alan M. Dershowitz, "Supreme Court Acknowledges Country's Other Rape Epidemic," *Boston Herald*, June 12, 1994.

The United States may already be guilty of violating at least the spirit of the prohibition against torture. In a recent case the Canadian Supreme Court refused to extradite an accused person to the United States because of threats made by a judge and a prosecutor regarding the treatment of those who did not voluntarily surrender themselves to the jurisdiction of the US court. First, as he was sentencing a coconspirator in the scheme, the American judge assigned to their trial commented that those fugitives who did not cooperate would get the "absolute maximum jail sentence." Then, the prosecuting attorney hinted during a television interview that uncooperative fugitives would be subject to homosexual rape in prison:

Zubrod [prosecutor]: I have told some of these individuals, "Look, you can come down and you can put this behind you by serving your time in prison and making restitution to victims, or you can wind up serving a great deal longer sentence under much more stringent conditions," and describe those conditions to them.

MacIntyre [reporter]: How would you describe those conditions?

Zubrod: *You're going to be the boyfriend of a very bad man if you wait out your extradition.*

MacIntyre: And does that have much of an impact on these people?

Zubrod: Well, out of the 89 people we've indicted so far, approximately 55 of them have said, "We give up."

After reading the transcripts, the Supreme Court of Canada held: "The pressures were not only inappropriate but also, in the case of the statements made by the prosecutor on the eve of the opening of the judicial hearing in Canada, unequivocally amounted to an abuse of the process of the court.

We do not condone the threat of sexual violence as a means for one party before the court to persuade any opponent to abandon his or her right to a hearing. Nor should we expect litigants to overcome well-founded fears of violent reprisals in order to be participants in a judicial process. Aside from such intimidation itself, it is plain that a committal order requiring a fugitive to return to face such an ominous climate—which was created by those who would play a large, if not decisive, role in determining the fugitive's ultimate fate—would not be consistent with the principles of fundamental justice." *United States v. Cobb*, 1 S.C.R. 587 (2001). (Thanks to Craig Jones, a student, for bringing this matter to my attention.)

17. John Langbein, *Torture and the Law of Proof* (Chicago: University of Chicago Press, 1977), p. 68. Voltaire generally opposed torture but favored it in some cases.

18. A special edition of the *Israel Law Review* in 1989 presented a written symposium on the report on the Landau Commission, which investigated interrogation practices of Israel's General Security Services from 1987 to 1989.

19. A fifth approach would be simply to never discuss the issue of torture—or to postpone any such discussion until after we actually experience a ticking bomb case—but I have always believed that it is preferable to consider and discuss tragic choices before we confront them, so that the issue can be debated without recriminatory emotions and after-the-fact finger-pointing.

20. "The Supreme Court of Israel left the security services a tiny window of opportunity in extreme cases. Citing the traditional common-law defense of necessity, the Supreme Court left open the possibility that a member of the security services who honestly believed that rough interrogation was the only means available to save lives in imminent danger could raise this defense. This leaves such an individual member of the security services in the position of having to guess how a court would ultimately resolve his case. That is extremely unfair to such investigators. It would have been far better had the court required any investigator who believed that torture was necessary in order to save lives to apply to a judge. The judge would then be in a position either to authorize or refuse to authorize a 'torture warrant.' Such a procedure would require judges to dirty their hands by authorizing torture warrants or bear the responsibility for failing to do so. Individual interrogators should not have to place their liberty at risk by guessing how a court might ultimately decide a close case. They should be able to get an advance ruling based on the evidence available at the time.

"Perhaps the legislature will create a procedure for advance judicial scrutiny. This would be akin to the warrant requirement in the Fourth Amendment to the United States Constitution. It is a traditional role for judges to play, since it is the job of the judiciary to balance the needs for security against the imperatives of liberty. Interrogators from the security services are not trained to strike such a delicate balance. Their mission is single-minded: to prevent terrorism. Similarly the mission of civil liberties lawyers who oppose torture is single-minded: to vindicate the individual rights of suspected terrorists. It is the role of the court to strike the appropriate balance. The Supreme Court of Israel took a giant step in the direction of striking that balance. But it—or the legislature—should take a further step of requiring the judiciary to assume responsibility in individual cases. The essence of a democracy is placing responsibility for difficult choices in a visible and neutral institution like the judiciary." Alan M. Dershowitz, *Shouting Fire: Civil Liberties in a Turbulent Age* (New York: Little Brown, 2002), pp. 476–77.

21. Charles M. Sennott, "Israeli High Court Bans Torture in Questioning; 10,000 Palestinians Subjected to Tactics," *Boston Globe*, September 7, 1999.

22. Osama Awadallah, a green-card holder living in San Diego, has made various charges of torture, abuse, and denial of access to a lawyer. Shira Scheindlin, a federal district court judge in New York, has confirmed the seriousness and credibility of the charges, saying Awadallah may have been "unlawfully arrested, unlawfully searched, abused by law enforcement officials, denied access to his lawyer and family." Anthony Lewis, "Taking Our Liberties," *New York Times*, March 9, 2002.

23. Drogin and Miller, "Spy Agencies Facing Questions of Tactics." Philip Heymann is the only person I have debated thus far who is willing to take the position that no form of torture should ever be permitted—or used—even if thousands of lives could be saved by its use. Philip B. Heymann, "Torture Should Not Be Authorized," *Boston Globe*, February 16, 2002. Whether he would act on that principled view if he were the responsible government official who was authorized to make this life and death choice—as distinguished from an academic with the luxury of expressing views without being accountable for their consequences—is a more difficult question. He has told me that he probably would authorize torture in an actual ticking bomb case, but that it would be wrong and he would expect to be punished for it.

24. The necessity defense is designed to allow interstitial action to be taken in the absence of any governing law and in the absence of time to

change the law. It is for the nonrecurring situation that was never anticipated by the law. The use of torture in the ticking bomb case has been debated for decades. It can surely be anticipated. See Dershowitz, *Shouting Fire*, pp. 474–76.

Indeed, there is already one case in our jurisprudence in which this has occurred and the courts have considered it. In the 1984 case of *Leon v. Wainwright*, Jean Leon and an accomplice kidnapped a taxicab driver and held him for ransom. Leon was arrested while trying to collect the ransom, but refused to disclose where he was holding the victim. At this point, several police officers threatened him and then twisted his arm behind his back and choked him until he told them the victim's whereabouts. Although the federal appellate court disclaimed any wish to "sanction the use of force and coercion, by police officers," the judges went out of their way to state that this was not the act of "brutal law enforcement agents trying to obtain a confession." "This was instead a group of concerned officers acting in a reasonable manner to obtain information they needed in order to protect another individual from bodily harm or death." Although the court did not find it necessary to invoke the "necessity defense," since no charges were brought against the policemen who tortured the kidnapper, it described the torture as having been "motivated by the immediate *necessity* to find the victim and save his life." *Leon v. Wainwright*, 734 F.2d 770, 772–73 (11th Cir. 1984). (Emphasis added.) If an appellate court would so regard the use of police brutality—torture—in a case involving one kidnap victim, it is not difficult to extrapolate to a situation in which hundreds or thousands of lives might hang in the balance.

25. Quoted in Twining and Twining, "Bentham on Torture," p. 345.

26. Sir Edward Coke was "designated in commissions to examine particular suspects under torture." Langbein, *Torture and the Law of Proof*, p. 73.

27. Ibid., p. 7.

28. Ibid., p. 90, quoting Bacon.

29. Ibid., pp. 136–37, 139.

30. When it is known that torture is a possible option, terrorists sometimes provide the information and then claim they have been tortured, in order to be able to justify their complicity to their colleagues.

31. *Korematsu v. United States*, 323 US 214, 245–46 (1944) (Jackson, J. dissenting).

16.

TORTURE SHOULD NOT BE AUTHORIZED

Philip B. Heymann

Authorizing torture is a bad and dangerous idea that can easily be made to sound plausible. There is a sublte fallacy embedded in the traditional "ticking bomb" argument for torture to save lives. That argument goes like this. First, I can imagine dangers so dire that I might torture or kill guilty or innocent persons if I was quite sure that was necessary and sufficient to prevent those dangers. Second, very many feel this way, although differing in the circumstances and the certainty level they would want. Therefore, the "ticking bomb" argument concludes, everyone wants a system for authorizing torture or murder; we need only debate the circumstances and the level of certainty.

This conclusion, leading to abandonment of one of the few worldwide legal prohibitions, leaves out the fact that I do not have faith in the authorizing system for finding the required circumstances with any certainty because the costs of errors are born by the suspect tortured, not by those who decide to torture him. The conclusion also ignores the high probability that the practice of torture will spread unwisely if acceptance of torture with the approval of judges is substituted for a flat, worldwide prohibition.

The use of torture would increase sharply if there were "torture warrants." Any law enforcement or intelligence official who tortures a prisoner in the United States now is very likely to be prosecuted and imprisoned.

Punches may be thrown, but anything we think of as "torture" is considered an inexcusable practice. That revulsion will disappear if we make torture acceptable and legal whenever a judge accepts the judgment of intelligence officials that: (1) there is a bomb; (2) the suspect knows where it is; (3) torture will get the truth, not a false story, out of him before the bomb explodes; (4) the bomb won't be moved in the meantime. Every individual who believes in his heart, however recklessly, that those conditions (or others he thinks are just as compelling) are met will think there is nothing seriously wrong with torture.

Prof. Alan Dershowitz wants to bet that judges will say "no" in a high enough percentage of cases of "ticking bombs" that whatever moral force their refusal has will offset the legitimating and demoralizing effects of authorizing occasional torture. It's a bad bet.

Judges have deferred to the last several thousand requests for national security wiretaps and they would defer here. The basis of their decisions, information revealing secret "sources and methods" of intelligence gathering, would not be public. And if the judge refused, overrode the judgment of agents who thought lives would be lost without torture, and denied a warrant, why would that decision be more likely to be accepted and followed by agents desperate to save lives than the flat ban on torture we now have?

How many false positives do you want to accept? You would get six false positives out of ten occasions of torture even in the extraordinarily unlikely event that the intelligence officers convince the judge that they were really 80 percent sure of each of the above four predictions.

And even if you would tolerate this number of false positives if torture were in fact the only way to get the needed information to defuse the bomb, there are frequently other promising ways (such as emergency searches or stimulating conversations over tapped phones) that will be abandoned or discounted if torture is available.

Finally, if we approve torture in one set of circumstances, isn't every country then free to define its own exceptions, applicable to Americans as well as its own citizens? Fear of that led us to accept the Geneva Convention prohibiting torture of a prisoner of war, although obtaining his information might save dozens of American lives.

As to preventing terrorism, torture is an equally bad idea. Torture is a prescription for losing a war for support of our beliefs in the hope of reducing the casualties from relatively small battles.

. . . I do not accept torture either "off the books" with a wink at the secret discretion of the torturers or on the open authority of the judges from whom they might seek authorization. I predict so many types of harms to so many people and to the nation from any system that authorizes torture, either secretly or openly, that I would prohibit it.

The overall, longer-term cost of any system authorizing torture, openly or tacitly, would far outweigh its occasional, short-term benefits.

17.

IN TORTURE WE TRUST?

Eyal Press

If patriotism has to precipitate us into dishonour, if there is no precipice of inhumanity over which nations and men will not throw themselves, then, why in fact do we go to so much trouble to become, or to remain, human?

—John-Paul Sartre

The recent capture of al Qaeda leader Khalid Shaikh Mohammed is the latest indication that the taboo on torture has been broken. In the days after Mohammed's arrest, an unnamed official told the *Wall Street Journal* that US interrogators may authorize "a little bit of smacky-face" while questioning captives in the war on terrorism. Others proposed that the United States ship Mohammed off to a country where laxer rules apply. "There's a reason why [Mohammed] isn't going to be near a place where he has *Miranda* rights or the equivalent," a senior federal law enforcer told the *Journal*. "You go to some other country that'll let us pistol-whip this guy."

Asked about this by CNN's Wolf Blitzer, Sen. Jay Rockefeller IV, a

Reprinted with permission from the March 31, 2003, issue of the *Nation*. "In Torture We Trust," by Eyal Press.

Democrat from West Virginia and vice chairman of the Senate Select Committee on Intelligence, replied, "I wouldn't take anything off the table where he is concerned, because this is the man who has killed hundreds and hundreds of Americans over the last ten years." (An aide to Rockefeller subsequently insisted that the senator did not condone turning Mohammed over to a regime that tortures.) In fact, sending US captives to abusive allies, and other policies that potentially implicate America in torture, have been in use for months.

On December 26 of last year, the *Washington Post* published a front-page story detailing allegations of torture and inhumane treatment involving thousands of suspects apprehended since the September 11 terrorist attacks. Al Qaeda captives held at overseas CIA interrogation centers, which are completely off limits to reporters, lawyers and outside agencies, are routinely "softened up"—that is, beaten—by US Army Special Forces before interrogation, as well as thrown against walls, hooded, deprived of sleep, bombarded with light and bound in painful positions with duct tape. "If you don't violate someone's human rights some of the time, you probably aren't doing your job," one official said to the *Post* of these methods, which at the very least constitute cruel and inhumane treatment and may rise to the level of "severe pain or suffering, whether physical or mental," the benchmark of torture.

The same article reported that approximately one hundred suspects have been transferred to US allies, including Saudi Arabia and Morocco, whose brutal torture methods have been amply documented in the State Department's own annual human rights reports. "We don't kick the [expletive] out of them," one official told the *Post*. "We send them to other countries so they can kick the [expletive] out of them." Many captives have been sent to Egypt, where, according to the State Department, suspects are routinely "stripped and blindfolded; suspended from a ceiling or door frame with feet just touching the floor; beaten with fists, whips, metal rods, or other objects; subjected to electric shocks." In at least one case, a suspect was sent to Syria, where, the State Department says, torture methods include "pulling out fingernails; forcing objects into the rectum . . . using a chair that bends backwards to asphyxiate the victim or fracture the spine." A story in *Newsday* published just after Mohammed's arrest quoted a former CIA official who, describing a detainee transferred from Guantanamo Bay to Egypt, said, "They promptly tore his fingernails out and he started telling things."

Just as pundits debated Mohammed's possible transfer, evidence emerged that remaining in US custody might not be any safer: death certificates released for two al Qaeda suspects who died while in US custody at the Bagram base in Afghanistan showed that both were killed by "blunt force injuries." Other detainees told of being hung from the ceiling by chains.

The Bush administration insists that the United States has not violated the UN Convention against Torture, which the Senate ratified in 1994. But the cascade of recent revelations has left human rights groups understandably alarmed. Shortly after the *Washington Post* article appeared, a coalition of organizations, including Amnesty International and Human Rights Watch, fired off a letter to Defense Secretary Paul Wolfowitz calling upon the Bush administration to unequivocally denounce torture and clarify that the United States will "neither seek nor rely upon intelligence obtained" through such practices. But few have echoed their call. "There's been a painful silence about this," says Human Rights Watch executive director Ken Roth. "I haven't heard anyone in Congress call for hearings or even speak out publicly." The silence extends to the media, where, until Mohammed's capture, no follow-up investigations and few editorials had appeared—not even in the *New York Times*.

The absence of debate may simply reflect a preoccupation with Iraq, but it may also signal that in these jittery times, many people see torture as justified. In the aftermath of the World Trade Center attack, numerous commentators did suggest that the absolute prohibition on torture should be reconsidered. Harvard law professor Alan Dershowitz famously proposed allowing US judges to issue "torture warrants" to prevent potentially catastrophic terrorist attacks. Writing in the *New Republic* last fall, Richard Posner, a judge on the US Court of Appeals for the Seventh Circuit, expressed reservations about Dershowitz's proposal but argued that "if the stakes are high enough, torture is permissible. No one who doubts that this is the case should be in a position of responsibility."

Lurking behind such comments is the specter of the so-called ticking bomb: the captive who knows of an imminent attack that will cost thousands of lives, imagined vividly on February 4 in the hit Fox series *24*, in which US agents used electroshock to extract a confession about an impending nuclear attack.

Should an exceptional captive such as Mohammed be tortured to extract potentially lifesaving information? The *Nation* spoke with several prominent theorists of ethics, human rights, and the law, all of whom acknowledged that this is very difficult emotional terrain, even if there is, in the end, only one truly ethical answer. Martha Nussbaum, a professor at the University of Chicago who has written several books on ethics and human rights, offered a frank—and somewhat jarring—admission. "I don't think any sensible moral position would deny that there might be some imaginable situations in which torture [of a particular individual] is justified," Nussbaum wrote in an e-mail to the *Nation*.

But as Nussbaum went on to note, in the real world, governments don't just torture ticking time bombs: they torture their enemies, under circumstances that routinely stray from the isolated, extreme scenario. Even the most scrupulous regime is bound to do so, for the simple reason that nobody can know for certain whether a suspect really is a ticking bomb. "There's an inevitable uncertainty," explains Georgetown law professor David Cole, the author of *Terrorism and the Constitution* and a forthcoming book on September 11 and civil liberties. "You can't know whether a person knows where the bomb is, or even if they're telling the truth. Because of this, you end up going down a slippery slope and sanctioning torture in general." So while Cole and Nussbaum can imagine scenarios where torture might constitute a lesser evil, both favor a "bright line," in Cole's words, banning the practice.

Henry Shue, a professor of politics and international relations at Oxford who has published an influential academic article on torture, points out that the French experience in Algeria is illustrative. Though justified as a rare measure to prevent imminent assaults on civilians, says Shue, torture quickly spread through the French security apparatus "like a cancer." "The problem is that torture is a shortcut, and everybody loves a shortcut," Shue says. "I think it's a fantasy to believe that the United States is that much better than anybody else in this respect."

The Algerian experience recurred in Israel, where, until the Israeli Supreme Court formally banned the practice in 1999, preventing "ticking bombs" from carrying out suicide attacks served as the justification for hooding, beating, and abusing hundreds of Palestinians. "Very quickly, from a rare exception torture in Israel became standard practice in part because the ticking bomb metaphor is infinitely expandable," says Human Rights Watch's Roth. "Why stop with the bomber? Why not torture the person who could introduce you to the cousin who knows someone who planted the bomb? Why not torture the wife and kids? Friends? All of this becomes justified."

And once torture becomes common practice, it severely undermines a society's democratic norms. As Shibley Telhami, a professor at the University of Maryland and an expert on the Middle East, writes in his new book, *The Stakes*, "We cannot defend what we stand for by subverting our own values in the process." In the current climate, conservatives may dismiss such talk as soft-minded idealism. In fact, nobody has more adamantly insisted that the war on terrorism is, at root, a conflict about values than George W. Bush. In his recent State of the Union address, the president catalogued the torture methods administered to prisoners in Iraq. "Electric shock, burning with hot irons, dripping acid on the skin, mutilation with electric drills," Bush said. "If this is not evil, then evil has no meaning."

For the same government that denounces such practices to soften the rules when its own interests are at stake sends a disturbing message: that American moralizing is meaningless. That the United States is willing to dehumanize its enemies in much the way that it complains Islamic terrorists dehumanize theirs.

The parallel between terrorism and torture is instructive. Proponents of each practice maintain that the ends justify the means. They explain away violence by framing it as a necessary "last resort." And they obscure the human impact of that violence by refusing to register the humanity of their victims.

For torture is—and has always been—a function not of brute

sadism but of the willingness to view one's enemies as something less than human. As Edward Peters, a professor of history at the University of Pennsylvania, has shown in his authoritative history of the subject, in ancient Greece only slaves and foreigners were subjected to *basanos* (torture). During the late eighteenth and early nineteenth centuries, as the Enlightenment swept across Europe, one nation after another abolished the practice, to the point where, by 1874, Victor Hugo could proclaim that "torture has ceased to exist." Yet torture was reinstated during the decades that followed—just as the European powers established colonial empires. It became acceptable to treat "natives" in ways that were unacceptable for "the civilized." In more recent decades, when torture has been employed—South Africa, Cambodia, Tibet—it has often been meted out to members of groups so demonized that their individual identities were erased. In this context, it is chilling that the names and identities of the captives in the war on terrorism are as unknown to us as the methods being used against them.

"For the torturers, the sheer and simple fact of human agony is made invisible, and the moral fact of inflicting that agony is made neutral," writes Elaine Scarry in her powerful book *The Body in Pain*. But those facts are neither invisible nor neutral to the victims. "Whoever has succumbed to torture can no longer feel at home in the world," the Holocaust survivor (and torture victim) Jean Amery observed in his searing memoir *At the Mind's Limits*. "It is fear that henceforth reigns. . . . Fear—and also what is called resentments. They remain, and have scarcely a chance to concentrate into a seething, purifying thirst for revenge." In a recent article in the London *Guardian*, Hafiz Abu Sa'eda, head of the Egyptian Organization for Human Rights, described how the experience of being tortured by Egyptian authorities has played a role in radicalizing members of Islamist groups such as the Muslim Brotherhood.

"Torture demonstrates that the regime deserves destroying because it does not respect the dignity of the people," Sa'eda explains. "[The Muslim Brotherhood] began to argue that society should be destroyed and rebuilt again on the basis of an Islamic state." Among those who have been transformed from relative moderates into hard-line fanatics through such a process, the *Guardian* noted, is Dr. Ayman al-Zawahiri, a surgeon who, after being tortured in Egypt, fled to Afghanistan to join the mujahedeen and eventually became Osama bin Laden's deputy. It's possible that Zawahiri would have followed this path independently, of course. But no regime has ever quelled the hatred of its enemies by engaging in torture. The abuses instead fuel this hatred and indelibly transform not only the victims but the torturers themselves. "The screaming I heard on Saturday morning . . . those were screams which until today, when I sleep at night, I hear them inside my ears all the time," an Israeli soldier who stood guard over tortured prisoners said in an oral history published in 1990. "It doesn't leave me, I can't get rid of it."

To insist that the ban on torture should be absolute ought not to lead one to deny that this position comes with certain costs. It is probable that Israeli security forces have prevented some suicide bombings over the years by subjecting Palestinians to beatings and shakings, just as the French crushed the National Liberation Front during the battle of Algiers partly by torturing (and killing) many of its members. In democratic societies, however, it is understood that, as the Israeli Supreme Court noted in its 1999 decision banning torture, "not all means are acceptable." Torture, in this sense, is hardly unique: Most rights—free speech, privacy, freedom of assembly— entail potential costs by limiting what governments can do to insure order. Holding the line on torture should thus be viewed in the context of a broad debate about where to draw the line between liberty and security, and whether, in the aftermath of September 11, America is willing to stand by its professed values.

Those who advocate crossing the line frequently invoke the famous warning from Supreme Court Justice Robert Jackson that, however much we value our liberties, the Bill of Rights should not become "a suicide pact." But as real as the danger of al Qaeda may be, few would argue that it constitutes an existential threat to the nation. As the world's wealthiest and most powerful country, the United States has enormous resources at its disposal and countless tools with which to wage its war on terror. In this respect, it's worth asking why brutal CIA interrogation methods could be considered necessary for our security—while adequately funding homeland security is not.

As a tool for collecting information, moreover, torture is notoriously ineffective (since people in pain have the unfortunate habit of lying to make it stop) and has done little to solve long-term security threats. Witness modern Israel—or for that matter France in Algeria.

A deeper problem is that, all too often, even the absolutist position goes unenforced. No government on earth admits to practicing torture, yet each year Amnesty International documents countless states that do. The disparity stems from the fact that torture nearly always takes place in private settings, and in societies loath to discuss the subject openly. In a forthcoming article, Sanford Levinson, a professor at the University of Texas Law School and a noted legal realist, argues that this gap between rhetoric and reality may bolster Dershowitz's proposal that torture should be brought out into the open and regulated.

As William Schulz has argued persuasively in these pages [see "The Torturer's Apprentice," May 13, 2002], there are many reasons why, far from limiting torture, such a policy would end up making the practice more ubiquitous than ever. Any country in the world, Schulz points out, would henceforth be able to issue similar warrants and torture at will, free of criticism from the nation that pioneered the practice.

Levinson is right that it won't do simply to pretend that torture is not being perpetrated, as CNBC news anchor Brian Williams did the day after Mohammed's capture, saying to his guest, "Now, the United States says it does not engage in torture, and certainly for the purposes of this conversation and beyond we will take the government at its word." What's needed instead are scholars, reporters, politicians, and citizens who are willing both to hold democracies such as the United States to their stated ideals, and to ask hard questions about what, in a democratic society, should constitute permissible methods of interrogation during wartime. If violence and the threat of violence are out, should prolonged interrogations be permitted? (The Supreme Court has ruled that any confession obtained after thirty-six hours of questioning is by definition coerced.)

Should captives have access to lawyers? Should solitary confinement be allowed? This entire area of the law, says David Cole, remains nebulous, perhaps because it is an unpleasant topic to discuss.

Accompanying this discussion should be an equally frank dialogue about the safeguards we need to insure that rampant violations don't occur. For torture, like all governmental abuses, thrives in the absence of openness and accountability. In January the International Secretariat of the World Organisation against Torture (OMCT), a coalition of nongovernmental organizations from more than sixty-five different countries, issued a press release urging Washington to allow the United Nations Special Rapporteur on Torture to visit the Bagram base in Afghanistan, where the practices the *Washington Post* described are taking place. The OMCT's recommendation was met with stony silence, not only in Washington but by the US media.

The chilled atmosphere is reminiscent of the cold war, when discussion of US support for regimes that engaged in torture (Pinochet's Chile, Suharto's Indonesia) was likewise swept beneath the rug of national security. A language of euphemism and evasion emerged that became so ingrained as to go unnoticed. On February 6, in a disturbing sign that the pattern is being repeated, the *New York Times* published a front-page story detailing the intelligence breakthrough that led US officials to connect the recent murder of a diplomat to an al Qaeda cell in Baghdad. "Critical information about the network emerged from interrogations of captured cell members conducted under *unspecified circumstances of psychological pressure* [emphasis added]," the *Times* reported, a phrase you would expect to find in the training manual of a South American police state, not the world's leading newspaper. In the days following Mohammed's arrest, the US media uncritically accepted the Bush administration's vow not to violate the UN Convention against Torture, while casually mentioning (sometimes in the same article) that America could persuade Mohammed to talk by reminding him that it has access to his two young children. (Any threat to physically harm a captive's children would constitute torture.) London's *Economist*, by contrast, has questioned whether the United States is "quietly sanctioning the use of some forms of torture" and called on Bush to stop "handing prisoners over to less scrupulous allies."

In early March, the same week that news broke of the cause of the captives' deaths in Afghanistan, the *Post* reported that some nineteen detainees have attempted suicide at the US Navy Prison at Guantanamo Bay, which Michael Ratner, president of the Center for Constitutional Rights, says "begs the question of the long-term psychological effects of the techniques that are being employed there." For Americans to accept their government's assurances in light of these and other recent disclosures is deeply disquieting. For, as historian Peters has noted, the source of torture throughout history has always been the same: not the depraved prison guard who relishes inflicting pain but the society that agrees to tolerate, or even encourage, his actions. "It is still civil society," Peters writes, "that tortures or authorizes torture or is indifferent to those wielding it on civil society's behalf."

America's unique stature encumbers it with a special responsibility in this regard. "For better or worse, the United States sets precedents and examples," Henry Shue says. "We're very visible. If the most powerful country in the world has to torture, how are we supposed to convince anyone else that they shouldn't torture?" In Iran, a group of reformists in Parliament recently submitted a bill calling on their country to sign the UN Convention against Torture. One can only hope that Teheran's hard-line clerics haven't been reading the *Washington Post*.

18.

INTERROGATING SUSPECTED TERRORISTS

SHOULD TORTURE BE AN OPTION?

John T. Parry and Welsh S. White

In the wake of the September 11 terrorist attacks on the United States, voices in and out of the government have called for allowing interrogators to use torture to obtain information from suspected terrorists. The magnitude and shock of the attacks, the difficulties of the investigation, and the need to prevent future attacks place immense pressure on law enforcement officials. When suspects refuse to talk, investigators will understandably consider using extreme methods to obtain desperately needed information.

Federal investigators' experience with suspects believed to be involved in the attacks provides one example of interrogators' frustration. Shortly after the attacks, FBI agents and Justice Department investigators detained suspects who were believed to be connected to the attacks either because they were traveling with "false passports" and were carrying "box cutters, hair dye, and $5,000 in cash,"

John T. Parry and Welsh S. White, "Interrogating Suspected Terrorists: Should Torture Be an Option?" *University of Pittsburgh Law Review* 63 (Summer 2002): 743–66.

or because they had "links to al Qaeda."[1] In seeking information from these suspects, FBI agents not only employed traditional interrogation tactics but also offered the suspects unusual incentives such as "a new identity and life in the United States for them and their family members."[2] When all such efforts proved unsuccessful, one agent stated, "We are known for humanitarian treatment, so basically we are stuck. . . . Usually there is some incentive, some angle to play, what you can do for them. But it could get to that spot where we could go to pressure . . . where we won't have a choice and we are probably getting there."[3]

When confronted with these difficult situations, what kinds of pressures should interrogators be permitted to use? Experts have suggested various strategies, including using drugs and extraditing suspects to allied countries where less humane interrogation tactics are employed. In extreme situations, moreover, even traditionally liberal commentators have advocated that US interrogators should be permitted to use physical force or other abusive interrogation methods in order to force the disclosure of vital information.

One prominent civil libertarian, Harvard law professor Alan Dershowitz, has argued that when lives are at stake interrogators should sometimes be allowed to torture suspects to obtain information.[4] As one example, Professor Dershowitz cites a case "in which . . . [t]he kidnapper refuse[s] to disclose" the location of "a kidnapped child [who has] been buried in a box with two hours of oxygen."[5] In this and related situations, Dershowitz suggests that judges should issue "torture warrants" so that interrogators will be permitted to employ torture in extraordinary cases within our legal system rather than "outside of the law."[6] Other commentators have made similar arguments or have admitted that torture cannot be ruled out categorically.

The United Nations Convention against Torture and Other Cruel, Inhuman, or Degrading Treatment or Punishment erects an absolute ban on torture, which it defines as: any act by which severe pain or suffering, whether physical or mental, is intentionally inflicted on a person for such purposes as obtaining from him or a third person information or a confession, punishing him for an act he or a third person has committed or is suspected of having committed, or intimidating or coercing him or a third person, or for any reason based on discrimination of any kind, when such pain or suffering is inflicted by or at the instigation of or with the consent or acquiescence of a public official or other person acting in an official capacity. It does not include pain or suffering arising only from, inherent in, or incidental to lawful sanctions.[7]

The United States has adopted a more restrictive definition of torture that requires specific intent and narrows the definition of mental harm but nonetheless covers most of the same territory.[8] International law also distinguishes between torture and other less precisely defined yet nonetheless illegal forms of "cruel, unhuman, or degrading" treatment.[9] Although the meaning of the latter phrase is unclear, the United States interprets it as equivalent to "the cruel, unusual, and inhumane treatment or punishment prohibited by the Fifth, Eighth, and Fourteenth Amendments to the Constitution of the United States."[10] In this article, we use "torture" in a more general sense to refer to any coercive interrogation practice that involves the infliction of pain or extreme discomfort.[11]

As Professor Dershowitz admits, the notion that interrogators will be permitted to torture or otherwise mistreat suspects to obtain information in any situation is "very troubling."[12] In deciding when, if ever, interrogators should be allowed to employ such extreme techniques, several questions relating to interrogation law and practice seem relevant. First, from a legal standpoint, what guidance do the Supreme Court's interrogation cases provide for determining the circumstances under which police interrogators should be permitted to employ torture? Second, from a pragmatic standpoint, will police interrogating suspected terrorists be more likely to obtain useful information through employing torture rather than interrogation techniques employed by the police in other serious cases? Third, assuming there are situations in which torture would be more effective than other interrogation techniques, when, if ever, should the police be permitted to employ it? . . .

We admit that torture may be understandable in extreme situations. Nonetheless, we argue torture should remain illegal under all circumstances and victims of torture should a have a full array of available remedies. At the same time, however, a government official accused of using torture should be able to raise the necessity defense in a subsequent criminal prosecution to the extent the defense would otherwise be available.

I. THE LAW OF TORTURE IN THE UNITED STATES

A. The Supreme Court's Prohibition on Interrogators' Use of Torture

In the early twentieth century, some police interrogators routinely employed torture to obtain information from criminal suspects. They subjected suspects to physical brutality with the aid of various instruments, including boxing gloves, rubber hoses, placing a rope around the suspect's neck, or using the "water cure," which involved slowly pouring water into the nostrils of a suspect who was held down on his back.[13] In addition, they employed other abusive practices, such as stripping the suspect of clothing, placing him in an airless, overcrowded unsanitary room, and subjecting him to protracted questioning without sleep.[14]

When practices of this type came under attack, police defended them on the ground that confessions induced by such practices were often the only means through which they could solve serious crimes.[15] They maintained that the truthfulness of the resulting confessions could be verified by requiring the suspect to provide details that would be known only to the perpetrator.[16] The end—obtaining reliable evidence necessary to solve serious crimes—justified the means of using abusive interrogation practices.

In 1931, however, the Wickersham Commission issued a report that unequivocally condemned police use of abusive interrogation practices.[17] The report disputed the claim that such practices promoted effective law enforcement, observing that the practies often produced false confessions, which sometimes led to wrongful convictions.[18] In addition, the report condemned interrogators' abusive practices not only because they violated suspects' rights but also because they degraded law enforcement officers, reducing them to the level of the criminals they were seeking to apprehend.[19]

The Wickersham Report significantly influenced the development of the law imposing constitutional restrictions on interrogators. Prior to the commission's report, the Supreme Court had not considered any state cases in which the admissibility of a defendant's confession was at issue. In a line of cases beginning in 1936,[20] however, the Supreme Court decided that the admission of a confession obtained as a result of abusive interrogation practices violated the due process clause of the Fourteenth Amendment. In three of these cases,[21] the Court not only cited the Wickersham Report, but made it clear that it fully endorsed the report's position: law enforcement's practice of obtaining confessions through torture or other abusive interrogation practices should be eliminated.

Although the Court's due process confession cases ostensibly decided only whether confessions obtained by police interrogators were properly admitted against criminal defendants, the Court nevertheless indicated that certain interrogations were unequivocally impermissible. In *Brown v. Mississippi*, the first in this line of cases, a white deputy sheriff obtained confessions from three black suspects by whipping them until they confessed. The Court stated that "[i]t would be difficult to conceive of methods more revolting to the sense of justice than those taken to procure the confessions." In *Ashcraft v. Tennessee*, decided six years later, Justice Jackson, while dissenting from the Court's holding that the admission of a confession obtained after thirty-six hours of virtually continuous interrogation violated due process, sought to distinguish between permissible and impermissible interrogation techniques by stating, "[i]nterrogation per se is not, while violence per se is, an outlaw." In other words, in deciding whether a confession obtained by prolonged police questioning would be inadmissible, courts would have to examine the questioning's effect on the suspect. When the police employed violence to produce a confession, however, no such inquiry would be necessary. The confession would be excluded because police interrogators are absolutely prohibited from using violence to obtain statements. . . .

At least two lessons can be drawn from the Court's due process confession cases. First, police interrogation practices that severely infringe on a suspect's mental or physical autonomy violate the due process clause regardless of whether they produce statements that are admitted against the suspect. An interrogator's torture of a suspect would thus ordinarily result in a violation of the suspect's constitutional rights—an issue we discuss again in the next section. Second, law enforcement officers' right to employ extreme interrogation practices apparently does not vary depending on law enforcement's need for information. Rather, interrogation practices that are prohibited because they impose too severe infringements on individual autonomy will be impermissible regardless of the law enforcement interest at stake.

B. Torture beyond Confessions

As we suggested in the previous section, the legal consequences of a coercive interrogation go beyond an inadmissible confession. The use of coercion in interrogation violates the victim's due process rights whether or not the government ever seeks to use the confession. Thus, the victims of coercive interrogation—whether or not it rises to the level of torture—may bring a Bivens or § 1983 action for damages against their interrogators.[22] . . .

In addition, state and federal law criminalizes all conduct that fits within the definition of torture, as well as most conduct that would fall under the more ambiguous category of "cruel, inhuman, and degrading treatment or punishment." . . .

In sum, a variety of laws and constitutional provisions indicate that torture is illegal and unconstitutional in any context. As the State Department recently summarized the law:

> Torture is prohibited by law throughout the United States. It is categorically denounced as a matter of policy and as a tool of state authority. Every act constituting torture under the [Convention against Torture] constitutes a criminal offense under the law of the United States. No official of the government, federal, state, or local, civilian or military, is authorized to commit or to instruct anyone

else to commit torture. Nor may any official condone or tolerate torture in any form. No exceptional circumstances may be invoked as a justification for torture. US law contains no provision permitting otherwise prohibited acts of torture or other cruel, inhuman or degrading treatment of punishment to be employed on grounds of exigent circumstances (for example, during a "state of public emergency") or on orders from a superior officer or public authority, and the protective mechanisms of an independent judiciary are not subject to suspension.[23]

The relevance of these statements and the case law should not be overestimated, however. US law on torture has developed in situations in which the individual interests at stake are to be weighed against law enforcement's general interest in solving or punishing a crime; it has not been tested against the more extreme circumstances presented by terrorism.

When government officials are seeking information from a suspected terrorist, they may be seeking to protect national security or even to prevent the imminent loss of life. When interests of this magnitude are involved, arguably the balance struck in cases like Chambers—where the government's only interest is in solving a completed crime—should be recalibrated. Nevertheless, the evolution of the Court's due process confession cases, as well as other discussions of torture, provide a clear warning that allowing police interrogators to employ torture in any situation would be contrary to safeguards that have become a part of our constitutional heritage.

II. MODERN INTERROGATION PRACTICES

In the wake of the Court's prohibition of abusive interrogation practices, interrogators developed sophisticated psychologically oriented interrogation techniques that were designed to convince suspects it was in their own best interest to make truthful statements to interrogators. As they refined these techniques, interrogators discovered that the new techniques were more effective than the old. Interrogators who skillfully employed psychologically oriented techniques were generally able to convince suspects that it was in their best interest to talk to the police. In contrast to the abusive tactics employed in the past, moreover, interrogators' proper use of the new techniques was generally likely to elicit truthful statements from suspects. . . .

Even with the addition of the protections afforded by the *Miranda* warnings, modern interrogators have been remarkably successful at convincing suspects that it is in their own best interest to make a statement to the police. Studies indicate that, in most jurisdictions, police interrogators are able to persuade suspects to waive their *Miranda* rights and to make a statement to the police in more than 80 percent of all cases.[24] Even when the police are not able to obtain a *Miranda* waiver, moreover, they are sometimes able to persuade suspects to make a statement that will assist the police in solving a crime, even if it cannot be introduced into evidence.

In some cases, of course, interrogators' use of standard interrogation techniques will not produce a statement. There is a small group of suspects—including professional criminals—who operate on the assumption that they will "say nothing" to the police.[25] If law enforcement officials wish to obtain statements from suspects in this category, they will have to employ more extreme interrogation tactics than those permitted in ordinary criminal cases. If suspected terrorists are likely to fit within this category, then it may be necessary to consider what types of interrogation tactics have the best chance of securing information from individuals who are determined not to disclose it.

Are suspected terrorists likely to be hard-core suspects in the sense that they will refuse to disclose information? Obviously, suspected terrorists cannot all be placed in a single category. Even aside from the fact that many of those suspected of terrorism may be innocent, some suspects who are connected with terrorist activity will be so naive and vulnerable that they may easily be induced to speak through psychologically oriented interrogation tactics. On the other hand, some individuals are undoubtedly so committed to terrorist objectives that they would be adamant in their refusal to disclose useful information to the police.

When dealing with the latter category of suspects, what interrogation methods are most likely to lead to the disclosure of useful information? Even with suspects who refuse to cooperate, practices short of torture would sometimes be likely to produce useful information. When interrogators believe it is critical to determine whether a suspect has knowledge of specific facts, using cutting-edge technology to evaluate suspects' brain waves may soon be effective. Moreover, although there is considerable debate regarding the efficacy of so-called truth serums, some experts believe that interrogators' use of sodium pentothal or other compounds will sometimes lead suspects to reveal secret information. And as in ordinary cases, when interrogators have sufficient time to employ the full range of psychologically oriented interrogation methods, their patient efforts to extract information through gaining the suspect's trust and establishing a rapport may be surprisingly likely to produce positive results.

In some cases, however, interrogators may reasonably believe that the only way in which they can obtain vital information from suspects is through the use of torture or other abusive interrogation practices. When cases of this type arise, what approach should courts take in regulating the conduct of interrogators?

III. TORTURE AND NECESSITY

The pressures of the war on terrorism have yet to test US laws against torture. Nonetheless, a precedent is available. For more than a decade, the Israeli legal system struggled to create a framework that would recognize the claims of basic human rights while also giving due regard to the needs of the government in its effort to foil terrorists who "have established as their goal Israel's annihilation."[26] Before considering the best framework for assessing whether government agents should be permitted to torture terrorists in the United States, therefore, we will briefly discuss the Israeli approach.

A. The Israeli Experience

Israel's General Security Service (GSS, also known as Shin Bet) was long suspected of employing torture. In 1987, a commission chaired by Moshe Landau, former president of the Supreme Court of Israel, examined the GSS's interrogation practices. The Landau Commission concluded that Israel's codified version of the necessity defense authorizes in advance the use of force in interrogation, so long as the interrogator reasonably believes the lesser evil of force is necessary to get information that would prevent the greater evil of loss of innocent lives.

Although the report generated controversy, its recommendations established the bureaucratic framework for torture in Israel. According to the Supreme Court of Israel: the decision to utilize physical means in a particular instance is based on internal regulations, which requires obtaining permission from various ranks of the GSS hierarchy. The regulations themselves were approved by a special Ministerial Committee on GSS interrogations. Among other guidelines, the committee set forth directives pertaining to the rank authorized to allow these interrogation practices. . . . Different interrogation methods are employed depending on the suspect, both in relation to what is required in that situation and to the likelihood of obtaining authorization. The GSS does not resort to every interrogation method at its disposal in each case.

In practice, however, GSS investators often disregarded the limits that the report attempted to put in place, and some commentators claim the GSS tortured as many as 85 percent of detained Palestinians. During the 1987–1994 period, between sixteen and twenty-five Palestinians died during or after interrogation. At the same time, however, the GSS's interrogation methods apparently helped to foil some terrorist attacks.

The Supreme Court of Israel heard a number of cases challenging GSS interrogation practices but did not provide a clear ruling until 1999. In 1996, for example, the court issued an order to prevent the use of physical force in a particular interrogation, but lifted the order the next day after the GSS claimed it sought information from the suspect that could prevent future terrorist attacks. According to the suspect's attorney, the court's decision reflected its usual practice of "grant[ing] injunctions only when the state made no objection, and allow[ing] the use of physical pressures when the state sought it."[27]

The 1996 decision led to a United Nations investigation of Israel's use of force in interrogations. Soon thereafter, the court—sitting as the High Court of Justice—began hearings in a case brought by six individual Palestinians and two Israeli human rights organizations.

The court issued its decision in 1999. In its ruling, the court made clear that any form of interrogation must be measured against a strong presumption of individual liberty: "An interrogation inevitably infringes upon the suspect's freedom, even if physical means are not used. Indeed, undergoing an interrogation infringes on both the suspect's dignity and his individual privacy. In a state adhering to the Rule of Law, interrogations are therefore not permitted in [the] absence of clear statutory authorization."[28]

The court found no legislative authorization for any of the coercive practices at issue, and accordingly held that each practice was prohibited. Moreover, the court rejected the government's claim (accepted by the Landau Commission) that torture is authorized in advance by the necessity defense because it leads to information that saves lives. As a remedy, the court entered the functional equivalent of a general injunction against the use of torture in interrogations.

Although the court banned torture, it also declared its willingness "to accept that in the appropriate circumstances, GSS investigators may avail themselves of the 'necessity' defence, if criminally indicted."[29] In particular, the court discussed the possible application of the necessity defense to a "ticking time bomb" situation, in which law enforcement officials torture a suspect who "holds information respecting the location of a bomb that was set and will imminently explode."[30] Public committee has had a significant impact on GSS interrogation practices. Indeed, Amnesty International has admitted that "the GSS ceased systematic use of these interrogation techniques" after the decision.[31] Reports of torture continue as the second Intifada rages, but with much less frequency than before the court's ruling.

B. Applying the Necessity Defense to the Torture of Terrorists

Consider the following hypothetical. Federal law enforcement officials receive credible information that a specific, known terrorist group has

planted a nuclear device in a major US city, and the device will detonate in a few hours. Time is so short that only a relatively small number
of those in the city could be evacuated to safety. Soon thereafter, officials apprehend in the vicinity of the targeted city an individual known
to be among the leadership of the terrorist group. After an interrogation employing as many standard techniques as possible in the limited
time available, the terrorist refuses to admit or deny that a nuclear
device has been planted and refuses to provide any other information.
With time running out, should torture be an option?

We believe the answer in that situation is yes, regardless of the
legal status of torture. That is, under extreme "ticking time bomb"
circumstances, torture may be the least worse choice. But this hypothetical proves little. Anyone can devise a fact pattern that would
convince nearly everyone to permit torture under the specific circumstances. The normal case—if there is such a thing—in which
officials will be tempted to torture is likely to depart significantly
from our hypothetical. For example, law enforcement rarely will
have specific information about the nature, location, and timing of
the attack, the group carrying it out, or the identities of those who
have knowledge of the attack. In fact, officials may not even know
whether there is a specific attack planned at all.

The more likely case is the one currently facing the federal government with some of those captured in the aftermath of September
11: law enforcement officials have captured someone whom they
have reason to believe is a member of a terrorist group, and they
seek information from that person about past attacks and possible
future attacks. Put differently, officials may interrogate for the purpose of solving past crimes, getting additional information about
past crimes whether or not they have already been solved, and
obtaining information that would help foil future attacks whether
or not any particular attacks are on the drawing board. Officials may
have reason to believe that the person they have captured knows
something about past attacks or future plans, but they cannot be
sure. If the suspect refuses to provide any information (or worse,
mocks their efforts), they may become frustrated and angry. In such
cases, should torture be an option?

In rough terms, we believe the Israeli approach provides the best answer. Torture is categorically illegal under international law, the federal Constitution and statutes, and state law. Regardless of the claimed purpose or need, it should remain so. No court, legislature, or executive official should encourage or condone torture in any way. In addition, victims of torture should have the full array of available remedies: criminal prosecutions, damages actions, and injunctive relief where appropriate.

Our rationales are both moral and pragmatic. We believe torture is wrong in nearly every circumstance. Moreover, legalizing torture would create administrative difficulties that would raise further moral issues. For example, if some form of torture were legal, Congress would have to craft legislative standards for when and how to torture (e.g., how long can interrogators hold someone's head under water?), delegate that task to the executive, or entrust the torture decision to executive branch discretion. If the executive branch drafted regulations, the courts would engage in Chevron review to make sure the executive's interpretations were reasonable and within the range of permitted activity, and would preside over any subsequent cases. All three branches would thus play a role in creating the framework for torture, and all three branches would become complicit in it. Finally, no matter how carefully the respective branches performed their appointed tasks, the resulting standards would inevitably be overinclusive, resulting in unnecessary torture.

Authorizing law enforcement officials to use torture even in extremely limited circumstances would also send a variety of undesirable messages. Once torture is available for terrorists in extreme circumstances, someone inevitably will demand it in less extreme circumstances, and then for suspected serial rapists or murderers, or even for those accused of lesser crimes. The slippery slope problem with torture and the related risk of abuse is real, and the harms that would inevitably result from a loosening of standards are significant. Authorizing torture would also betray well-established constitutional values and teach citizens that principles are among the first things to be jettisoned in an emergency.

A claim by the United States that it may torture in extreme circumstances would have serious international consequences as well. Such a claim would undermine the "painfully won and still fragile consensus" against torture. Absent an absolute ban on torture, other countries or even terrorist groups could claim they were simply following the example of the United States. The frequency of torture in many countries could increase, which would also increase the chance that a US national would be tortured if kidnapped or captured by terrorists or the military forces of another country.

For these reasons, the government should not have the authority to torture even in the extreme-circumstances scenario discussed above, in which we conceded that torture could be permitted. Rather, the best approach is to place the decision squarely on the shoulders of the individuals who order or carry out torture. Government agents should use torture only when it provides the last remaining chance to save lives that are in imminent peril. If interrogators know that they act at their peril, because the law provides no authority for torture under any circumstances, then they are likely to be deterred from acting except when the choice—however distasteful—seems obvious.

When a government agent uses torture to gain information that would avert a future terrorist act, the necessity defense should be available in any resulting criminal prosecution. A successful necessity claim requires proof that the defendant reasonably believed his harmful actions were necessary to avert a greater, imminent harm. A better—though less popular—description of the defense is that necessity claims turn on whether the defendant's conduct, however harmful, was "right and proper . . . under the circumstances."[32] Under either formulation, a government agent who tortures to save lives has a fair chance of mounting a successful defense.

Allowing the necessity defense in torture cases is consistent with providing strong deterrence against torture. Most officials probably believe that torture is prohibited, but they are less likely to know that the necessity defense could be available despite that prohibition. Ignorance of the exception to the rule would promote deterrence. Even if interrogators know that the necessity defense is available, they will not be able to predict with certainty before they act whether the defense would be successful, and the resulting uncertainty would also foster deterrence. The primary obstacle to deterrence is prosecutorial discretion. An interrogator might assume that the government will not prosecute if torture reveals critical information. For that reason, the Department of Justice should have a clear and public policy of prosecuting without exception any law enforcement official who uses torture. . . .

IV. CONCLUSION

To paraphrase Justice Jackson, torture is an "outlaw." Our experience with abusive police interrogation practices during the past century taught us that police use of torture to obtain confessions is not the best way to obtain reliable evidence. More importantly, torture violates fundamental human rights protected by the Constitution and international law and degrades law enforcement by reducing it to the level of the criminals it seeks to apprehend. During the pre-*Miranda* era, Supreme Court decisions regulating police interrogation thus held that the government is absolutely prohibited from using torture to obtain incriminating statements. Over the past decade, this principle has been confirmed and expanded. Under our current law, torture is absolutely prohibited. Moreover, state-sponsored torture cannot be justified by any exceptional circumstances.

These principles were formulated before the attacks of September 11 precipitated our present concern with protecting innocent people from imminent terrorist attacks. Nevertheless, we believe these principles provide the framework within which government officials interrogating suspected terrorists should be required to operate. There will, of course, be "ticking bomb" hypotheticals in which an officer's decision to use torture to obtain vital information would be viewed by everyone as the best choice under the circumstances. But such situations will rarely, if ever, arise in practice. In the great majority of cases, an officer will not plausibly be able to claim that he believed that torturing a suspected terrorist was the only means through which he could avert an imminent loss of life.

Accordingly, whenever a government officer employs torture, he should be subjected to criminal prosecution. If the officer claims that he reasonably believed his criminal behavior was immediately necessary to avert a greater harm (such as the loss of innocent lives), he should be allowed to raise a necessity defense which can be evaluated by a judge or jury. Through this means, officers who torture in true "ticking bomb" situations may be relieved of criminal liability, a result that seems consistent with normative standards of fairness. At the same time, however, through maintaining the principle that torture is prohibited, we will provide maximum deterrence against government use of torture and thereby, to the extent possible, prevent the government from degrading itself by engaging in behavior that is inconsistent with our constitutional heritage and condemned by civilized nations.

NOTES

1. Walter Pincus, "Silence of 4 Terror Probe Suspects Poses a Dilemma for FBI," *Washington Post*, October 21, 2001, p. A6.
2. Ibid.
3. Ibid.
4. See Alan M. Dershowitz, "Is There a Torturous Road to Justice?" *Los Angeles Times*, November 8, 2001, p. B19. See also Alan M. Dershowitz, *Shouting Fire: Civil Liberties in a Turbulent Age* (New York: Little Brown, 2002), p. 477; Alan M. Dershowitz, "Is It Necessary to Apply 'Physical Pressure' to Terrorists—And to Lie About It?" *Israel Law Review* 23 (1989): 192; Alan M. Dershowitz, "Want to Torture? Get a Warrant," *San Francisco Chronicle*, January 22, 2002, p. A19.
5. Dershowitz, "Is There a Torturous Road to Justice?"
6. Ibid.
7. UN General Assembly, *Convention against Torture and Other Cruel, Inhuman, or Degrading Treatment or Punishment*, Resolution. 39/46, annex, 39 UN GAOR Supp. (No. 51) at 197, UN Doc. A/39/51 (1984), entered into force June 26, 1987.
8. The Senate's reservations to the UN *Convention against Torture* state: [T]he United States understands that, in order to constitute torture, an act must be specifically intended to inflict severe physical or mental pain or

suffering and that mental pain or suffering refers to prolonged mental harm caused by or resulting from: (1) the intentional infliction or threatened infliction of severe physical pain or suffering; (2) the administration or application, or threatened administration or application, of mind-altering substances or other procedures calculated to disrupt profoundly the senses or the personality; (3) the threat of imminent death; or (4) the threat that another person will imminently be subject to death, severe physical pain or suffering, or the administration or application of mind-altering substances calculated to disrupt profoundly the senses or personality. "U.S. Reservations, Declarations, and Understandings and Convention against Torture and Other Forms of Cruel, Inhuman, or Degrading Treatment or Punishment, *Congressional Record* II(1)(a), 136 S 17491–92 (1994); see also *Federal Criminal Code–Crimes–Torture, U.S. Code*, vol. 18, sec, 2340 (2002) (providing a nearly identical definition for criminalization of torture committed outside the United States by US nationals or persons later found in the United States); *Torture Victim Protection Act, U.S. Code*, vol. 28, sec. 1350 (2002) (same for civil remedy against torturers acting under color of law of a foreign nation). For more expansive discussions of torture from a variety of perspectives, see J. Herman Burgers and Hans Danelius, *The United Nations Convention against Torture: A Handbook on the Convention against Torture and Other Cruel, Inhuman, and Degrading Treatment or Punishment*, Kluver Law International (Dordrecht/Boston/London: Martinus Nijhoff Publishers, 1998); John Conroy, *Unspeakable Acts, Ordinary People* (New York: Knopf, 2000); Alan Hyde, *Bodies of Law* (Princeton, NJ: Princeton University Press, 1997), pp. 187–91; John H. Langbein, *Torture and the Law of Proof* (Chicago: University of Chicago Press, 1977); Edward Peters, *Torture*, exp. ed. (Philadelphia: University of Pennsylvania Press, 1996); Ronald D. Crelinsten and Alex P. Schmid, eds., *The Politics of Pain: Torturers and Their Masters* (Boulder, CO: Westview Press, 1995); Nigel S. Rodley, *The Treatment of Prisoners under International Law*, 2nd ed. (Oxford: Clarendon Press, 1999); Elaine Scarry, *The Body in Pain: The Making and Unmaking of the World* (Oxford: Oxford University Press, 1985), pp. 35–59; Robert M. Cover, "Violence and the Word," *Yale Law Journal* 95 (1986): 1601, 1603; Mordechai Kremnitzer, "The Landau Commission Report—Was the Security Service Subordinated to the Law, or the Law to the 'Needs' of the Security Service?" *Israel Law Review* 23 (1989): 216, 250–51; Henry Shue, "Torture," *Philosophy and Public Affairs* 7 (1978): 124.

9. UN General Assembly, *Convention against Torture*, article 16 (proscribing but not defining "other acts of cruel, inhuman, or degrading treat-

ment or punishment which do not amount to torture"). For overviews of the distinction between "torture" and "cruel, inhuman, or degrading treatment of punishment" under international and European law see Rodley, *Treatment of Prisoners*, pp. 75–106; Malcolm D. Evans, "Getting to Grips with Torture," *International and Comparative Law Quarterly* 51 (2002): 365.

10. U.S. Reservations, Declarations, *Congressional Record* at I(1).

11. Compare Conroy, *Unspeakable Acts*, pp. 34–38 (discussing the use of hunger, sleep deprivation, humiliation, and psychological methods as a means of torture); Scarry, *Body in Pain*, pp. 47–48 (describing how even ordinary movements or postures qualify as torture when prolonged); and Kremnitzer, "Landau Commission Report," p. 250 ("A cold shower may be commonplace, but it can be degrading treatment when forced upon a person as a means of breaking down his resistance.").

12. Dershowitz, "Torturous Road to Justice," p. 19. Indeed Professor Dershowitz appears to have backed away from his proposal: "My personal hope is that no torture warrant would ever be issued, because the criteria for obtaining one would be so limited and rigorous." Alan M. Dershowitz, "Letter to the Editor," *San Francisco Chronicle*, January 28, 2002, p. B4. Compare Dershowitz, "Is It Necessary," 199–200 ("I am personally convinced that there are some circumstances—at least in theory—under which extraordinary means, including physical pressure, may properly be authorized; I am also convinced that these circumstances are present far less frequently than law enforcement would claim.").

13. Welsh S. White, *Miranda's Waning Protections: Police Interrogation Practices after Dickerson* (Ann Arbor: University of Michigan Press, 2001), p. 18.

14. Ibid.

15. Ibid., p. 17.

16. Ibid., see p. 19. (Observing that the Wickersham Commission's Report concluded that abusive interrogation practices "produced a danger of false confessions that in some cases resulted in wrongful convictions.")

17. National Commission on Law Observance and Enforcement (Wickersham Commission), *Report on Lawlessness in Law Enforcement* (Washington, DC: Government Printing Office, 1931), p. 169.

18. White, *Miranda's Waning Protections*, p. 19. For a contemporary example, see *60 Minutes: Torture?* (CBS television broadcast, January 20, 2002) describing a case in which a terrorist confessed to the Oklahoma City bombing while being tortured by Philippine authorities.

19. White, *Miranda's Waning Protections*, p. 19 (citing Wickersham Report, p. 191).

20. See *Brown v. Mississippi*, 297 US 278 (1936).

21. See *Culombe v. Connecticut*, 367 US 568, 571–72n.2, 572n.3, 573–74n.6, 574n.8 (1961); *Ashcraft v. Tennessee*, 322 US 143, 150n.4 (1944); *Chambers v. Florida*, 309 US 227, 238n.11, 240–41n.15 (1940).

22. See *Bivens v. Six Unknown Named Federal Agents*, 403 US 388 (1971) (allowing action against federal officials for violation of constitutional rights); *Civil Action for Deprivation of Rights*, U.S. *Code*, vol. 42, sec. 1983 (2002) (creating cause of action against persons who violate constitutional rights while acting under color of state law).

23. See US Department of State, Initial Report of the United States of America to the UN Committee against Torture (1999) at http://www.state .gov/www/global/human-rights/torture_articles.html.

24. Richard A. Leo and Welsh S. White, "Adapting to Miranda: Modern Interrogators' Strategies for Dealing with the Obstacles Posed by Miranda," *Minnesota Law Review* 84, no. 2 (1999): 397, 468.

25. David Simon, *Homicide: A Year on the Killing Streets* (New York: Houghton Mifflin, 1991), p. 198. ("The professionals say nothing.")

26. *Public Committee against Torture in Israel v. The State of Israel*, 38 I.L.M. 1471 (1999) court case: H.C. 5100/94.

27. See Serge Schmemann, "Israel Allows Use of Physical Force in Arab's Interrogation," *New York Times*, November 16, 1996, p. 8. See also George C. Christie, "The Defense of Necessity Considered from the Legal and Moral Point of View," *Duke Law Journal* 48 (1999): 975, 1031n.306. (discussing the 1996 decision and assuming it allowed the Israeli government to use torture at least where it could result in a net saving of lives); Catherine M. Grosso, "International Law in the Domestic Arena: The Case of Torture in Israel," *Iowa Law Review* 86 (2000): 321–23 (discussing the pre–Public Committee cases).

28. *Public Committee against Torture in Israel v. The State of Israel*, 1478.

29. Ibid., 1486, 1488.

30. Ibid., 1485.

31. Amnesty International, "Torture in Israel: Amnesty International Oral Statement," UN Commission on Human Rights Concerning Israel and the Occupied Territories (March 2000), http://www.angelfire.com/ia/ palestinefoever/amnestytorture.html.

32. *United States v. Schoon*, 971 F.2d 193, 200 (9th Cir. 1991) (Fernandez, J. concurring).

PART 5.

HABEAS CORPUS AND "ENEMY COMBATANTS"

19.

Ex Parte Quirin

US Supreme Court

Decided July 31, 1942.
Extended opinion filed October 29, 1942.

M r. Chief Justice Stone delivered the opinion of the Court.
. . . The question for decision is whether the detention of petitioners by respondent for trial by Military Commission, appointed by Order of the President of July 2, 1942, on charges preferred against them purporting to set out their violations of the law of war and of the Articles of War, is in conformity to the laws and Constitution of the United States.

After denial of their applications by the District Court, petitioners asked leave to file petitions for habeas corpus in this Court. In view of the public importance of the questions raised by their petitions and of the duty which rests on the courts, in time of war as well as in time of peace, to preserve unimpaired the constitutional safeguards of civil liberty, and because in our opinion the public interest required that we consider and decide those questions without any avoidable delay, we directed that petitioners' applications be set down for full oral argument at a special term of this Court, convened on July 29, 1942. . . .

On July 31, 1942, after hearing argument of counsel and after full consideration of all questions raised, this Court affirmed the orders of the District Court and denied petitioners' applications for leave to file petitions for habeas corpus. . . .

The following facts appear from the petitions or are stipulated. Except as noted they are undisputed.

All the petitioners were born in Germany; all have lived in the United States. All returned to Germany between 1933 and 1941. All except petitioner Haupt are admittedly citizens of the German Reich, with which the United States is at war. Haupt came to this country with his parents when he was five years old; it is contended that he became a citizen of the United States by virtue of the naturalization of his parents during his minority and that he has not since lost his citizenship. The Government, however, takes the position that on attaining his majority he elected to maintain German allegiance and citizenship, or in any case that he has by his conduct renounced or abandoned his United States citizenship. For reasons presently to be stated we do not find it necessary to resolve these contentions.

After the declaration of war between the United States and the German Reich, petitioners received training at a sabotage school near Berlin, Germany, where they were instructed in the use of explosives and in methods of secret writing. Thereafter petitioners, with a German citizen, Dasch, proceeded from Germany to a seaport in Occupied France, where petitioners Burger, Heinck, and Quirin, together with Dasch, boarded a German submarine which proceeded across the Atlantic to Amagansett Beach on Long Island, New York. The four were there landed from the submarine in the hours of darkness, on or about June 13, 1942, carrying with them a supply of explosives, fuses, and incendiary and timing devices. While landing they wore German Marine Infantry uniforms or parts of uniforms. Immediately after landing they buried their uniforms and the other articles mentioned, and proceeded in civilian dress to New York City.

The remaining four petitioners at the same French port boarded another German submarine, which carried them across the Atlantic to Ponte Vedra Beach, Florida. On or about June 17, 1942, they came ashore during the hours of darkness, wearing caps of the German Marine Infantry and carrying with them a supply of explosives, fuses, and incendiary and timing devices. They immediately buried their caps and the other articles mentioned, and proceeded in civilian dress to Jacksonville, Florida, and thence to various points in the United States. All were taken into custody in New York or Chicago by agents of the Federal Bureau of Investigation. All had received instructions in Germany from an officer of the German High Command to destroy war industries and war facilities in the United States, for which they or their relatives in Germany were to receive salary payments from the German government. They also had been paid by the German government during their course of training at the sabotage school and had received substantial sums in United States currency, which were in their possession when arrested. The currency had been handed to them by an officer of the German High Command, who had instructed them to wear their German uniforms while landing in the United States.

The President, as President and Commander in Chief of the Army and Navy, by Order of July 2, 1942, appointed a Military Commission and directed it to try petitioners for offenses against the law of war and the Articles of War, and prescribed regulations for the procedure on the trial and for review of the record of the trial and of any judgment or sentence of the Commission. On the same day, by Proclamation the President declared that "all persons who are subjects, citizens, or residents of any nation at war with the United States or who give obedience to or act under the direction of any such nation, and who during time of war enter or attempt to enter the United States . . . through coastal or boundary defenses, and are charged with committing or attempting or preparing to commit sabotage, espionage, hostile or warlike acts, or violations of the law of war, shall be subject to the law of war and to the jurisdiction of military tribunals."

The Proclamation also stated in terms that all such persons were denied access to the courts. . . .

On July 3, 1942, the Judge Advocate General's Department of

the Army prepared and lodged with the Commission the following charges against petitioners, supported by specifications:

1. Violation of the law of war.
2. Violation of Article 81 of the Articles of War, defining the offense of relieving or attempting to relieve, or corresponding with or giving intelligence to, the enemy.
3. Violation of Article 82, defining the offense of spying.
4. Conspiracy to commit the offenses alleged in charges 1, 2, and 3.

The Commission met on July 8, 1942, and proceeded with the trial, which continued in progress while the causes were pending in this Court. On July 27th, before petitioners' applications to the District Court, all the evidence for the prosecution and the defense had been taken by the Commission and the case had been closed except for arguments of counsel. . . .

Petitioners' main contention is that the President is without any statutory or constitutional authority to order the petitioners to be tried by military tribunal for offenses with which they are charged; that in consequence they are entitled to be tried in the civil courts with the safeguards, including trial by jury, which the Fifth and Sixth Amendments guarantee to all persons charged in such courts with criminal offenses. . . .

The Government challenges each of these propositions. But regardless of their merits, it also insists that petitioners must be denied access to the courts, both because they are enemy aliens or have entered our territory as enemy belligerents, and because the President's Proclamation undertakes in terms to deny such access to the class of persons defined by the Proclamation, which aptly describes the character and conduct of petitioners. It is urged that if they are enemy aliens or if the Proclamation has force, no court may afford the petitioners a hearing. But there is certainly nothing in the Proclamation to preclude access to the courts for determining its applicability to the particular case. And neither the Proclamation nor the fact that they are enemy aliens forecloses consideration by the courts of petitioners' contentions that the Constitution and laws of the United States constitutionally enacted forbid their trial by military commission. . . .

We are not here concerned with any question of the guilt or innocence of petitioners. Constitutional safeguards for the protection of all who are charged with offenses are not to be disregarded in order to inflict merited punishment on some who are guilty. But the detention and trial of petitioners—ordered by the President in the declared exercise of his powers as Commander in Chief of the Army in time of war and of grave public danger—are not to be set aside by the courts without the clear conviction that they are in conflict with the Constitution or laws of Congress constitutionally enacted.

Congress and the President, like the courts, possess no power not derived from the Constitution. But one of the objects of the Constitution, as declared by its preamble, is to "provide for the common defence." As a means to that end, the Constitution gives to Congress the power to "provide for the common Defence," "To raise and support Armies," "To provide and maintain a Navy," and "To make Rules for the Government and Regulation of the land and naval forces." Congress is given authority "To declare War, grant Letters of Marque and Reprisal, and make Rules concerning Captures on Land and Water" and "To define and punish Piracies and Felonies committed on the high Seas, and Offences against the Law of Nations." And finally, the Constitution authorizes Congress "To make all Laws which shall be necessary and proper for carrying into Execution the foregoing Powers, and all other Powers vested by this Constitution in the Government of the United States, or in any Department or Officer thereof."

The Constitution confers on the President the "executive Power," and imposes on him the duty to "take Care that the Laws be faithfully executed." It makes him the Commander in Chief of the Army and Navy, and empowers him to appoint and commission officers of the United States.

The Constitution thus invests the President, as Commander in Chief, with the power to wage war which Congress has declared, and to carry into effect all laws passed by Congress for the conduct of war and for the government and regulation of the Armed Forces, and all laws defining and punishing offenses against the law of nations, including those which pertain to the conduct of war.

By the Articles of War, Congress has provided rules for the government of the Army. It has provided for the trial and punishment, by courts-martial, of violations of the Articles by members of the armed forces and by specified classes of persons associated or serving with the Army. But the Articles also recognize the "military commission" appointed by military command as an appropriate tribunal for the trial and punishment of offenses against the law of war not ordinarily tried by court-martial. Articles 38 and 46 authorize the President, with certain limitations, to prescribe the procedure for military commissions. Articles 81 and 82 authorize trial, either by court-martial or military commission, of those charged with relieving, harboring, or corresponding with the enemy and those charged with spying. And Article 15 declares that "the provisions of these articles conferring jurisdiction upon courts-martial shall not be construed as depriving military commissions . . . or other military tribunals of concurrent jurisdiction in respect of offenders or offenses that by statute or by the law of war may be triable by such military commissions . . . or other military tribunals." . . .

From the very beginning of its history this Court has recognized and applied the law of war as including that part of the law of nations which prescribes, for the conduct of war, the status, rights, and duties of enemy nations as well as of enemy individuals. By the Articles of War, and especially Article 15, Congress has explicitly provided, so far as it may constitutionally do so, that military tribunals shall have jurisdiction to try offenders or offenses against the law of war in appropriate cases. Congress, in addition to making rules for the government of our Armed Forces, has thus exercised its authority to define and punish offenses against the law of nations by sanctioning, within constitutional limitations, the jurisdiction of military commissions to try persons for offenses which, according to the rules and precepts of the law of nations, and more particularly the law of war, are cognizable by such tribunals. And the President, as Commander in Chief, by his Proclamation in time of war has invoked that law. By his Order creating the present Commission he has undertaken to exercise the authority conferred upon him by Congress, and also such authority as the Constitution itself gives the Commander in Chief, to direct the performance of those functions which may constitutionally be performed by the military arm of the nation in time of war.

An important incident to the conduct of war is the adoption of measures by the military command not only to repel and defeat the enemy, but to seize and subject to disciplinary measures those enemies who in their attempt to thwart or impede our military effort have violated the law of war. It is unnecessary for present purposes to determine to what extent the President as Commander in Chief has constitutional power to create military commissions without the support of Congressional legislation. For here Congress has authorized trial of offenses against the law of war before such commissions. We are concerned only with the question whether it is within the constitutional power of the National Government to place petitioners upon trial before a military commission for the offenses with which they are charged. We must therefore first inquire whether any of the acts charged is an offense against the law of war cognizable before a military tribunal, and if so whether the Constitution prohibits the trial. We may assume that there are acts regarded in other countries, or by some writers on international law, as offenses against the law of war which would not be triable by military tribunal here, either because they are not recognized by our courts as violations of the law of war or because they are of that class of offenses constitutionally triable only by a jury. It was upon such grounds that the Court denied the right to proceed by military tribunal in *Ex parte Milligan*. But as we shall show, these petitioners were charged with an offense against the law of war which the Constitution does not require to be tried by jury.

It is no objection that Congress in providing for the trial of such offenses has not itself undertaken to codify that branch of international law or to mark its precise boundaries, or to enumerate or define by statute all the acts which that law condemns. . . . Congress had the choice of crystallizing in permanent form and in minute detail every offense against the law of war, or of adopting the system of common law applied by military tribunals so far as it should be recognized and deemed applicable by the courts. It chose the latter course.

By universal agreement and practice, the law of war draws a distinction between the armed forces and the peaceful populations of belligerent nation and also between those who are lawful and unlawful combatants. Lawful combatants are subject to capture and detention as prisoners of war by opposing military forces. Unlawful combatants are likewise subject to capture and detention, but in addition they are subject to trial and punishment by military tribunals for acts which render their belligerency unlawful. The spy who secretly and without uniform passes the military lines of a belligerent in time of war, seeking to gather military information and communicate it to the enemy, or an enemy combatant who without uniform comes secretly through the lines for the purpose of waging war by destruction of life or property are familiar examples of belligerents who are generally deemed not to be entitled to the status of prisoners of war, but to be offenders against the law of war subject to trial and punishment by military tribunals.

Such was the practice of our own military authorities before the adoption of the Constitution, and during the Mexican and Civil Wars. . . .

Our Government, by . . . defining lawful belligerents entitled to be treated as prisoners of war, has recognized that there is a class of unlawful belligerents not entitled to that privilege, including those who, though combatants, do not wear "fixed and distinctive emblems." And by Article 15 of the Articles of War Congress has made provision for their trial and punishment by military commission, according to "the law of war."

By a long course of practical administrative construction by its military authorities, our Government has likewise recognized that those who during time of war pass surreptitiously from enemy territory into our own, discarding their uniforms upon entry, for the commission of hostile acts involving destruction of life or property, have the status of unlawful combatants punishable as such by military commission. This precept of the law of war has been so recognized in practice both here and abroad, and has so generally been accepted as valid by authorities on international law that we think it must be regarded as a rule or principle of the law of war recognized by this Government by its enactment of the Fifteenth Article of War.

Specification 1 of the first charge is sufficient to charge all the petitioners with the offense of unlawful belligerency, trial of which is within the jurisdiction of the Commission, and the admitted facts affirmatively show that the charge is not merely colorable or without foundation.

Specification 1 states that petitioners, "being enemies of the United States and acting for . . . the German Reich, a belligerent enemy nation, secretly and covertly passed, in civilian dress, contrary to the law of war, through the military and naval lines and defenses of the United States . . . and went behind such lines, contrary to the law of war, in civilian dress . . . for the purpose of committing . . . hostile acts, and, in particular, to destroy certain war industries, war utilities, and war materials within the United States."

This specification so plainly alleges violation of the law of war as to require but brief discussion of petitioners' contentions. As we have seen, entry upon our territory in time of war by enemy belligerents, including those acting under the direction of the armed forces of the enemy, for the purpose of destroying property used or useful in prosecuting the war, is a hostile and warlike act. It subjects those who participate in it without uniform to the punishment prescribed by the law of war for unlawful belligerents. . . .

Citizenship in the United States of an enemy belligerent does not relieve him from the consequences of a belligerency which is unlawfiul because in violation of the law of war. Citizens who associate themselves with the military arm of the enemy government, and with its aid, guidance, and direction enter this country bent on hostile acts, are enemy belligerents within the meaning of the Hague Convention and the law of war. It is as an enemy belligerent that petitioner Haupt is charged with entering the United States, and unlawful belligerency is the gravamen of the offense of which he is accused. . . .

But petitioners insist that, even if the offenses with which they are charged are offenses against the law of war, their trial is subject to the requirement of the Fifth Amendment that no person shall be held to answer for a capital or otherwise infamous crime unless on a presentment or indictment of a grand jury, and that such trials by Article III, §2, and the Sixth Amendment must be by jury in a civil court. . . .

Presentment by a grand jury and trial by a jury of the vicinage where the crime was committed were at the time of the adoption of the Constitution familiar parts of the machinery for criminal trials in the civil courts. But they were procedures unknown to military tribunals, which are not courts in the sense of the Judiciary Article, and which in the natural course of events are usually called upon to function under conditions precluding resort to such procedures. As this Court has often recognized, it was not the purpose or effect of § 2 of Article III, read in the light of the common law, to enlarge the then existing right to a jury trial. The object was to preserve unimpaired trial by jury in all those cases in which it had been recognized by the common law and in all cases of a like nature as they might arise in the future, but not to bring within the sweep of the guaranty those cases in which it was then well understood that a jury trial could not be demanded as of right.

The Fifth and Sixth Amendments, while guaranteeing the continuance of certain incidents of trial by jury which Article III, § 2, had left unmentioned, did not enlarge the right to jury trial as it had been established by that Article. . . .

Section 2 of the Act of Congress of April 10, 1806, derived from the Resolution of the Continental Congress of August 21, 1776, imposed the death penalty on alien spies "according to the law and usage of nations, by sentence of a general court martial." This enactment must be regarded as a contemporary construction of both Article III, § 2, and the Amendments as not foreclosing trial by military tribunals, without a jury, of offenses against the law of war committed by enemies not in or associated with our Armed Forces. It is a construction of the Constitution which has been followed since the founding of our Government, and is now continued in the 82nd Article of War. Such a construction is entitled to the greatest respect. It has not hitherto been challenged, and, so far as we are advised, it has never been suggested in the very extensive literature of the subject that an alien spy, in time of war, could not be tried by military tribunal without a jury. . . .

We conclude that the Fifth and Sixth Amendments did not restrict whatever authority was conferred by the Constitution to try offenses against the law of war by military commission, and that petitioners, charged with such an offense not required to be tried by jury at common law, were lawfully placed on trial by the Commission without a jury.

Petitioners, and especially petitioner Haupt, stress the pronouncement of this Court in the *Milligan* case, that the law of war "can never be applied to citizens in states which have upheld the authority of the government, and where the courts are open and their process unobstructed." Elsewhere in its opinion, the Court was at pains to point out that Milligan, a citizen twenty years resident in Indiana, who had never been a resident of any of the states in rebellion, was not an enemy belligerent either entitled to the status of a prisoner of war or subject to the penalties imposed upon unlawful belligerents. We construe the Court's statement as to the inapplicability of the law of war to Milligan's case as having particular reference to the facts before it. From them the Court concluded that Milligan, not being a part of or associated with the armed forces of the enemy, was a nonbelligerent, not subject to the law of war save as—in circumstances found not there to be present, and not involved here—martial law might be constitutionally established.

The Court's opinion is inapplicable to the case presented by the present record. We have no occasion now to define with meticulous care the ultimate boundaries of the jurisdiction of military tribunals to try persons according to the law of war. It is enough that petitioners here, upon the conceded facts, were plainly within those boundaries, and were held in good faith for trial by military commission, charged with being enemies who, with the purpose of destroying war materials and utilities, entered, or after entry remained in, our territory without uniform—an offense against the law of war. We hold only that those particular acts constitute an offense against the law of war which the Constitution authorizes to be tried by military commission. . . .

20.

PADILLA V. RUMSFELD

Second Circuit Court of Appeals

Argued November 17, 2003.
Decided December 18, 2003.

INTRODUCTION

This habeas corpus appeal requires us to consider a series of questions raised by Secretary of Defense Donald Rumsfeld and by Donna R. Newman, Esq., on behalf of Jose Padilla, an American citizen held by military authorities as an enemy combatant. Padilla is suspected of being associated with al Qaeda and planning terrorist attacks in this country. The questions were certified by the United States District Court for the Southern District of New York (Michael B. Mukasey, C.J.) and involve, among others: whether the Secretary of Defense is Padilla's "custodian" for habeas purposes, whether the Southern District of New York had jurisdiction over the petition, and whether the President has the authority to detain Padilla as an enemy combatant. We conclude that the Secretary of Defense is a proper respondent and that the District Court had jurisdiction. We also conclude that Padilla's detention was not authorized by Congress, and absent such authorization, the President does not have the power under Article II of the Constitution to detain as an enemy combatant an American citizen seized on American soil outside a zone of combat.

As this Court sits only a short distance from where the World Trade Center once stood, we are as keenly aware as anyone of the threat al Qaeda poses to our country and of the responsibilities the President and law enforcement officials bear for protecting the nation. But presidential authority does not exist in a vacuum, and this case involves not whether those responsibilities should be aggressively pursued, but whether the President is obligated, in the circumstances presented here, to share them with Congress.

Where, as here, the President's power as Commander in Chief of the armed forces and the domestic rule of law intersect, we conclude that clear congressional authorization is required for detentions of American citizens on American soil because 18 U.S.C. § 4001(a) (2000) (the "Non-Detention Act") prohibits such detentions absent specific congressional authorization. Congress's Authorization for Use of Military Force Joint Resolution (2001) ("Joint Resolution"), passed shortly after the attacks of September 11, 2001, is not such an authorization, and no exception to section 4001(a) otherwise exists. In light of this express prohibition, the government must undertake to show that Padilla's detention can nonetheless be grounded in the President's inherent constitutional powers. We conclude that it has not made this showing. In reaching this conclusion, we do not address the detention of an American citizen seized within a zone of combat in Afghanistan, such as the court confronted in *Hamdi v. Rumsfeld* (*"Hamdi III"*). Nor do we express any opinion as to the hypothetical situation of a congressionally authorized detention of an American citizen.

Accordingly, we remand to the District Court with instructions to issue a writ of habeas corpus directing Secretary Rumsfeld to release Padilla from military custody within thirty days, at which point the government can act within its legislatively conferred authority to take further action. For example, Padilla can be transferred to the appropriate civilian authorities who can bring criminal charges against him. If appropriate, he can also be held as a material witness in connection with grand jury proceedings. Under any scenario, Padilla will be entitled to the constitutional protections extended to other citizens.

BACKGROUND

I. The Initial Detention

On May 8, 2002, Jose Padilla, an American citizen, flew on his American passport from Pakistan, via Switzerland, to Chicago's O'Hare International Airport. There he was arrested by FBI agents pursuant to a material witness warrant issued by the Chief Judge of the Southern District of New York in connection with a grand jury investigation of the terrorist attacks of September 11. Padilla carried no weapons or explosives.

The agents brought Padilla to New York where he was held as a civilian material witness in the maximum security wing of the Metropolitan Correctional Center (MCC). At that point, Padilla was under the control of the Bureau of Prisons and the United States Marshal Service. Any immediate threat he posed to national security had effectively been neutralized. On May 15, 2002, he appeared before Chief Judge Mukasey, who appointed Donna R. Newman, Esq., to represent Padilla. Newman "conferred with [Padilla] over a period of weeks in . . . an effort to end [his] confinement." *Padilla ex rel. Newman v. Bush.* (*"Padilla I"*). She also conferred with Padilla's relatives and with government representatives on Padilla's behalf.

On May 22, Newman moved to vacate the material witness warrant. By June 7, the motion had been submitted for decision. A conference on the motion was scheduled for June 11. However, on June 9, the government notified the court ex parte that (1) it wished to withdraw its subpoena and (2) the President had issued an Order (the "June 9 Order") designating Padilla as an enemy combatant and directing Secretary Rumsfeld to detain him. Chief Judge

Mukasey vacated the warrant, and Padilla was taken into custody by Department of Defense (DOD) personnel and transported from New York to the high-security Consolidated Naval Brig in Charleston, South Carolina. At the scheduled June 11 conference, Newman, unable to secure Padilla's signature on a habeas corpus petition, nonetheless filed one on his behalf as "next friend."

For the past eighteen months, Padilla has been held in the Brig in Charleston. He has not been permitted any contact with his counsel, his family, or any other nonmilitary personnel. During this period he has been the subject of ongoing questioning regarding the al Qaeda network and its terrorist activities in an effort to obtain intelligence.

II. The Order Authorizing the Detention

In his June 9 Order, the President directed Secretary Rumsfeld to detain Padilla based on findings that Padilla was an enemy combatant who (1) was "closely associated with al Qaeda, an international terrorist organization with which the United States is at war"; (2) had engaged in "warlike acts, including conduct in preparation for acts of international terrorism" against the United States; (3) had intelligence that could assist the United States to ward off future terrorist attacks; and (4) was a continuing threat to United States security. As authority for the detention, the President relied on "the Constitution and . . . the laws of the United States, including the [Joint Resolution]."

In an unsealed declaration submitted to the District Court, Michael H. Mobbs, a special advisor to the Undersecretary of Defense for Policy (who claims no direct knowledge of Padilla's actions or of the interrogations that produced the information discussed in his declaration), set forth the information the President received before he designated Padilla as an enemy combatant. According to the declaration, Padilla was born in New York, was convicted of murder in 1983, and remained incarcerated until his eighteenth birthday. In 1991, he was convicted on a handgun charge and again sent to prison. He moved to Egypt in 1998 and traveled to several countries in the Middle East and Southwest Asia between 1999 and 2000. During this period, he was closely associated with known members and leaders of al Qaeda. While in Afghanistan in 2001, Padilla became involved with a plan to build and detonate a "dirty bomb" within the United States, and went to Pakistan to receive training on explosives from al Qaeda operatives. There he was instructed by senior al Qaeda officials to return to the United States to conduct reconnaissance and/or other attacks on behalf of al Qaeda. He then traveled to Chicago, where he was arrested upon arrival into the United States on May 8, 2002. Notwithstanding Padilla's extensive contacts with al Qaeda members and his actions under their direction, the government does not allege that Padilla was a member of al Qaeda.

The government also offered for the District Court's review Mobbs's sealed declaration, which the District Court characterized as "identifying one or more of the sources referred to only in cryptic terms in the [unsealed] Mobbs Declaration" and "set[ting] forth objective circumstantial evidence that corroborates the factual allegations in the [unsealed] Mobbs Declaration." *Padilla I.*

III. District Court Proceedings on the Habeas Petition

On June 26, 2002, the government moved to dismiss Padilla's habeas petition on the grounds that Newman lacked standing to act as Padilla's next friend, that Secretary Rumsfeld was not a proper respondent, and that, in any event, the District Court lacked personal jurisdiction over him. On the merits, the government contended that each Mobbs declaration contained sufficient evidence of Padilla's association with al Qaeda and his intention to engage in terrorist acts in this country on behalf of al Qaeda to establish the legality of holding Padilla in military custody as an enemy combatant. Padilla contended that the President lacked authority to detain an American citizen taken into custody in the United States. At a minimum, he sought access to counsel.

In a comprehensive and thorough opinion, the District Court determined that (1) Newman could bring the habeas petition as Padilla's next friend; (2) Secretary Rumsfeld was a proper respondent and the District Court had jurisdiction over him; (3) the Constitution and statutory law give the President authority to detain American citizens as enemy combatants; (4) Padilla was entitled to consult with counsel to pursue his habeas petition "under conditions that will minimize the likelihood that he [could] use his lawyers as unwilling intermediaries for the transmission of information to others"; (5) Padilla could present facts and argument to the court to rebut the government's showing that he was an enemy combatant; and (6) the court would "examine only whether the President had some evidence to support his finding that Padilla was an enemy combatant, and whether that evidence has been mooted by events subsequent to his detention." *Padilla I*. The court did not rely on the sealed Mobbs declaration in making its ruling.

The District Court's order directed the parties to set conditions under which Padilla could meet with his counsel, but Secretary Rumsfeld declined to do so. Instead, more than a month after the *Padilla I* decision, the government moved for reconsideration of the portion of *Padilla I* that allowed him access to counsel, on the ground that no conditions could be set that would protect the national security. *Padilla ex rel Newman v. Rumsfeld* ("*Padilla II*"). Although Chief Judge Mukasey expressed doubts as to the procedural regularity of the motion, he nonetheless entertained it on the merits and denied it.

The government then moved for certification of the issues which it had lost. Chief Judge Mukasey certified the following questions as "involv[ing] . . . controlling question[s] of law as to which there is substantial ground for difference of opinion" and the resolution of which "may materially advance the ultimate termination of the litigation." 28 U.S.C. § 1292(b) (2000) *Padilla ex rel Newman v. Rumsfeld* ("*Padilla III*"):

(1) Is the Secretary of Defense, Donald Rumsfeld, a proper respondent in this case?

(2) Does this court have personal jurisdiction over Secretary Rumsfeld?

(3) Does the President have the authority to designate as an enemy combatant an American citizen captured within the United States, and, through the Secretary of Defense, to detain him for the duration of armed conflict with al Qaeda?

(4) What burden must the government meet to detain petitioner as an enemy combatant?

(5) Does petitioner have the right to present facts in support of his habeas corpus petition?

(6) Was it a proper exercise of this court's discretion and its authority under the All Writs Act to direct that petitioner be afforded access to counsel for the purpose of presenting facts in support of his petition?

On June 10, 2003, this Court granted the parties' application for an interlocutory appeal.

DISCUSSION

I. Preliminary Issues

[The court here concluded that Padilla's attorney was an appropriate person to bring the habeas petition, that Secretary of Defense Rumsfeld was an appropriate respondent and that the court had jurisdiction over Secretary Rumsfeld.]

II. Power to Detain

A. Introduction

The District Court concluded, and the government maintains here, that the indefinite detention of Padilla was a proper exercise of the President's power as Commander in Chief. The power to detain Padilla is said to derive from the President's authority, settled by *Ex parte Quirin* (1942) to detain enemy combatants in wartime— authority that is argued to encompass the detention of United States citizens seized on United States soil. This power, the court below reasoned, may be exercised without a formal declaration of war by Congress and "even if Congressional authorization were deemed necessary, the Joint Resolution, passed by both houses of Congress, . . . engages the President's full powers as Commander in Chief." *Padilla I*.

Specifically, the District Court found that the Joint Resolution acted as express congressional authorization under 18 U.S.C. § 4001(a) which prohibits the detention of American citizens absent such authorization. In addition, the government claims that 10 U.S.C. § 956(5), a statute that allows the military to use authorized funds for certain detentions, grants authority to detain American citizens.

These alternative arguments require us to examine the scope of the President's inherent power and, if this is found insufficient to support Padilla's detention, whether Congress has authorized such detentions of American citizens. We reemphasize, however, that our review is limited to the case of an American citizen arrested in the United States, not on a foreign battlefield or while actively engaged in armed conflict against the United States. As the Fourth Circuit recently—and accurately—noted in *Hamdi v. Rumsfeld*, "[t]o compare this battlefield capture [of Hamdi] to the domestic arrest in *Padilla v. Rumsfeld* is to compare apples and oranges." (*"Hamdi IV"*) (Wilkinson, J., concurring).

B. The Youngstown Analysis

Our review of the exercise by the President of war powers in the domestic sphere starts with the template the Supreme Court constructed in *Youngstown* (Jackson, J., concurring). *Youngstown* involved the validity of President Truman's efforts during the Korean War to seize the country's steel mills on the eve of a nationwide strike by steelworkers. Writing for the majority, Justice Black explained that the President's power "must stem either from an act of Congress or from the Constitution itself." The Court held that the seizure could not be justified as a function of the President's Commander in Chief powers and that it had not been authorized by Congress. Justice Jackson's concurrence, which provides the framework for reviewing the validity of executive action, posits three categories for evaluating the exercise of emergency powers by the President.

First, when the President acts pursuant to an express or implied authorization from Congress, "his authority is at its maximum, for it includes all that he possesses in his own right plus all that Congress can delegate." *Youngstown* (Jackson, J., concurring). This category is exemplified by the power exercised by the President in *Quirin* and in *United States v. Curtis-Wright Export Corp.* (1936). Second, when the President acts in the absence of either a congressional grant or denial of authority, "he can only rely upon his own independent powers, but there is a zone of twilight in which he and Congress may have concurrent authority, or in which its distribution is uncertain." *Youngstown* Finally, the third category includes those situations where the President takes measures incompatible with the express or implied will of Congress. In such cases, "his power is at its lowest ebb, for then he can rely only upon his own constitutional powers minus any constitutional powers of Congress over the matter." The [c]ourts can sustain exclusive presidential control [in this situation] only by disabling the Congress from acting upon the subject [Youngstown].

Here, we find that the President lacks inherent constitutional authority as Commander in Chief to detain American citizens on American soil outside a zone of combat. We also conclude that the Non-Detention Act serves as an explicit congressional "denial of authority" within the meaning of *Youngstown*, thus placing us in *Youngstown*'s third category. Finally, we conclude that because the Joint Resolution does not authorize the President to detain American citizens seized on American soil, we remain within *Youngstown*'s third category.

i. Inherent Power

The government contends that the President has the inherent authority to detain those who take up arms against this country pursuant to Article II, Section 2, of the Constitution, which makes him the Commander in Chief, and that the exercise of these powers domestically does not require congressional authorization. Moreover, the argument goes, it was settled by *Quirin* that the military's authority to detain enemy combatants in wartime applies to American citizens as well as to foreign combatants. There the Supreme Court explained that "universal agreement and practice" under "the law of war" holds that "[l]awful combatants are subject to capture and detention as prisoners of war by opposing military forces" and "[u]nlawful combatants are likewise subject to capture and detention, but in addition they are subject to trial and punishment by military tribunals for acts which render their belligerency unlawful." Finally, since the designation of an enemy combatant bears the closest imaginable connection to the President's constitutional responsibilities, principles of judicial deference are said by the government to assume heightened significance.

We agree that great deference is afforded the President's exercise of his authority as Commander in Chief. We also agree that whether a state of armed conflict exists against an enemy to which the laws of war apply is a political question for the President, not the courts. See *Johnson v. Eisentrager* (1950). . . . Because we have no authority to do so, we do not address the government's underlying assumption that an undeclared war exists between al Qaeda and the United States. We have no quarrel with the former chief of the Justice Department's Criminal Division, who said:

> For [al Qaeda] chose not to violate the law but to attack the law and its institutions directly. Their proclaimed goal, however unrealistic, was to destroy the United States. They used powerful weapons of destructive force and openly declared their willingness to employ even more powerful weapons of mass destruction if they could lay hold of them. They were as serious a threat to the national security of the United States as one could envision.
> (Michael Chertoff, "Law, Loyalty, and Terror:
> Our Legal Response to the Post-9/11 World,"
> *Wkly. Standard*, December 1, 2003, p. 15)

However, it is a different proposition entirely to argue that the President even in times of grave national security threats or war, whether declared or undeclared, can lay claim to any of the powers, express or implied, allocated to Congress. The deference due to the Executive in its exercise of its war powers therefore only starts the inquiry; it does not end it. Where the exercise of Commander in Chief powers, no matter how well intentioned, is challenged on the ground that it collides with the powers assigned by the Constitution to Congress, a fundamental role exists for the courts. See *Marbury v. Madison* (1803). To be sure, when Congress and the President act together in the conduct of war, "it is not for any court to sit in review of the wisdom of their action or substitute its judgment for theirs." *Hirabayashi v. United States* (1943). But when the Executive acts, even in the conduct of war, in the face of apparent congressional disapproval, challenges to his authority must be examined and resolved by the Article III courts. See *Youngstown* (Jackson, J., concurring).

These separation of powers concerns are heightened when the Commander in Chief's powers are exercised in the domestic sphere. The Supreme Court has long counseled that while the Executive should be "indulge[d] the widest latitude of interpretation to sustain his exclusive function to command the instruments of national force, at least when turned against the outside world for the security of our society," he enjoys "no such indulgence" when "it is turned inward." *Youngstown* (Jackson, J., concurring). This is because "the federal power over external affairs [is] in origin and essential character different from that over internal affairs," and "congressional legislation which is to be made effective through negotiation and inquiry within the international field must often accord to the President a degree of discretion and freedom from statutory restriction which would not be admissible were domestic affairs alone involved." *Curtis-Wright*. But, "Congress, not the Executive, should control utilization of the war power as an instrument of domestic policy." *Youngstown* (Jackson, J., concurring). Thus, we do not concern ourselves with the Executive's inherent wartime power, generally, to detain enemy combatants on the battlefield. Rather, we are called on to decide whether the Constitution gives the President the power to detain an American citizen seized in this country until the war with al Qaeda ends.

The government contends that the Constitution authorizes the President to detain Padilla as an enemy combatant as an exercise of inherent executive authority. Padilla contends that, in the absence of express congressional authorization, the President, by his June 9 Order denominating Padilla an enemy combatant, has engaged in the "lawmaking" function entrusted by the Constitution to Congress in violation of the separation of powers. In response, no argument is made that the Constitution expressly grants the President the power to name United States citizens as enemy combatants and order their detention. Rather, the government contends that the Commander in Chief Clause implicitly grants the President the power to detain enemy combatants domestically during times of national security crises such as the current conflict with al Qaeda. US Const. art. II, § 2.

As an initial matter, we note that in its explicit vesting of powers in Articles I and II, the Constitution circumscribes and defines the respective functions of the political branches. The Constitution gives Congress the full legislative powers of government and at the same time, gives the President full executive authority and responsibility to "take care" that the laws enacted are faithfully executed. US Const. art. I § 1 art. II, § § 1, 3. Thus, while the President has the obligation to enforce laws passed by Congress, he does not have the power to legislate.

The propriety of a given branch's conduct does not turn on the labeling of activity as "legislative" or "executive." Legislative action depends "not on form but upon whether [it] contain[s] matter which is properly to be regarded as legislative in its character and effect." *Chadha*. . . .

The Constitution entrusts the ability to define and punish offenses against the law of nations to the Congress, not the Executive. US Const. art. II, § 8, cl. 10. Padilla contends that the June 9 Order mandating his detention as an "enemy combatant" was not the result of congressional action defining the category of "enemy combatant." He also argues that there has been no other legislative articulation of what constitutes an "enemy combatant," what circumstances trigger the designation, or when it ends. As in *Youngstown*, Padilla maintains that "[t]he President's order does not direct that a congressional policy be executed in a manner prescribed by Congress—it directs that a presidential policy be executed in a manner prescribed by the President." *Youngstown*.

The Constitution envisions grave national emergencies and contemplates significant domestic abridgements of individual liberties during such times. Here, the Executive lays claim to the inherent emergency powers necessary to effect such abridgements, but we agree with Padilla that the Constitution lodges these powers with Congress, not the President.

First, the Constitution explicitly provides for the suspension of the writ of habeas corpus "when in Cases of Rebellion or Invasion the public Safety may require it." US Const. art. 1, § 9 cl. 2. This power, however, lies only with Congress. Furthermore, determinations about the scope of the writ are for Congress.

Moreover, the Third Amendment's prohibition on the quartering of troops during times of peace reflected the Framers' deep-seated beliefs about the sanctity of the home and the need to prevent military intrusion into civilian life. At the same time they understood that in times of war—of serious national crisis—military concerns prevailed and such intrusions could occur. But significantly, decisions as to the nature and scope of these intrusions were to be made "in a manner to be prescribed by law." US Const. amend. III. The only valid process for making "law" under the Constitution is, of course, via bicameral passage and presentment to the President, whose possible veto is subject to congressional override, provided in Article I, Section 7.

The Constitution's explicit grant of the powers authorized in the Offenses Clause, the Suspension Clause, and the Third Amendment, to Congress is a powerful indication that, absent express congressional authorization, the President's Commander in Chief powers do not support Padilla's confinement. The level of specificity with which the Framers allocated these domestic powers to Congress and the lack of any even near-equivalent grant of authority in Article II's catalogue of executive powers compels us to decline to read any such power into the Commander in Chief Clause. In sum, while Congress —otherwise acting consistently with the Constitution—may have the power to authorize the detention of United States citizens under the circumstances of Padilla's case, the President, acting alone, does not.

The government argues that *Quirin* established the President's inherent authority to detain Padilla. In *Quirin*, the Supreme Court reviewed the habeas petitions of German soldiers captured on United

States soil during World War II. All of the petitioners had lived in the United States at some point in their lives and had been trained in the German Army in the use of explosives. These soldiers, one of whom would later claim American citizenship, landed in the United States and shed their uniforms intending to engage in acts of military sabotage. They were arrested in New York and Chicago, tried by a military commission as "unlawful combatants," and sentenced to death. The Court denied the soldiers' petitions for habeas corpus, holding that the alleged American citizenship of one of the saboteurs was immaterial to its judgment: "Citizenship in the United States of an enemy belligerent does not relieve him from the consequences of a belligerency which is unlawful because in violation of the law of war." The government contends that *Quirin* conclusively establishes the President's authority to exercise military jurisdiction over American citizens.

We do not agree that *Quirin* controls. First, and most importantly, the *Quirin* Court's decision to uphold military jurisdiction rested on express congressional authorization of the use of military tribunals to try combatants who violated the laws of war. Specifically, the Court found it "unnecessary for present purposes to determine to what extent the President as Commander in Chief has constitutional power to create military commissions without the support of Congressional legislation." Accordingly, *Quirin* does not speak to whether, or to what degree, the President may impose military authority upon United States citizens domestically without clear congressional authorization. We are reluctant to read into *Quirin* a principle that the *Quirin* Court itself specifically declined to promulgate.

Moreover, there are other important distinctions between *Quirin* and this case. First, when *Quirin* was decided in 1942, section 4001(a) had not yet been enacted. The *Quirin* Court consequently had no occasion to consider the effects of legislation prohibiting the detention of American citizens absent statutory authorization. As a result, *Quirin* was premised on the conclusion—indisputable at the time—that the Executive's domestic projection of military authority had been authorized by Congress. Because the *Quirin* Court did not have to contend with section 4001(a) its usefulness is now sharply attenuated.

Second, the petitioners in *Quirin* admitted that they were soldiers in the armed forces of a nation against whom the United States had formally declared war. The *Quirin* Court deemed it unnecessary to consider the dispositive issue here—the boundaries of the Executive's military jurisdiction—because the *Quirin* petitioners "upon the conceded facts, were plainly within those boundaries." Padilla makes no such concession. To the contrary, he, from all indications, intends to dispute his designation as an enemy combatant, and points to the fact that the civilian accomplices of the *Quirin* saboteurs—citizens who advanced the sabotage plots but who were not members of the German armed forces—were charged and tried as civilians in civilian courts, not as enemy combatants subject to military authority.

In *Ex Parte Milligan* (1866), the government unsuccessfully attempted to prosecute before a military tribunal a citizen who, never having belonged to or received training from the Confederate Army, "conspired with bad men" to engage in acts of war and sabotage against the United States. Although *Quirin* distinguished *Milligan* on the ground that "Milligan, not being a part of or associated with the armed forces of the enemy, was a nonbelligerent, [and] not subject to the law of war," a more germane distinction rests on the different statutes involved in *Milligan* and *Quirin*. During the Civil War, Congress authorized the President to suspend the writ of habeas corpus. *Milligan*. However, it also limited his power to detain indefinitely "citizens of States in which the administration of the laws had continued unimpaired in the federal courts, who were then held, or might thereafter be held, as prisoners of the United States, under the authority of the President, otherwise than as prisoners of war."

This limitation was embodied in a requirement that the Executive furnish a list of such prisoners to the district and circuit courts and, upon request by a prisoner, release him if the grand jury failed to return an indictment. The grand jury sitting when Milligan was detained failed to indict him. The Court concluded that because "Congress could grant no . . . power" to authorize the military trial of a civilian in a state where the courts remained open and functioning, Milligan could not be tried by a military tribunal. Thus, both *Quirin* and *Milligan* are consistent with the principle that primary authority for imposing military jurisdiction upon American citizens lies with Congress. Even though *Quirin* limits to a certain extent the broader holding in *Milligan* that citizens cannot be subjected to military jurisdiction while the courts continue to function, *Quirin* and *Milligan* both teach that—at a minimum—an Act of Congress is required to expand military jurisdiction.

The government's argument for the legality of Padilla's detention also relies heavily on the Fourth Circuit's decisions in *Hamdi II* and *Hamdi III*. These decisions are inapposite. The Fourth Circuit directly predicated its holdings on the undisputed fact that Hamdi was captured in a zone of active combat in Afghanistan. . . .

The dissent also relies on *The Prize Cases*, which, like *Milligan*, arose out of the Civil War, to conclude that the President has the inherent constitutional authority to protect the nation when met with belligerency and to determine what degree of responsive force is necessary. We believe that neither the facts of *The Prize Cases* nor their holding support such a broad construction.

First, *The Prize Cases* dealt with the capture of enemy property-not the detention of persons. The Court had no occasion to address the strong constitutional arguments against deprivations of personal liberty, or the question of whether the President could infringe upon individual liberty rights through the exercise of his wartime powers outside a zone of combat.

Second, the dissent would have us read *The Prize Cases* as resolving any question as to whether the President may detain Padilla as an enemy combatant without congressional authorization. The Court did not, however, rest its decision upholding the exercise of the President's military authority solely on his constitutional powers without regard to congressional authorization. Rather, it noted that the President's authority to "call out the militia and use the military and naval forces of the United States in case of invasion by foreign nations, and to suppress insurrection against the government" stemmed from "the Acts of Congress of February 28th, 1795, and 3d of March, 1807." In any event, Congress's subsequent ratification of the President's wartime orders mooted any questions of presidential authority.

Finally, the Court in *The Prize Cases* was not faced with the Non-Detention Act specifically limiting the President's authority to detain American citizens absent express congressional authorization.

Based on the text of the Constitution and the cases interpreting it, we reject the government's contention that the President has inherent constitutional power to detain Padilla under the circumstances presented here. Therefore, under *Youngstown*, we must now consider whether Congress has authorized such detentions.

ii. Congressional Acts

a. THE NON-DETENTION ACT

As we have seen, the Non-Detention Act provides: "No citizen shall be imprisoned or otherwise detained by the United States except pursuant to an Act of Congress." 18 U.S.C. § 4001(a) The District Court held that this language "encompasses all detentions of United States citizens." *Padilla I.* . . .

We read the plain language of section 4001(a) to prohibit all detentions of citizens—a conclusion first reached by the Supreme Court. Not only has the government not made an extraordinary showing of contrary intentions, but the legislative history of the Non-Detention Act is fully consistent with our reading of it. Both the sponsor of the Act and its primary opponent repeatedly confirmed that the Act applies to detentions by the President during war and other times of national crisis. The legislative history is replete with references to the detentions of American citizens of Japanese descent during World War II, detentions that were authorized both by congressional acts and by orders issued pursuant to the President's war power. This context convinces us that military detentions were intended to be covered. Finally, the legislative history indicates that Congress understood that exceptions to the Non-Detention Act must specifically authorize *detentions*.

Section 4001(a) was enacted in 1971 and originated as an amendment to legislation repealing the Emergency Detention Act of 1950, which authorized the detention by the Attorney General during an invasion, a declared war, or "an insurrection within the United States in aid of a foreign enemy" of "each person as to whom there is reasonable ground to believe that such person probably will engage in, or probably will conspire with others to engage in, acts of espionage or of sabotage." Congress referred to section 4001(a) as the Railsback amendment for its drafter, Representative Railsback. The Railsback amendment emerged from the House Judiciary Committee and was opposed by the House Internal Security Committee, which offered other alternatives.

Congressman Ichord, the chair of the House Internal Security Committee and the primary opponent of the Railsback amendment, argued that it would tie the President's hands in times of national emergency or war. He characterized the amendment as "this most dangerous committee amendment" and as "depriv[ing] the President of his emergency powers and his most effective means of coping with sabotage and espionage agents in war-related crises." Representative Ichord's alarm stemmed from his belief that *Youngstown* "teaches that where the Congress has acted on a subject within its jurisdiction, sets forth its policy, and asserts its authority, the President might not thereafter act in a contrary manner." . . .

No proponent of the Railsback amendment challenged Representative Ichord's interpretation. In fact, in a striking exchange between Representatives Ichord and Railsback, he ratified Representative Ichord's interpretation. Representative Ichord asked: "Does [Representative Railsback] believe that in this country today there are people who are skilled in espionage and sabotage that might pose a possible threat to this Nation in the event of a war with nations of which those people are nationals or citizens?" Representative Railsback responded, "Yes." Representative Ichord then asked: "Does the gentleman believe then that if we were to become engaged in a war with the country of those nationals, that we would permit those people to run at large without apprehending them, and wait until after the sabotage is committed?" Railsback answered:

> I think what would happen is what J. Edgar Hoover thought could
> have happened when he opposed the actions that were taken in

1942. He suggested the FBI would have under surveillance those people in question and those persons they had probable cause to think would commit such actions. Does the gentleman know that J. Edgar Hoover was opposed to detention camps, because he thought he had sufficient personnel to keep all these potential saboteurs under surveillance, and that they could prosecute the guilty in accordance with due process?

Railsback also suggested to Congress that the President could seize citizens only pursuant to an Act of Congress or during a time of martial law when the courts are not open.

Congress's passage of the Railsback amendment by a vote of 257 to 49 after ample warning that both the sponsor of the amendment and its primary opponent believed it would limit detentions in times of war and peace alike is strong evidence that the amendment means what it says, that is that no American citizen can be detained without a congressional act authorizing the detention.

In addition, almost every representative who spoke in favor of repeal of the Emergency Detention Act or adoption of the Railsback amendment or in opposition to other amendments, described the detention of Japanese American citizens during World War II as the primary motivation for their positions. Because the World War II detentions were authorized pursuant to the President's war making powers as well as by a congressional declaration of war and by additional congressional acts, the manifest congressional concern about these detentions also suggests that section 4001(a) limits military as well as civilian detentions. . . .

Based primarily on the plain language of the Non-Detention Act but also on its legislative history and the Supreme Court's interpretation, we conclude that the Act applies to all detentions and that precise and specific language authorizing the detention of American citizens is required to override its prohibition.

Despite its plain language, the government argues that section 4001(a) is intended to preclude only detentions by the Attorney General, not by the military. Its first argument is a constitutional one: to construe section 4001(a) to include military detentions would, in the government's view, risk construing it as an unconstitutional abridgement of the President's war powers. Its second argument is a statutory "placement" argument, which the government claims is supported in two ways. First, it contends that because section 4001(a) appears in a section governing the management of prisons, it does not constrain the President's war power. Second, it maintains that because section 4001(a) immediately precedes section 4001(b)(1) which vests authority to manage prisons in the Attorney General but specifically excludes military prisons from his purview, section 4001(a) must be read to exclude military detentions.

The District Court correctly declined to construe section 4001(a) to apply only to civilian detentions in order to avoid a construction of the statute that would unconstitutionally limit the President's war power. It held that the "doctrine of constitutional avoidance 'has no application in the absence of statutory ambiguity.'" *Padilla I*. We agree. For the reasons discussed above, we have found that the statute is unambiguous. Moreover, this interpretation poses no risk of unconstitutionally abridging the President's war powers because, as we have also discussed above, the President, acting alone, possesses no inherent constitutional authority to detain American citizens seized within the United States, away from a zone of combat, as enemy combatants.

Nor are we persuaded by the government's statutory placement argument. No accepted canon of statutory interpretation permits "placement" to trump text, especially where, as here, the text is clear and our reading of it is fully supported by the legislative history. While we, of course, as the government argues, read statutes as a whole to determine the most likely meaning of particular provisions or terms, this principle has no application here. Section 4001(b)(1) was enacted many decades prior to the Emergency Detention Act as part of entirely different legislation. . . .

b. Specific Statutory Authorization

Since we conclude that the Non-Detention Act applies to military detentions such as Padilla's, we would need to find specific statutory authorization in order to uphold the detention. The government claims that both the Joint Resolution, which authorized the use of force against the perpetrators of the September 11 terrorist attacks, and 10 U.S.C. § 956(5) passed in 1984, which provides funding for military detentions, authorize the detention of enemy combatants. It is with respect to the Joint Resolution that we disagree with the District Court, which held that it must be read to confer authority for Padilla's detention. It found that the "language [of the Joint Resolution] authorizes action against not only those connected to the subject organizations who are directly responsible for the September 11 attacks, but also against those who would engage in 'future acts of international Terrorism' as part of 'such . . . organizations.'" *Padilla I.*

We disagree with the assumption that the authority to use military force against these organizations includes the authority to detain American citizens seized on American soil and not actively engaged in combat. First, we note that the Joint Resolution contains no language authorizing detention. It provides

That the President is authorized to use all necessary and appropriate force against those nations, organizations, or persons he determines planned, authorized, committed, or aided the terrorist attacks that occurred on September 11, 2001, or harbored such organizations or persons, in order to prevent any future acts of international terrorism against the United States by such nations, organizations or persons.

Joint Resolution § 2(a).

Because the government seeks to read into the Joint Resolution authority to detain American citizens on American soil, we interpret its language in light of the principles enunciated in *Ex parte Endo.* The *Endo* Court first recognized that "the Constitution when it committed to the Executive and to Congress the exercise of the war power necessarily gave them wide scope for the exercise of judgment and discretion so that war might be waged effectively and successfully." It then said: "At the same time, however, the Constitution is as specific in its enumeration of many of the civil rights of the individual as it is in its enumeration of the powers of his government. Thus it has prescribed procedural safeguards surrounding the arrest, detention and conviction of individuals." Therefore, the Court held: "[i]n interpreting a war-time measure we must assume that [the purpose of Congress and the Executive] was to allow for the greatest possible accommodation between those liberties and the exigencies of war." The Court added: "We must assume, when asked to find implied powers in a grant of legislative or executive authority, that the law makers intended to place no greater restraint on the citizen than was *clearly* and *unmistakably* indicated by the language they used."

The plain language of the Joint Resolution contains nothing authorizing the detention of American citizens captured on United States soil, much less the express authorization required by section 4001(a) and the "clear," "unmistakable" language required by *Endo*. While it may be possible to infer a power of detention from the Joint Resolution in the battlefield context where detentions are necessary to carry out the war, there is no reason to suspect from the language of the Joint Resolution that Congress believed it would be authorizing the detention of an American citizen already held in a federal correctional institution and not "arrayed against our troops" in the field of battle. *Hamdi III.*

Further, the Joint Resolution expressly provides that it is "intended to constitute specific statutory authorization within the meaning of . . . the War Powers Resolution." The War Powers Resolution requires the President to cease military operations within sixty days unless Congress has declared war or specifically authorized the use of the armed forces. It is unlikely—indeed, inconceivable—that Congress would expressly provide in the Joint Resolution an authorization required by the War Powers Resolution but, at the same time, leave unstated and to inference something so significant and unprecedented as authorization to detain American citizens under the Non-Detention Act.

Next, the Secretary argues that Padilla's detention is authorized by 10 U.S.C. § 956(5), which allows the use of appropriated funds for "expenses incident to the maintenance, pay, and allowances of prisoners of war, other persons in the custody of the Army, Navy or Air Force whose status is determined by the Secretary concerned to be similar to prisoners of war, and persons detained in the custody of [the Armed Services] pursuant to Presidential proclamation." The Fourth Circuit found that section 956(5) along with the Joint Resolution sufficed to authorize Hamdi's detention. *Hamdi III*. With respect to section 956(5) the court said: "It is difficult if not impossible to understand how Congress could make appropriations for the detention of persons 'similar to prisoners of war' without also authorizing their detention in the first instance."

At least with respect to American citizens seized off the battlefield, we disagree. Section 965(5) authorizes nothing beyond the expenditure of money. *Endo* unquestionably teaches that an authorization of funds devoid of language "clearly" and "unmistakably" authorizing the detention of American citizens seized here is insufficient. In light of *Endo*, the Non-Detention Act's requirement that Congress specifically authorize detentions of American citizens, and the guarantees of the Fourth and Fifth Amendments to the Constitution, we decline to impose on section 956(5) loads it cannot bear.

CONCLUSION

In sum, we hold that (1) Donna Newman, Esq., may pursue habeas relief on behalf of Jose Padilla; (2) Secretary of Defense Rumsfeld is a proper respondent to the habeas petition and the District Court had personal jurisdiction over him; (3) in the domestic context, the President's inherent constitutional powers do not extend to the detention as an enemy combatant of an American citizen seized within the country away from a zone of combat; (4) the Non-Detention Act prohibits the detention of American citizens without express congressional authorization; and (5) neither the Joint Resolution nor 10 U.S.C. § 956 (5) constitutes such authorization under section 4001(a) These conclusions are compelled by the constitutional and statutory provisions we have discussed above. The offenses Padilla is alleged to have committed are heinous crimes severely punishable under the criminal laws. Further, under those laws the Executive has the power to protect national security and the classified information upon which it depends. And if the President believes this authority to be insufficient, he can ask Congress—which has shown its responsiveness—to authorize additional powers. To reiterate, we remand to the District Court with instructions to issue a writ of habeas corpus directing the Secretary of Defense to release Padilla from military custody within thirty days. The government can transfer Padilla to appropriate civilian authorities who can bring criminal charges against him. Also, if appropriate, Padilla can be held as a material witness in connection with grand jury proceedings. In any case, Padilla will be entitled to the constitutional protections extended to other citizens. . . .

WESLEY, Circuit Judge, concurring in part, dissenting in part.

I respectfully dissent from that aspect of the majority's opinion that concludes the President is without authority from Congress or the Constitution to order the detention and interrogation of Mr. Padilla. In my view, the President as Commander in Chief has the inherent authority to thwart acts of belligerency at home or abroad that would do harm to United States citizens. But even if Mr. Padilla's status as a United States citizen on United States soil somehow changes the constitutional calculus, I cannot see how the Non-Detention Act precludes an affirmance.

Because I would affirm the thoughtful and thorough decision of Chief Judge Mukasey, a brief examination of his opinion is appropriate. After examining the President's inherent powers under the Constitution, the district court held Padilla's detention is not unlawful, as the President is authorized under the Constitution to repel belligerent acts that threaten the safety of United States citizens. The court also held that the detention is authorized by Congress' Authorization for Use of Military Force ("Joint Resolution"). Chief Judge Mukasey noted that 18 U.S.C. § 4001(a) did not preclude this result in that the Joint Resolution identified a specific group of belligerents.

Relying on the Third Geneva Convention, the district court examined the distinction between lawful and unlawful combatants and ultimately concluded that either could be detained. The court concluded that the President's ability to detain Padilla as an unlawful enemy combatant was not altered by Padilla's citizenship. The court distinguished *Ex parte Milligan* (1866), by noting that the citizens in *Milligan* were neither part of, nor associated with, the armed forces of the Confederacy. Thus, they were not enemy combatants subject to the laws of war.

Much of Chief Judge Mukasey's work is not the focus of the majority's analytical resolution of this case. I offer that not as a criticism but merely as a note of limitation. Our task here is confined to the interplay between the President's Article II responsibilities as Commander in Chief and the authority of Congress to regulate domestic activity, even in a time of war, pursuant to Article I of the Constitution.

My disagreement with the majority is two-fold. In my view, the President, as Commander in Chief, has inherent authority to thwart acts of belligerency on US soil that would cause harm to US citizens, and, in this case, Congress through the Joint Resolution specifically and directly authorized the President to take the actions herein contested. The majority concludes the President is without inherent authority to detain Padilla. They agree that "great deference is afforded the President's exercise of his authority as Commander in Chief," and concede the judiciary has no authority to determine the political question of whether the nation is at war. They recognize that the President and Congress often work cooperatively during times of armed conflict. However, the majority contends that separation of powers concerns are heightened when the President's powers are exercised in the "domestic sphere" and that Congress, not the Executive, controls utilization of war powers when invoked as an instrument of domestic policy.

It is true that Congress plays the primary role in domestic policy even in a time of war. Congress does have the power to define and punish offenses committed on US soil, *see* US Const. art. I § 8 cl. 10, to suspend the Writ of Habeas Corpus, *see* US Const. art. I § 9 cl. 2 and to determine when and if soldiers are to be quartered in private homes during a time of war, *see* US Const. amend. III. But none of those powers are in question here nor does the majority cite a specific constitutional provision in which Congress is given exclusive constitutional authority to determine how our military forces will deal with the acts of a belligerent on American soil. There is no well traveled road delineating the respective constitutional powers and limitations in this regard.

The majority relies on *Youngstown Sheet & Tube Co. v. Sawyer* (1952) as its analytical guide in determining the President's constitutional authority in this matter. However, this is a different case. In *Youngstown*, the Supreme Court was confronted with two opposing claims of constitutional authority. The President argued he had the authority to seize the steel mills in question by virtue of his constitutional responsibilities as Commander in Chief and as Chief Executive. The President contended that a steady supply of steel was necessary to sustain the war effort in Korea. The steel mills argued that at its core the dispute was a labor matter—an area clearly reserved for congressional regulation. The Court sided with the steel mills, and with good reason—the President's attempt to link the seizure to prosecuting the war in Korea was far too attenuated. In this case the President's authority is directly tied to his responsibilities as Commander in Chief.

In *The Prize Cases* the Supreme Court rejected a challenge to the President's authority to impose a blockade on the secessionist states absent a declaration of war. As I read *The Prize Cases*, it is clear that common sense and the Constitution allow the Commander in Chief to protect the nation when met with belligerency and to determine what degree of responsive force is necessary. The President has "no power to initiate or declare a war" but "[i]f a war be made by invasion . . . , the President is not only authorized but bound to resist force by force. He . . . is bound to accept the challenge without waiting for any special legislative authority. Regardless the title given the force, the President, in fulfilling his duties as Commander in Chief to suppress insurrection and to deal with belligerents aligned against the nation, is entitled to determine the appropriate response.

In reaching this conclusion the Court noted the President's decision regarding the level of force necessary is a political not a judicial decision. Thus, as courts have previously recognized, *The Prize Cases* stands "for the proposition that the President has independent authority to repel aggressive acts by third parties even without specific congressional authorization, and courts may not review the level of force selected." *Campbell v. Clinton*, (D.C.Cir.2000) (Silberman, J., concurring); *The Prize Cases* demonstrates that congressional authorization is not necessary for the Executive to exercise his constitutional authority to prosecute armed conflicts when, as on September 11, 2001, the United States is attacked.

My colleagues appear to agree with this premise but conclude that somehow the President has *no* power to deal with acts of a belligerent on US soil "away from a zone of combat" absent express authorization from Congress. That would seem to imply that the President does have some war power authority to detain a citizen on US soil if the "zone of combat" was the United States. The majority does not tell us who has the authority to define a "zone of combat" or to designate a geopolitical area as such. Given the majority's view that "the Constitution lodges . . . [inherent national emergency powers] with Congress, not the President," it would seem that the majority views this responsibility as also the singular province of Congress. That produces a startling conclusion. The President would be without any authority to detain a terrorist citizen dangerously close to a violent or destructive act on US soil unless Congress declared the area in question a zone of combat *or* authorized the detention. Curiously, even Mr. Padilla's attorney conceded that the President could detain a terrorist without Congressional authorization if the attack were imminent.

But the scope of the President's inherent war powers under Article II does not end the matter, for in my view Congress clearly and specifically authorized the President's actions here. Chief Judge Mukasey noted, the Joint Resolution, passed by both houses of Congress, "authorizes the President to use necessary and appropriate force in order, among other things, 'to prevent any future acts of international terrorism against the United States,' and thereby engages the President's full powers as Commander in Chief." . . . *Youngstown* fully supports that view. "When the President acts pursuant to an *express* or *implied* authorization of Congress, his authority is at its maximum, for it includes all that he possesses in his own right plus all that Congress can delegate." The Joint Resolution authorized the President to take the action herein challenged; his powers were at their apogee.

Following the attacks of 9/11, the President declared a national emergency. On September 18, 2001, Congress passed Public Law 107-40 as a joint resolution. That resolution, entitled "Authorization for Use of Military Force," notes the "acts of treacherous violence committed against the United States and its citizens," and the danger those acts posed to national security. Moreover, the resolution recognizes "the President has authority *under the Constitution* to take action to deter and prevent acts of international terrorism against the United States." It provides:

> That the President is authorized to use all necessary and appropriate force against those nations, organizations, or persons he determines planned, authorized, committed, or aided the terrorist attacks that occurred on September 11, 2001, or harbored such organizations or persons, in order to prevent any future acts of international terrorism against the United States by such nations, organizations or persons.

Some of the belligerents covered by the Joint Resolution are not nation states, they have no armies in the traditional sense—their "membership" consists of "soldiers" who rely on subterfuge and surprise. Congress recognized that these organizations are waging a war different from any our nation has faced. It authorized the President to employ the necessary and appropriate force to prevent future terrorist attacks.

It is quite clear from the President's Order of June 9, 2002 that Mr. Padilla falls within the Joint Resolution's intended sweep. As relevant here, the Joint Resolution authorizes the President (1) to use appropriate and necessary force—detention would seem to be an appropriate level of force in Mr. Padilla's situation, (2) against those organizations that planned, authorized, or committed the terrorist attacks of 9/11—none of us disputes al Qaeda is responsible for the carnage of that day, (3) in order to prevent future attacks of terrorism against the United States—Padilla is alleged to be closely associated with an al Qaeda plan to carry out an attack in the United States *and* to possess information that if obtained by the US would prevent future terrorist attacks.

The Joint Resolution has limits; it applies only to those subsets of persons, organizations and nations "[the President] determines planned, authorized, committed, or aided the terrorist attacks. The President is not free to detain US citizens who are merely sympathetic to al Qaeda. Nor is he broadly empowered to detain citizens based on their ethnic heritage. Rather, the Joint Resolution is a specific and direct mandate from Congress to stop al Qaeda from killing or harming Americans here or abroad. The Joint Resolution is quite clear in its mandate. Congress noted that the 9/11 attacks made it "both necessary and appropriate that the United States exercise its rights to self-defense and to protect Unites States citizens both at home and abroad." It seems clear to me that Congress understood that in light of the 9/11 attacks the United States had become a zone of combat.

Organizations such as al Qaeda are comprised of people. Congress could not have intended to limit the President's authority to only those al Qaeda operatives who actually planned or took part in 9/11. That would do little to prevent future attacks. The fate of the participants is well known. And surely Congress did not intend to limit the President to pursue only those individuals who were al Qaeda operatives as of September 11, 2001. But even if it did, Mr. Padilla fits within the class for by September of 2001, he had already been under the tutelage and direction of senior al Qaeda officers for three years. Clearly, Congress recognized that al Qaeda and those who now do its bidding are a continuing threat to the United States. Thus, the Joint Resolution does have teeth and whether Padilla is a loaded weapon of al Qaeda would appear to be a fact question. A hearing, as ordered by the district court, would have settled the matter.

The majority suggests, however, that the President's actions are ultra vires because "the Joint Resolution does not specifically authorize detentions." To read the resolution as the majority suggests would create a false distinction between the use of force and the ability to detain. It would be curious if the resolution authorized the interdiction and shooting of an al Qaeda operative but not the detention of that person.

The majority contends that 18 U.S.C. § 4001(a) prohibits detention of US citizens on US soil as enemy combatants absent a precise and specific statutory authorization from Congress. They offer a detailed history of the statute's enactment, which effectuated a repeal of the Emergency Detention Act of 1950. I share their view that the plain language of the statute appears to apply to military and civil detentions and that its placement in the U.S.Code does not rebut that conclusion. However, I find it somewhat puzzling that despite the statute's obvious and conceded clarity, the majority, based solely on the statement of one Member of Congress, sees fit to add a condition not found in the words of the section. The statute is quite clear: "No citizen shall be imprisoned or otherwise detained by the United States except pursuant to an Act of Congress." 18 U.S.C. § 4001(a) The section neither defines an "Act of Congress" nor contains a requirement that the authorizing enactment use the word "detention." The majority does not contest that the Joint Resolution is an Act of Congress. However, they chafe at its lack of specificity. As noted above, I think it would be quite difficult to conclude that Congress did not envision that detaining a terrorist was a possibility. It is apparent from the legislative record of § 4001(a) and the Joint Resolution that the efforts of Congress in each instance meant and implied many different things to individual Members. That is not unusual. It would be quite a surprise to see that Congress was of one mind on any issue; that is the nature of a representative democracy. But one thing is clear, both enactments have the force of law. It is the words used, not the individual motives of legislators, that should serve as the guide. Thus, I think it best to trace a course of legislative intent using the plain and powerful language employed.

The problem with the majority's view of the Joint Resolution of September 18, 2001, is that it reduces the legislative efforts contained therein to a general policy statement notwithstanding the resolution's declaration invoking the War Powers Resolution of 1973. Following the events of 9/11 the President declared a national emergency, thus triggering the President's war powers authority under the War Powers

Resolution. Nothing in the War Powers Resolution of 1973 constrains the President's utilization of his war powers. Congress passed the Joint Resolution and agreed that the President should utilize his war powers with regard to an identified threat. Of course, identifying the threat made sense. Only days earlier the nation had been attacked—American lives had been lost on American soil. Congress responded and invested the President with authority to pursue those responsible for the attacks in order to prevent future attacks. Contrary to the implication of the majority, the Joint Resolution was *not* limited in geographic scope. It did not limit the President's authority to foreign theaters. Congress clearly recognized that the events of 9/11 signaled a war with al Qaeda that could be waged on U S. soil.

The President's authority to detain an enemy combatant in wartime is undiminished by the individual's US citizenship. *Quirin.* Consequently, Padilla's citizenship here is irrelevant. Moreover, the fact that he was captured on US soil is a distinction without a difference. While Mr. Padilla's conduct may have been criminal, it was well within the threat identified in the Joint Resolution. The resolution recognizes the painful reality of 9/11; it seeks to protect US citizens from terrorist attacks at home and abroad. "[E]ntry upon our territory in time of war by enemy belligerents, including those acting under the direction of armed forces of the enemy . . . is a warlike act." *Quirin.*

Congress presumably was aware of 4001(a) when it passed the Joint Resolution. The resolution was congressional confirmation that the nation was in crisis. Congress called upon the President to utilize his Article II war powers to deal with the emergency. By authorizing the President to use necessary and appropriate force against al Qaeda and its operatives, Congress had to know the President might detain someone who fell within the categories of identified belligerents in carrying out his charge. A different view requires a strained reading of the plain language of the resolution and cabins the theater of the President's powers as Commander in Chief to foreign soil. If that was the intent of Congress it was masked by the strong and direct language of the Joint Resolution. And if, as the majority asserts, 4001(a) is an impenetrable barrier to the President detaining a US citizen who is alleged to have ties to the belligerent and who is part of a plan for belligerency on US soil, then § 4001(a) in my view, is unconstitutional.

Sadly, the majority's resolution of this matter fails to address the real weakness of the government's appeal. Padilla presses to have his day in court to rebut the government's factual assertions that he falls within the authority of the Joint Resolution. The government contends that Mr. Padilla can be held incommunicado for eighteen months with no serious opportunity to put the government to its proof by an appropriate standard. The government fears that to do otherwise would compromise its ability both to gather important information from Mr. Padilla and to prevent him from communicating with other al Qaeda operatives in the United States.

While those concerns may be valid, they cannot withstand the force of another clause of the Constitution on which all three of us could surely agree. No one has suspended the Great Writ. *See* U.S Const. art. I § 9 cl. 2 Padilla's right to pursue a remedy through the writ would be meaningless if he had to do so alone. I therefore would extend to him the right to counsel as Chief Judge Mukasey did. At the hearing, Padilla, assisted by counsel, would be able to contest whether he is actually an enemy combatant thereby falling within the President's constitutional and statutory authority.

One of the more troubling aspects of Mr. Padilla's detention is that it is undefined by statute or Presidential Order. Certainly, a court could inquire whether Padilla continues to possess information that was helpful to the President in prosecuting the war against al Qaeda. Presumably, if he does not, the President would be required to charge Padilla criminally or delineate the appropriate process by which Padilla would remain under the President's control.

Mr. Padilla's case reveals the unique dynamics of our constitutional government. Padilla is alleged to be a member of an organization that most Americans view with anger and distrust. Yet his legal claims receive careful and thoughtful attention and are examined not in the light of his cause—whatever it may be—but by the constitutional and statutory validity of the powers invoked against him. See *Youngstown* (Jackson, J., concurring).

21.

NO PRESIDENT IS ABOVE THE US CONSTITUTION

Nat Hentoff

On December 18, the Second Circuit Court of Appeals sent a fundamental message to President Bush and all Americans who depend on the separation of powers that undergirds our democracy.

In the case of American citizen Jose Padilla, held—solely on the authority of the president—for eighteen months in a Charleston, South Carolina, brig without charges, indefinitely and without access to a lawyer as an enemy combatant, the Second Circuit ruled:

"The president, acting alone, possesses no inherent constitutional authority to detain American citizens seized within the United States, away from the zone of combat, as enemy combatants."

In the 2–1 decision, the majority cited a 1971 Non-Detention Act by Congress, which itself was a reaction to the widely criticized imprisonment of Japanese Americans in detention camps during World War II. The act unequivocally states that "no citizen shall be . . . detained by the United States except pursuant to an act of Congress."

Actually, back in 1936 (in *Valentine v. United States*), the Supreme

From the *Kalamazoo Gazette*, December 30, 2003. Reprinted by permission of the Newspaper Enterprise Association, Inc.

Court had declared that "the Constitution creates no executive prerogative to dispose of the liberty of the individual. Proceedings against him must be authorized by law." The case involved the extradition of US citizens to France for crimes allegedly committed there.

In the *Padilla* case, the Second Circuit Court of Appeals emphasized that Congress has not passed, in our war on terrorism, a law giving the president, as commander in chief, the unilateral power to hold Padilla without the fundamental rights to due process to which all American citizens are entitled.

Fundamental to the protection of our liberties is the system of checks and balances between the three branches of government that is enshrined in our Constitution. As James Madison emphasized in the Federalist Papers: "The accumulation of all powers, legislative, executive, and judiciary, in the same hands' . . . may justly be pronounced the very definition of tyranny."

We are nowhere near a state of tyranny.

The press is free. The civilian courts are open. There are increasing bipartisan measures in Congress to roll back the USA PATRIOT Act—specifically the section that dangerously limits judicial supervision over certain acts of the executive branch, particularly the Justice Department.

Nor does the administration and its supporters seem to have even the remotest intention of verging on tyranny. I have come to know, for example, Viet Dinh, who, as a close adviser to John Ashcroft in the Justice Department, was the principal drafter of the PATRIOT Act. He is now a law professor at George Washington University Law Center.

Dinh and I disagree on a number of actions the administration has taken in the name of security, but he experienced actual tyranny, having been born in Vietnam, and does not want to see it emerge anywhere. After he and I debated the PATRIOT Act at the National Press Foundation in Washington (while he was still at the Justice Department) Dinh said to me "keep us honest."

I've been doing the best that I can. So has the Second Circuit.

The administration's argument from the beginning has been that the *Padilla* case does not belong in the courts at all because of the president's inherent power as commander in chief, during a time of war, to do what he has done to Padilla.

After being brought to the courts, the administration, still holding that view, claims that Congress' Authorization for Use of Military Force Joint resolution soon after September 11 does give the president this authority over enemy combatants. But the Second Circuit found that this resolution "contains no language authorizing detention." The president has no power to act on his own without a specific law by Congress.

The court's decision, of course, is being appealed; but until that is decided, Padilla, the Second Circuit says, "will be entitled to constitutional protections" of all other citizens. Worth noting is that the dissenting judge, Richard Wesley, while agreeing with the government that the congressional resolution supports the president's position—also believes that Padilla, like any American citizen, has the right to see his lawyer. Will the Supreme Court deny him that and the rest of due process to which a citizen is entitled?

On the day of the Second Circuit decision, *New York Times* reporter David Stout wrote about the bedrock question before the Supreme Court: "the delicate balance between personal freedoms and the security of the nation, especially, in wartime." Especially in wartime, the Constitution must stand upright for the freedoms we are fighting to defend against the terrorists.

22.

ERRING ON ENEMY COMBATANTS

Chicago Tribune Editorial

O n September 12, 2001, no American could have doubted the nation was at war. The United States had not declared war on anyone, but an enemy known as al Qaeda had unmistakably declared war on the United States. After twenty-six months without another major terrorist attack on American soil, though, it's easy to get the idea that the war is over or isn't really a war. That dangerous mistake lies at the heart of a federal appeals court decision ordering the release of a suspected confederate of al Qaeda.

Jose Padilla, a US citizen, was arrested in May 2002 after arriving from Pakistan at O'Hare International Airport. The government says he met with al Qaeda operatives and returned to the United States after proposing to steal radioactive material to make a "dirty bomb." He was eventually declared an enemy combatant and has been held in a brig ever since.

But Thursday, the US Court of Appeals for the 2nd Circuit said the president lacks the power to detain Padilla as an enemy combatant—and must free him from military custody within thirty days.

Editorial reprinted with permission from the December 22, 2003, issue of the *Chicago Tribune*.

If the government sees him as a threat, says the court, it can file criminal charges.

The decision is hard to fathom. In time of war, presidents have broad powers to attack the enemy and protect Americans, from sending hundreds of thousands of American troops in harm's way to launching nuclear missiles. The war-making power entrusted to the president in the Constitution obviously includes the right to capture and hold anyone fighting on the other side even if he's an American seized on American soil. During World War II, the Supreme Court upheld the military trial of several German saboteurs caught in the United States, including one who claimed American citizenship.

The appeals court, however, dismissed the notion that the Constitution grants the president this power outside what the court called "a zone of combat"—as if the fifty states were off-limits to attack. It said that in addition, he disregarded a law barring detentions of citizens.

But that law says detentions may indeed be carried out "pursuant to an act of Congress"—such as the one adopted September 18, 2001, authorizing the president to "use all necessary and appropriate force" against those who carried out the September 11 attacks. What part of "all" does the appeals court not understand? Even if the Constitution didn't grant the president wide latitude in waging war, which it does, that resolution left no doubt about his power to go after al Qaeda wherever it might be found.

It's true that the administration went too far in claiming unfettered power over an American captured on American soil. For that reason, a federal district court was right to insist that Padilla be allowed to challenge the evidence that he is, in fact, an enemy combatant, and have access to a lawyer to do so. But it refused to buy the crazy idea that someone accused of plotting to slaughter Americans on behalf of a foreign power should be treated like a shoplifter.

If the administration was guilty of overreaching, the appeals court has more than matched its error. The criminal justice system is no place for enemy combatants. The Supreme Court should waste no time affirming that fact of life.

PART 6.

RECENT DEVELOPMENTS

23.

MEMORANDUM FOR ALBERTO R. GONZALES,

COUNSEL TO THE PRESIDENT

US Department of Justice
Office of Legal Counsel

Office of the Assistant Attorney General   Washington, DC 20530

August 1, 2002

Re: Standards of Conduct for Interrogation
Under 18 U.S.C. §§ 2340–2340A

You have asked for our Office's views regarding the standards of conduct under the Convention against Torture and Other Cruel, Inhuman, and Degrading Treatment or Punishment as implemented by Sections 2340–2340A of title 18 of the United States Code. As we understand it, this question has arisen in the context of the conduct of interrogations outside of the United States. We conclude below that Section 2340A proscribes acts inflicting, and that are specifically intended to inflict, severe pain or suffering, whether mental or physical. Those acts must be of an extreme nature to rise to the level of torture within the meaning of Section 2340A and the Convention. We further conclude that certain acts may be cruel, inhuman, or degrading, but still not produce pain and suffering of the requisite intensity to fall within Section 2340A's proscription against torture. We conclude by examining possible defenses that would negate any claim that certain interrogation methods violate the statute.

In Part I, we examine the criminal statute's text and history. We conclude that for an act to constitute torture as defined in Section 2340, it must inflict pain that is difficult to endure. Physical pain amounting to torture must be equivalent in intensity to the pain accompanying serious physical injury, such as organ failure, impairment of bodily function, or even death. For purely mental pain or suffering to amount to torture under Section 2340, it must result in serious psychological harm of significant duration, for example, lasting for months or even years. . . .

. . . In Part IV, we examine international decisions regarding the use of sensory deprivation techniques. These cases make clear that while many of these techniques may amount to cruel, inhuman, or degrading treatment, they do not produce pain or suffering of the necessary intensity to meet the definition of torture. From these decisions, we conclude that there is a wide range of such techniques that will not rise to the level of torture.

In Part V, we discuss whether Section 2340A may be unconstitutional if applied to interrogations undertaken of enemy combatants pursuant to the President's Commander in Chief powers. We find that in the circumstances of the current war against al Qaeda and its allies, prosecution under Section 2340A may be barred because enforcement of the statute would represent an unconstitutional infringement of the President's authority to conduct war. In Part VI, we discuss defenses to an allegation that an interrogation method might violate the statute. We conclude that, under the current circumstances, necessity or self-defense may justify interrogation methods that might violate Section 2340A.

I. 18 U.S.C. §§ 2340–2340A

Section 2340A makes it a criminal offense for any person "outside the United States [to] commit or [attempt] to commit torture." Section 2340 defines the act of torture as an:

> act committed by a person acting under the color of law specifically intended to inflict severe physical or mental pain or suffering (other than pain or suffering incidental to lawful sanctions) upon another person within his custody or physical control.

. . . The key statutory phrase in the definition of torture is the statement that acts amount to torture if they cause "severe physical or mental pain or suffering." In examining the meaning of a statute, its text must be the starting point. . . . The statute does not, however, define the term "severe." "In the absence of such a definition, we construe a statutory term in accordance with its ordinary or natural meaning." *FDIC v. Meyer* (1994). The dictionary defines "severe" as "[u]nsparing in exaction, punishment, or censure" or "[I]nflicting discomfort or pain hard to endure; sharp; afflictive; distressing; violent; extreme; as *severe* pain, anguish, torture." *Webster's New International Dictionary* 2295 (2d ed. 1935). . . . Thus, the adjective "severe" conveys that the pain or suffering must be of such a high level of intensity that the pain is difficult for the subject to endure.

Congress's use of the phrase "severe pain" elsewhere in the United States Code can shed more light on its meaning. . . . Significantly, the phrase "severe pain" appears in statutes defining an emergency medical condition for the purpose of providing health benefits. . . . They treat severe pain as an indicator of ailments that are likely to result in permanent and serious physical damage in the absence of immediate medial treatment. Such damage must rise to the level of death, organ failure, or the permanent impairment of a significant body function. These statutes suggest that "severe pain," as used in Section 2340, must rise to a similarly high level—the level that would ordinarily be associated with a sufficiently serious physical condition or injury such as death, organ failure, or serious impairment of body functions—in order to constitute torture. . . .

Section 2340 gives further guidance as to the meaning of "severe mental pain or suffering," as distinguished from severe physical pain and suffering. The statute defines "severe mental pain or suffering" as:

the prolonged mental harm caused by or resulting from—

(A) the intentional infliction or threatened infliction of severe physical pain or suffering;

(B) the administration or application, or threatened administration or application, of mind-altering substances or other procedures calculated to disrupt profoundly the senses or the personality;

(C) the threat of imminent death; or

(D) the threat that another person will imminently be subjected to death, severe physical pain or suffering, or the administration or application of mind-altering substances or other procedures calculated to disrupt profoundly the senses or personality.

18 U.S.C. § 2340(2). In order to prove "severe mental pain or suffering," the statute requires proof of "prolonged mental harm" that was caused by or resulted from one of four enumerated acts. . . .

IV. INTERNATIONAL DECISIONS

International decisions can prove of some value in assessing what conduct might rise to the level of severe mental pain or suffering. Although decisions by foreign or international bodies are in no way binding authority upon the United States, they provide guidance about how other nations will likely react to our interpretation of the CAT [Convention against Torture] and Section 2340. As this part will discuss, other Western nations have generally used a high standard in determining whether interrogation techniques violate the international prohibition on torture. In fact, these decisions have found various aggressive interrogation methods to, at worst, constitute cruel, inhuman, and degrading treatment, but not torture. These decisions only reinforce our view that there is a clear distinction between the two standards and that only extreme conduct, resulting in pain that is of an intensity often accompanying serious physical injury, will violate the latter.

A. European Court of Human Rights

An analogue to CAT's provisions can be found in the European Convention on Human Rights and Fundamental Freedoms (the "European Convention"). This convention prohibits torture, though it offers no definition of it. It also prohibits cruel, inhuman, or degrading treatment or punishment. By barring both types of acts, the European Convention implicitly distinguishes between them and further suggests that torture is a grave act beyond cruel, inhuman, or degrading treatment or punishment. Thus, while neither the European Convention nor the European Court of Human Rights decisions interpreting that convention would be authority for the interpretation of Sections 2340–2340A, the European Convention decisions concerning torture nonetheless provide a useful barometer of the international view of what actions amount to torture.

The leading European Court of Human Rights case explicating the differences between torture and cruel, inhuman, or degrading treatment or punishment is *Ireland v. the United Kingdom* (1978). . . . Careful attention to this case is worthwhile . . . also because the Reagan administration relied on this case in reaching the conclusion that the term torture is reserved in international usage for "extreme, deliberate, and unusually cruel practices." (S. Treaty Doc. 100-20, at 4).

The methods at issue in *Ireland* were:

(1) Wall Standing. The prisoner stands spread eagle against the wall, with fingers high above his head, and feet back so that he is standing on his toes such that all of his weight falls on his fingers.

(2) Hooding. A black or navy hood is placed over the prisoner's head and kept there except during the interrogation.

(3) Subjection to Noise. Pending interrogation, the prisoner is kept in a room with a loud and continuous hissing noise.

(4) Sleep Deprivation. Prisoners are deprived of sleep pending interrogation.

(5) Deprivation of Food and Drink. Prisoners receive a reduced diet during detention and pending interrogation.

The European Court of Human Rights concluded that these techniques used in combination, and applied for hours at a time, were inhuman and degrading but did not amount to torture. In analyzing whether these methods constituted torture, the court treated them as part of a single program. The court found that this program caused "if not actual bodily injury, at least intense physical and mental suffering to the person subjected thereto and also led to acute psychiatric disturbances during the interrogation." Thus, this program "fell into the category of inhuman treatment." The court further found that "[t]he techniques were also degrading since they were such as to arouse in their victims feeling of fear, anguish, and inferiority capable of humiliating and debasing them and possible [*sic*] breaking their physical or moral resistance." Yet, the court ultimately concluded:

> Although the five techniques, as applied in combination, undoubtedly amounted to inhuman and degrading treatment, although their object was the extraction of confession, the naming of others and/or information and although they were used systematically, they did not occasion suffering of the particular *intensity* and *cruelty* implied by the word torture. . . .

Thus, even though the court had concluded that the techniques produce "intense physical and mental suffering" and "acute psychiatric disturbances," they were not sufficient intensity or cruelty to amount to torture.

The court reached this conclusion based on the distinction the European Convention drew between torture and cruel, inhuman, or degrading treatment or punishment. The court reasoned that by expressly distinguishing between these two categories of treatment, the European Convention sought to "attach a special stigma to deliberate inhuman treatment causing very serious and cruel suffering." According to the court, "this distinction derives principally from a difference in the intensity of the suffering inflicted." The court further noted that this distinction paralleled the one drawn in the UN Declaration on the Protection from Torture, which specifically defines torture as "an aggravated and deliberate form of cruel, inhuman, or degrading treatment or punishment."

The court relied on this same "intensity/cruelty" distinction to conclude that some physical maltreatment fails to amount to torture. For example, four detainees were severely beaten and forced to stand spread eagle up against a wall. Other detainees were forced to stand spread eagle while an interrogator kicked them "continuously on the inside of the legs." Those detainees were beaten, some receiving injuries that were "substantial," and others received "massive" injuries. Another detainee was "subjected to . . . 'comparatively trivial' beatings" that resulted in a perforation of the detainee's eardrum and some "minor bruising." The court concluded that none of these situations "attain[ed] the particular level [of severity] inherent in the notion of torture." . . .

V. THE PRESIDENT'S COMMANDER IN CHIEF POWER

Even if an interrogation method arguably were to violate Section 2340A, the statute would be unconstitutional if it impermissibly encroached on the President's constitutional power to conduct a military campaign. As Commander in Chief, the President has the constitutional authority to order interrogations of enemy combatants to gain intelligence information concerning the military plans of the enemy. The demands of the Commander in Chief power are especially pronounced in the middle of a war in which the nation has already suffered a direct attack. In such a case, the information gained from interrogations may prevent future attacks by foreign enemies. Any effort to apply Section 2340A in a manner that interferes with the President's direction of such core war matters as the detention and interrogation of enemy combatants thus would be unconstitutional.

A. The War with al Qaeda

At the outset, we should make clear the nature of the threat presently posed to the nation. While your request for legal advice is not specifically limited to the current circumstances, we think it is useful to discuss this question in the context of the current war against the al Qaeda terrorist network. The situation in which these issues arise is unprecedented in recent American history. Four coordinated terrorist attacks, using hijacked commercial airliners as guided missiles, took place in rapid succession on the morning of September 11, 2001. These attacks were aimed at critical government buildings in the nation's capital and landmark buildings in its financial center. . . . They caused thousands of deaths. . . . Moreover, these attacks are part of a violent campaign against the United States. . . .

In response, the government has engaged in a broad effort at home and abroad to counter terrorism. . . .

Despite these efforts, numerous upper-echelon leaders of al Qaeda and the Taliban, with access to active terrorist cells and other resources, remain at large. . . .

Al Qaeda continues to plan further attacks, such as destroying American civilian airliners and killing American troops, which have fortunately been prevented. It is clear that bin Laden and his organization have conducted several violent attacks on the United States and its nationals, and that they seek to continue to do so. Thus, the capture and interrogation of such individuals is clearly imperative to our national security and defense. Interrogation of captured al Qaeda operatives may provide information concerning the nature of al Qaeda plans and the identities of its personnel, which may prove invaluable in preventing further direct attacks on the United States and its citizens. Given the massive destruction and loss of life caused by the September 11 attacks, it is reasonable to believe that information gained from al Qaeda personnel could prevent attacks of a similar (if not greater) magnitude from occurring in the United States. The case of Jose Padilla, a.k.a. Abdullah al Mujahir, illustrates the importance of such information. Padilla allegedly had journeyed to Afghanistan and Pakistan, met with senior al Qaeda leaders, and hatched a plot to construct and detonate a radioactive dispersal device in the United States. After allegedly receiving training in wiring explosives and with a substantial amount of currency in his [possession], Padilla attempted in May 2002 to enter the United States to further his scheme. Interrogation of captured al Qaeda operatives allegedly allowed US intelligence and law enforcement agencies to track Padilla and to detain him upon his entry into the United States.

B. Interpretation to Avoid Constitutional Problems

. . . In order to respect the President's inherent constitutional authority to manage a military campaign against al Qaeda and its allies, Section 2340A must be construed as not applying to interrogations undertaken pursuant to his Commander in Chief authority. As our Office has consistently held during this administration and previous administrations, Congress lacks authority under Article I to set the terms and conditions under which the President may exercise his authority as Commander in Chief to control the conduct of operations during a war. . . .

C. The Commander in Chief Power

. . . The text, structure, and history of the Constitution establish that the Founders entrusted the President with the primary responsibility, and therefore the power, to ensure the security of the United States in situations of grave and unforeseen emergencies. . . . [T]he structure of the Constitution demonstrates that any power traditionally understood as pertaining to the executive—which includes the conduct of warfare and the defense of the nation—unless expressly assigned in the Constitution to Congress, is vested in the President. Article II, Section 1 makes this clear by stating that the "executive Power shall be vested in a President of the United States of America." That sweeping grant vests in the President an unenumerated "executive power" and contrasts with the specific enumeration of the powers—those "herein"—granted to Congress in Article I. The implications of constitutional text and structure are confirmed by the practical consideration that national security decisions require the unity in purpose and energy in action that characterize the presidency rather than Congress. . . .

One of the core functions of the Commander in Chief is that of capturing, detaining, and interrogating members of the enemy. . . . It is well settled that the President may seize and detain enemy combatants, at least for the duration of the conflict, and the laws of war make clear that prisoners may be interrogated for information concerning the enemy, its strength, and its plans. Numerous Presidents have ordered the capture, detention, and questioning of enemy combatants during virtually every major conflict in the nation's history, including recent conflicts such as the Gulf, Vietnam, and Korean wars. Recognizing this authority, Congress has never attempted to restrict or interfere with the President's authority on this score.

Any effort by Congress to regulate the interrogation of battlefield combatants would violate the Constitution's sole vesting of the Commander in Chief authority in the President. There can be little doubt that intelligence operations, such as the detention and interrogation of enemy combatants and leaders, are both necessary and proper for the effective conduct of a military campaign. . . .

VI. DEFENSES

. . . Even if an interrogation method . . . might arguably cross the line drawn in Section 2340, and application of the statute was not held to be an unconstitutional infringement of the President's Commander in Chief authority, we believe that under the current circumstances certain justification defenses might be available that would potentially eliminate criminal liability. Standard criminal law defenses of necessity and self-defense could justify interrogation methods needed to elicit information to prevent a direct and imminent threat to the United States and its citizens.

A. Necessity

We believe that a defense of necessity could be raised, under the current circumstances, to an allegation of a Section 2340A violation. Often referred to as the "choice of evils" defense, necessity has been defined as follows:

> Conduct that the actor believes to be necessary to avoid a harm or evil to himself or to another is justifiable, provided that:
>
> (a) the harm or evil sought to be avoided by such conduct is greater than that sought to be prevented by the law defining the offense charged; and
> (b) neither the Code nor other law defining the offense provides exceptions or defenses dealing with the specific situation involved; and
> (c) a legislative purpose to exclude the justification claimed does not otherwise plainly appear.

Model Penal Code § 3.02.

. . . It appears to us that under the current circumstances the necessity defense could be successfully maintained in response to an allegation of a Section 2340A violation. On September 11, 2001, al Qaeda launched a surprise covert attack on civilian targets in the United States that led to the deaths of thousands and losses in the billions of dollars. According to public and governmental reports, al Qaeda has other sleeper cells within the United States that may be planning similar attacks. Indeed, al Qaeda plans apparently include efforts to develop and deploy chemical, biological, and nuclear weapons of mass destruction. Under these circumstances, a detainee may possess information that could enable the United States to prevent attacks that potentially could equal or surpass the September 11 attacks in their magnitude. Clearly, any harm that might occur during an interrogation would pale to insignificance compared to the harm avoided by preventing such an attack, which could take hundreds or thousands of lives.

Under this calculus, two factors will help indicate when the necessity defense could appropriately be invoked. First, the more certain that government officials are that a particular individual has information needed to prevent an attack, the more necessary interrogation will be. Second, the more likely it appears to be that a terrorist attack is likely to occur, and the greater the amount of damage expected from such an attack, the more that an interrogation to get information would become necessary. Of course, the strength of the necessity defense depends on the circumstances that prevail, and the knowledge of the government actors involved, when the interrogation is conducted. While every interrogation that might violate Section 2340A does not trigger a necessity defense, we can say that certain circumstances could support such a defense. . . .

B. Self-Defense

Even if a court were to find that a violation of Section 2340A was not justified by necessity, a defendant could still appropriately raise a claim of self-defense. The right to self-defense, even when it involves the use of deadly force, is deeply embedded in our law, both as to individuals and as to the nation as a whole. . . .

CONCLUSION

For the foregoing reasons, we conclude that torture as defined in and proscribed by Sections 2340–2340A, covers only extreme acts. Severe pain is generally of the kind difficult for the victim to endure. Where the pain is physical, it must be of an intensity akin to that which accompanies serious physical injury such as death or organ failure. Severe mental pain requires suffering not just at the moment of infliction but it also requires lasting psychological harm, such as seen in mental disorders like posttraumatic stress disorder. Additionally, such severe mental pain can arise only from the predicate acts listed in Section 2340. Because the acts inflicting torture are extreme, there is significant range of acts that though they might constitute cruel, inhuman, or degrading treatment or punishment fail to rise to the level of torture.

Further, we conclude that under the circumstances of the current war against al Qaeda and its allies, application of Section 2340A to interrogations undertaken pursuant to the President's Commander in Chief powers may be unconstitutional. Finally, even if an interrogation method might violate Section 2340A, necessity or self-defense could provide justifications that would eliminate any criminal liability.

Please let us know if we can be of further assistance.

[signed]
Jay S. Bybee
Assistant Attorney General

Editor's Note: A copy of the signed August 2, 2002, memorandum, with some small redactions, was obtained via an Internet link from the *Washington Post*. I have made substantial edits to the memo in the interest of space and have eliminated most internal citations and all footnotes. MKBD

24.

A PLUNGE FROM THE MORAL HEIGHTS

Richard Cohen

Come and sit with me for a moment. I am in a room, in a Middle Eastern country, and I am talking to a government official. He mentions the abuses at Abu Ghraib, the US-run prison outside Baghdad, and what this has done to America's image in his region. He smiles at what he says, for he is a man who appreciates irony. Of course, this same thing happens in his country, he says. Inwardly, I smile back, smug in my confidence that Abu Ghraib or no Abu Ghraib, America is a different sort of nation. It now seems I was a bit too smug.

The recent revelations that the Justice Department prepared memos parsing what is and what is not torture brings to mind regimes that, well, I would rather not bring to mind. These are the torturers of the world, although they deny it, and to bolster their lie they produce copious laws against the practice.

Attorney General John Ashcroft, whose Justice Department prepared the memos—one of them running to fifty pages and signed by Jay S. Bybee, then head of the Office of Legal Counsel—assured the Senate the other day that the memos are of no consequence. They were only internal Justice Department stuff, the scribblings of lawyers, and—most important—the president has not "directed or ordered" torture, Ashcroft said. In another administration, such an assurance would be enough for me, but given this one's cavalier approach to civil liberties, I have to note that "directed" or "ordered" is not the same as condoned. That's what I wonder about.

I wonder, too, why the much-pressed Justice Department—all those news releases to get out extolling Ashcroft—went to all the trouble of coming up with definitions of torture that might be permissible under US law when no one was supposedly considering torturing al Qaeda prisoners in the first place. A fifty-page memo is not an hour's work. It's clear someone had torture in mind. The Defense Department and the CIA were looking for guidance.

In a way, you can understand why. The memos followed—sometimes by more than a year—the terrorist attacks of September 11, 2001. What if the CIA got its hands on a terrorist who it thought might have information about coming attacks? What should it do? What could it do? Could it, say, torture the guy a little bit—not too much, mind you—so he would cough up the information? In one of the memos leaked to the *Post*, the Justice Department said yes, precisely—torture, but only a bit. "For purely mental pain or suffering to amount to torture, it must result in significant psychological harm of significant duration, e.g., lasting for months or even years." This is a very odd—shall we say "tortured"—definition.

My dictionary, compiled by lexicographers and not, thank God, by lawyers, knows precisely what torture is. "To bring great physical or mental pain upon another," is one of several definitions. Simple. Had the CIA or the Pentagon turned to a Boy Scout troop or a gathering of Future Farmers of America, they would have said something similar. They also might say that, given human nature, it is as preposterous to talk about a little bit of torture as it is to talk about a little bit pregnant. This sort of stuff isn't possible to contain, and before you know it, a little torture is a lot of torture—and who's to say at the moment whether the psychological "harm" cited in the memo is going to last a week or a lifetime? A little bit of torture can go a long, long way.

The Bush administration constantly reminds us that there's a war on. That's wrong. There are two. One is being fought by soldiers in combat, and the other is being fought for the hearts and minds of people who are not yet our enemies. However badly the administration has botched the first war—where, oh where, is Osama bin Laden?—it has done even worse with the second. It has jutted its chin to the world, appeared pugnacious and unilateralist, permitted the abuse of POWs and others at Abu Ghraib, and now toyed in some fashion with torture. The Bush administration has shamed us all, reducing us to the level of those governments that also have wonderful laws forbidding torture, but condone it anyway.

It is commonly said that we are a nation of laws, not men. And we are. But beyond the laws, we are also a nation of men and women with a common ethic. Some things are not American. Torture, for damned sure, is one of them.

25.

A CRUCIAL LOOK AT TORTURE LAW

John C. Yoo

Among the Justice Department memos released by the Bush administration, the one that generated the most criticism, dated August 1, 2002, considered the definition of torture under federal criminal laws.

Its critics have attacked the differences between the memo's conclusions and the definition of torture in the 1984 Convention against Torture. They've attacked its discussion of possible defenses against prosecution and of the scope of the commander in chief's power. Most of all, they have attacked the fact that it did not consider policy or moral issues.

The Justice Department's office of legal counsel, in which I served, produced the memo. It is important to understand the memo's function so that future administrations may receive such candid advice on the most delicate and important kinds of legal questions.

First, there is a clear and necessary difference between law and policy. The memo did not advocate or recommend torture; indeed,

John C. Yoo, Professor of Law, University of California at Berkeley School of Law (Boalt Hall); Visiting Scholar, American Enterprise Institute.

it did not discuss the pros and cons of any interrogation tactic. Rather, the memo sought to answer a discrete question: What is the meaning of "torture" under the federal criminal laws? What the law permits and what policymakers chose to do are entirely different things. Second, there was nothing wrong—and everything right—with analyzing a law that establishes boundaries on interrogation in the war on terrorism. Unlike previous wars, our enemy now is a stateless network of religious extremists. They do not obey the laws of war; they hide among peaceful populations and launch surprise attacks on civilians. They have no armed forces per se, no territory or citizens to defend, and no fear of dying during their attacks. Information is our primary weapon against this enemy, and intelligence gathered from captured operatives is perhaps the most effective means of preventing future attacks.

An American leader would be derelict of duty if he did not seek to understand all his options in such unprecedented circumstances. Presidents Lincoln during the Civil War and Roosevelt in the lead-up to World War II sought legal advice about the outer bounds of their power—even if they did not always use it. Our leaders should ask legal questions first, before setting policy or making decisions in a fog of uncertainty.

Third, there are no easy legal questions about torture, despite the moral certitude displayed by the administration's critics. The Reagan and first Bush administrations developed a strict test for torture—the "specific intent" to inflict "severe physical or mental pain or suffering" —that was adopted by Congress and the Clinton administration in 1994. It uses words rare in the federal code, no prosecutions have been brought under it, and it has never been interpreted by a court.

As a result, the 2002 memo looked to other federal laws, domestic and international judicial decisions, legislative history, and presidential and diplomatic records, which reinforced the conclusion that the United States intentionally defined torture strictly.

It is easy now for critics to claim that the work was poor; they haven't produced their own analyses or confronted any of the hard questions. For example, would they say that no technique beyond shouted questions could be used to interrogate a high-level terrorist leader, such as Osama bin Laden, who knows of planned attacks on the United States?

Lawyers who must answer such questions must also explain possible defenses. For example, if a police officer were to ask when the use of force is allowed, a lawyer would first explain that killing constitutes murder or manslaughter, but he should also explain when self-defense or necessity would permit the use of force without criminal sanctions.

Self-defense and necessity are long-accepted defenses to criminal prosecution, and Congress chose not to preclude them in its statute barring torture, despite language in the Torture Convention to the contrary. Similarly, precedent and history support the idea that the president, as commander in chief, may have to take measures in extreme wartime situations that might run counter to Congress's wishes. To ignore these issues would deny policymakers a view of the entire playing field.

Our system has a place for the discussion of morality and policy. Our elected and appointed officials must weigh these issues in deciding on how it will conduct interrogations. Ultimately, they must answer to the American people for their choices. A lawyer must not read the law to be more restrictive than it is just to satisfy his own moral goals, to prevent diplomatic backlash, or to advance the cause of international human rights law.

However valid those considerations, they simply do not rest within the province of the lawyer who must make sure the government understands what the law permits before it decides what it should do.

26.

RUMSFELD V. PADILLA

US Supreme Court

Donald H. RUMSFELD, Secretary of Defense, Petitioner,

v.

Jose PADILLA and Donna R. Newman,
as next friend of Jose Padilla

Argued April 28, 2004.
Decided June 28, 2004.

Rehnquist, C.J., delivered the opinion of the Court, in which O'Connor, Scalia, Kennedy, and Thomas, JJ., joined. Kennedy, J., filed a concurring opinion, in which O'Connor, J., joined. Stevens, J., filed a dissenting opinion, in which Souter, Ginsburg, and Breyer, JJ., joined.

ON WRIT OF CERTIORARI TO THE UNITED STATES COURT OF APPEALS FOR THE SECOND CIRCUIT

Chief Justice Rehnquist delivered the opinion of the Court.

Respondent Jose Padilla is a United States citizen detained by the

Department of Defense pursuant to the President's determination that he is an "enemy combatant" who conspired with al Qaeda to carry out terrorist attacks in the United States. We confront two questions: First, did Padilla properly file his habeas petition in the Southern District of New York; and second, did the President possess authority to detain Padilla militarily. We answer the threshold question in the negative and thus do not reach the second question presented.

Because we do not decide the merits, we only briefly recount the relevant facts. On May 8, 2002, Padilla flew from Pakistan to Chicago's O'Hare International Airport. As he stepped off the plane, Padilla was apprehended by federal agents executing a material witness warrant issued by the United States District Court for the Southern District of New York (Southern District) in connection with its grand jury investigation into the September 11 terrorist attacks. Padilla was then transported to New York, where he was held in federal criminal custody. On May 22, acting through appointed counsel, Padilla moved to vacate the material witness warrant.

Padilla's motion was still pending when, on June 9, the President issued an order to Secretary of Defense Donald H. Rumsfeld designating Padilla an "enemy combatant" and directing the Secretary to detain him in military custody. In support of this action, the President invoked his authority as "Commander in Chief of the US armed forces" and the Authorization for Use of Military Force Joint Resolution (AUMF), enacted by Congress on September 18, 2001. The President also made several factual findings explaining his decision to designate Padilla an enemy combatant. Based on these findings, the President concluded that it is "consistent with US law and the laws of war for the Secretary of Defense to detain Mr. Padilla as an enemy combatant."

That same day, Padilla was taken into custody by Department of Defense officials and transported to the Consolidated Naval Brig in Charleston, South Carolina. He has been held there ever since.

On June 11, Padilla's counsel, claiming to act as his next friend, filed in the Southern District a habeas corpus petition under 28 U.S.C. § 2241. The petition, as amended, alleged that Padilla's military detention violates the Fourth, Fifth, and Sixth Amendments and

the Suspension Clause, Art. I, § 9, cl. 2, of the United States Consti-
tution. The amended petition named as respondents President
Bush, Secretary Rumsfeld, and Melanie A. Marr, Commander of the
Consolidated Naval Brig.

The Government moved to dismiss, arguing that Commander
Marr, as Padilla's immediate custodian, is the only proper respondent
to his habeas petition, and that the District Court lacks jurisdiction
over Commander Marr because she is located outside the Southern
District. On the merits, the Government contended that the President
has authority to detain Padilla militarily pursuant to the Commander
in Chief Clause of the Constitution, Art. II, § 2, cl. 1, the congressional
AUMF, and this Court's decision in *Ex parte Quirin* (1942). The District Court issued its decision in December 2002. The court held that
the Secretary's "personal involvement" in Padilla's military custody
renders him a proper respondent to Padilla's habeas petition, and that
it can assert jurisdiction over the Secretary under New York's long-arm
statute, notwithstanding his absence from the Southern District. On
the merits, however, the court accepted the Government's contention
that the President has authority to detain as enemy combatants citizens captured on American soil during a time of war.

The Court of Appeals for the Second Circuit reversed. The court
agreed with the District Court that Secretary Rumsfeld is a proper
respondent, reasoning that in cases where the habeas petitioner is
detained for "other than federal criminal violations, the Supreme
Court has recognized exceptions to the general practice of naming
the immediate physical custodian as respondent." The Court of
Appeals concluded that on these "unique" facts Secretary Rumsfeld
is Padilla's custodian because he exercises "the legal reality of control" over Padilla and because he was personally involved in
Padilla's military detention. The Court of Appeals also affirmed the
District Court's holding that it has jurisdiction over the Secretary
under New York's long-arm statute.

Reaching the merits, the Court of Appeals held that the President
lacks authority to detain Padilla militarily. The court concluded that
neither the President's Commander in Chief power nor the AUMF
authorizes military detentions of American citizens captured on

American soil. To the contrary, the Court of Appeals found in both our case law and in the Non-Detention Act, 18 U.S.C. § 4001(a), a strong presumption against domestic military detention of citizens absent explicit congressional authorization. Accordingly, the court granted the writ of habeas corpus and directed the Secretary to release Padilla from military custody within thirty days.

We granted the Government's petition for certiorari to review the Court of Appeals' rulings with respect to the jurisdictional and the merits issues, both of which raise important questions of federal law.

The question whether the Southern District has jurisdiction over Padilla's habeas petition breaks down into two related subquestions. First, who is the proper respondent to that petition? And second, does the Southern District have jurisdiction over him or her? We address these questions in turn.

I

The federal habeas statute straightforwardly provides that the proper respondent to a habeas petition is "the person who has custody over [the petitioner]" 28 U.S.C. § 2242; see also § 2243 ("The writ, or order to show cause shall be directed to the person having custody of the person detained"). The consistent use of the definite article in reference to the custodian indicates that there is generally only one proper respondent to a given prisoner's habeas petition. This custodian, moreover, is "the person" with the ability to produce the prisoner's body before the habeas court. We summed up the plain language of the habeas statute over one hundred years ago in this way: "[T]hese provisions contemplate a proceeding against some person who has the *immediate custody* of the party detained, with the power to produce the body of such party before the court or judge, that he may be liberated if no sufficient reason is shown to the contrary" *Wales v. Whitney* (1885); see also *Braden v. 30th Judicial Circuit Court of Ky.* (1973). . . .

In accord with the statutory language and *Wales's* immediate custodian rule, longstanding practice confirms that in habeas challenges to present physical confinement—"core challenges"—the default rule is that the proper respondent is the warden of the facility where the prisoner is being held, not the Attorney General or some other remote supervisory official. No exceptions to this rule, either recognized or proposed, apply here.

If the *Wales* immediate custodian rule applies in this case, Commander Marr—the equivalent of the warden at the military brig—is the proper respondent, not Secretary Rumsfeld. . . . Neither Padilla, nor the courts below, nor Justice Stevens's dissent deny the general applicability of the immediate custodian rule to habeas petitions challenging physical custody. They argue instead that the rule is flexible and should not apply on the "unique facts" of this case. We disagree.

. . . [T]he cases cited by Padilla stand for the simple proposition that the immediate physical custodian rule, by its terms, does not apply when a habeas petitioner challenges something other than his present physical confinement. . . .

In *Braden* . . . the immediate custodian rule did not apply because *there was no* immediate physical custodian with respect to the "custody" being challenged. That is not the case here: Commander Marr exercises day-to-day control over Padilla's physical custody. We have never intimated that a habeas petitioner could name someone other than his immediate physical custodian as respondent simply because the challenged physical custody does not arise out of a criminal conviction. Nor can we do so here just because Padilla's physical confinement stems from a military order by the President.

. . . In challenges to present physical confinement, we reaffirm that the immediate custodian, not a supervisory official who exercises legal control, is the proper respondent. If the "legal control" test applied to physical-custody challenges, a convicted prisoner would be able to name the State or the Attorney General as a respondent to a § 2241 petition. As the statutory language, established practice, and our precedent demonstrate, that is not the case. . . .

Padilla's argument reduces to a request for a new exception to the immediate custodian rule based upon the "unique facts" of this case. While Padilla's detention is undeniably unique in many respects, it is at bottom a simple challenge to physical custody imposed by the

Executive—the traditional core of the Great Writ. There is no indication that there was any attempt to manipulate behind Padilla's transfer—he was taken to the same facility where other al Qaeda members were already being held, and the Government did not attempt to hide from Padilla's lawyer where it had taken him. His detention is thus not unique in any way that would provide arguable basis for a departure from the immediate custodian rule. Accordingly, we hold that Commander Marr, not Secretary Rumsfeld, is Padilla's custodian and the proper respondent to his habeas petition.

II

We turn now to the second subquestion. District courts are limited to granting habeas relief "within their respective jurisdictions" 28 U.S.C. § 2241(a). We have interpreted this language to require "nothing more than that the court issuing the writ have jurisdiction over the custodian" *Braden*. Thus, jurisdiction over Padilla's habeas petition lies in the Southern District only if it has jurisdiction over Commander Marr. We conclude it does not.

Congress added the limiting clause—"within their respective jurisdictions"—to the habeas statute in 1867 to avert the "inconvenient [and] potentially embarrassing" possibility that "every judge anywhere [could] issue the Great Writ on behalf of applicants far distantly removed from the courts whereon they sat" *Carbo v. United States* (1961). Accordingly, with respect to habeas petitions "designed to relieve an individual from oppressive confinement," the traditional rule has always been that the Great Writ is "issuable only in the district of confinement."

Other portions of the habeas statute support this commonsense reading of § 2241(a). . . .

The plain language of the habeas statute thus confirms the general rule that for core habeas petitions challenging present physical confinement, jurisdiction lies in only one district: the district of confinement. . . .

The proviso that district courts may issue the writ only "within their respective jurisdictions" forms an important corollary to the immediate custodian rule in challenges to present physical custody under § 2241. Together they compose a simple rule that has been consistently applied in the lower courts, including in the context of military detentions: Whenever a § 2241 habeas petitioner seeks to challenge his present physical custody within the United States, he should name his warden as respondent and file the petition in the district of confinement. . . .

The District of South Carolina, not the Southern District of New York, was the district court in which Padilla should have brought his habeas petition. We therefore reverse the judgment of the Court of Appeals and remand the case for entry of an order of dismissal without prejudice.

It is so ordered.

Editor's Note: This opinion has been heavily edited, and concurring and dissenting opinions have been omitted. MKBD

27.

HAMDI V. RUMSFELD

US Supreme Court

Yaser Esam HAMDI and Esam Fouad Hamdi, as next friend of
Yaser Esam Hamdi, Petitioners,

v.

Donald H. RUMSFELD, Secretary of Defense, et al.

Argued April 28, 2004.
Decided June 28, 2004.

J ustice O'Connor announced the judgment of the Court and
delivered an opinion, in which the Chief Justice, Justice Kennedy,
and Justice Breyer join.

At this difficult time in our nation's history, we are called upon
to consider the legality of the Government's detention of a United
States citizen on United States soil as an "enemy combatant" and to
address the process that is constitutionally owed to one who seeks
to challenge his classification as such. The United States Court of
Appeals for the Fourth Circuit held that petitioner's detention was
legally authorized and that he was entitled to no further opportunity
to challenge his enemy-combatant label. We now vacate and

remand. We hold that although Congress authorized the detention of combatants in the narrow circumstances alleged here, due process demands that a citizen held in the United States as an enemy combatant be given a meaningful opportunity to contest the factual basis for that detention before a neutral decisionmaker.

I

On September 11, 2001, the al Qaeda terrorist network used hijacked commercial airliners to attack prominent targets in the United States. Approximately three thousand people were killed in those attacks. One week later, in response to these "acts of treacherous violence," Congress passed a resolution authorizing the President to "use all necessary and appropriate force against those nations, organizations, or persons he determines planned, authorized, committed, or aided the terrorist attacks" or "harbored such organizations or persons, in order to prevent any future acts of international terrorism against the United States by such nations, organizations, or persons." Authorization for Use of Military Force ("the AUMF"). Soon thereafter, the President ordered United States Armed Forces to Afghanistan, with a mission to subdue al Qaeda and quell the Taliban regime that was known to support it.

This case arises out of the detention of a man whom the Government alleges took up arms with the Taliban during this conflict. His name is Yaser Esam Hamdi. Born an American citizen in Louisiana in 1980, Hamdi moved with his family to Saudi Arabia as a child. By 2001, the parties agree, he resided in Afghanistan. At some point that year, he was seized by members of the Northern Alliance, a coalition of military groups opposed to the Taliban government, and eventually was turned over to the United States military. The Government asserts that it initially detained and interrogated Hamdi in Afghanistan before transferring him to the United States Naval Base in Guantanamo Bay in January 2002. In April 2002, upon learning that Hamdi is an American citizen, authorities transferred him to a naval brig in Norfolk, Virginia, where he remained until a recent transfer to a brig in Charleston, South Carolina. The Government contends that Hamdi is an "enemy combatant," and that this status justifies holding him in the United States indefinitely—without formal charges or proceedings—unless and until it makes the determination that access to counsel or further process is warranted.

In June 2002, Hamdi's father, Esam Fouad Hamdi, filed the present petition for a writ of habeas corpus under 28 U.S.C. § 2241 in the Eastern District of Virginia, naming as petitioners his son and himself as next friend. The elder Hamdi alleges in the petition that he has had no contact with his son since the Government took custody of him in 2001, and that the Government has held his son "without access to legal counsel or notice of any charges pending against him." The petition contends that Hamdi's detention was not legally authorized. It argues that "[a]s an American citizen, . . . Hamdi enjoys the full protections of the Constitution," and that Hamdi's detention in the United States without charges, access to an impartial tribunal, or assistance of counsel "violated and continue[s] to violate the Fifth and Fourteenth Amendments to the United States Constitution." The habeas petition asks that the court, among other things, (1) appoint counsel for Hamdi; (2) order respondents to cease interrogating him; (3) declare that he is being held in violation of the Fifth and Fourteenth Amendments; (4) "[t]o the extent Respondents contest any material factual allegations in this Petition, schedule an evidentiary hearing, at which Petitioners may adduce proof in support of their allegations"; and (5) order that Hamdi be released from his "unlawful custody." Although his habeas petition provides no details with regard to the factual circumstances surrounding his son's capture and detention, Hamdi's father has asserted in documents found elsewhere in the record that his son went to Afghanistan to do "relief work," and that he had been in that country less than two months before September 11, 2001, and could not have received military training. The twenty-year-old was traveling on his own for the first time, his father says, and "[b]ecause of his lack of experience, he was trapped in Afghanistan once that military campaign began."

The District Court found that Hamdi's father was a proper next friend, appointed the federal public defender as counsel for the petitioners, and ordered that counsel be given access to Hamdi. The United States Court of Appeals for the Fourth Circuit reversed that order, holding that the District Court had failed to extend appropriate deference to the Government's security and intelligence interests. It directed the District Court to consider "the most cautious procedures first," and to conduct a deferential inquiry into Hamdi's status. It opined that "if Hamdi is indeed an 'enemy combatant' who was captured during hostilities in Afghanistan, the government's present detention of him is a lawful one."

On remand, the Government filed a response and a motion to dismiss the petition. It attached to its response a declaration from one Michael Mobbs (hereinafter "Mobbs Declaration"), who identified himself as Special Advisor to the Undersecretary of Defense for Policy. Mobbs indicated that in this position, he has been "substantially involved with matters related to the detention of enemy combatants in the current war against the al Qaeda terrorists and those who support and harbor them (including the Taliban)." He expressed his "familiar[ity]" with Department of Defense and United States military policies and procedures applicable to the detention, control, and transfer of al Qaeda and Taliban personnel, and declared that "[b]ased upon my review of relevant records and reports, I am also familiar with the facts and circumstances related to the capture of . . . Hamdi and his detention by US military forces."

Mobbs then set forth what remains the sole evidentiary support that the Government has provided to the courts for Hamdi's detention. The declaration states that Hamdi "traveled to Afghanistan" in July or August 2001, and that he thereafter "affiliated with a Taliban military unit and received weapons training." It asserts that Hamdi "remained with his Taliban unit following the attacks of September 11" and that, during the time when Northern Alliance forces were "engaged in battle with the Taliban," "Hamdi's Taliban unit surrendered" to those forces, after which he "surrender[ed] his Kalishnikov assault rifle" to them. The Mobbs Declaration also states that, because al Qaeda and the Taliban "were and are hostile forces engaged in armed conflict with the armed forces of the United States," "individuals associated with" those groups "were and continue to be enemy combatants." Mobbs states that Hamdi was labeled an enemy combatant "[b]ased upon his interviews and in light of his association with the Taliban." According to the declaration, a series of "US military screening team[s]" determined that Hamdi met "the criteria for enemy combatants," and "a subsequent interview of Hamdi has confirmed that he surrendered and gave his firearm to Northern Alliance forces, which supports his classification as an enemy combatant."

After the Government submitted this declaration, the Fourth Circuit directed the District Court to proceed in accordance with its earlier ruling and, specifically, to " 'consider the sufficiency of the Mobbs Declaration as an independent matter before proceeding further.' " The District Court found that the Mobbs Declaration fell "far short" of supporting Hamdi's detention. It criticized the generic and hearsay nature of the affidavit, calling it "little more than the government's 'say-so.'" It ordered the Government to turn over numerous materials for *in camera* review, including copies of all of Hamdi's statements and the notes taken from interviews with him that related to his reasons for going to Afghanistan and his activities therein; a list of all interrogators who had questioned Hamdi and their names and addresses; statements by members of the Northern Alliance regarding Hamdi's surrender and capture; a list of the dates and locations of his capture and subsequent detentions; and the names and titles of the United States Government officials who made the determinations that Hamdi was an enemy combatant and that he should be moved to a naval brig. The court indicated that all of these materials were necessary for "meaningful judicial review" of whether Hamdi's detention was legally authorized and whether Hamdi had received sufficient process to satisfy the Due Process Clause of the Constitution and relevant treaties or military regulations.

The Government sought to appeal the production order, and the District Court certified the question of whether the Mobbs Declaration, "'standing alone, is sufficient as a matter of law to allow meaningful judicial review of [Hamdi's] classification as an enemy combatant.'" The Fourth Circuit reversed, but did not squarely answer the certified question. It instead stressed that, because it was "undisputed that Hamdi was captured in a zone of active combat in a foreign theater of conflict," no factual inquiry or evidentiary hearing allowing Hamdi to be heard or to rebut the Government's assertions was necessary or proper. Concluding that the factual averments in the Mobbs Declaration, "if accurate," provided a sufficient basis upon which to conclude that the President had constitutionally detained Hamdi pursuant to the President's war powers, it ordered the habeas petition dismissed. The Fourth Circuit emphasized that the "vital purposes" of the detention of uncharged enemy combatants—preventing those combatants from rejoining the enemy while relieving the military of the burden of litigating the circumstances of wartime captures halfway around the globe—were interests "directly derived from the war powers of Articles I and II." In that court's view, because "Article III contains nothing analogous to the specific powers of war so carefully enumerated in Articles I and II," separation of powers principles prohibited a federal court from "delv[ing] further into Hamdi's status and capture." Accordingly, the District Court's more vigorous inquiry "went far beyond the acceptable scope of review."

On the more global question of whether legal authorization exists for the detention of citizen enemy combatants at all, the Fourth Circuit rejected Hamdi's arguments that 18 U.S.C. § 4001(a) and Article 5 of the Geneva Convention rendered any such detentions unlawful. The court expressed doubt as to Hamdi's argument that § 4001(a), which provides that "[n]o citizen shall be imprisoned or otherwise detained by the United States except pursuant to an Act of Congress," required express congressional authorization of detentions of this sort. But it held that, in any event, such authorization was found in the post–September 11 Authorization for Use of Military Force. Because "capturing and detaining enemy combatants is an inherent part of warfare," the court held, "the 'necessary and appropriate force' referenced in the congressional resolution necessarily includes the capture and detention of any and all hostile forces arrayed against our troops." . . . The court likewise rejected Hamdi's Geneva Convention claim, concluding that the convention is not self-executing and that, even if it were, it would not preclude the Executive from detaining Hamdi until the cessation of hostilities.

Finally, the Fourth Circuit rejected Hamdi's contention that its legal analyses with regard to the authorization for the detention scheme and the process to which he was constitutionally entitled should be altered by the fact that he is an American citizen detained on American soil. Relying on *Ex parte Quirin*, the court emphasized that "[o]ne who takes up arms against the United States in a foreign theater of war, regardless of his citizenship, may properly be designated an enemy combatant and treated as such." "The privilege of citizenship," the court held, "entitles Hamdi to a limited judicial inquiry into his detention, but only to determine its legality under the war powers of the political branches. At least where it is undisputed that he was present in a zone of active combat operations, we are satisfied that the Constitution does not entitle him to a searching review of the factual determinations underlying his seizure there."

The Fourth Circuit denied rehearing en banc, and we granted certiorari. We now vacate the judgment below and remand.

II

The threshold question before us is whether the Executive has the authority to detain citizens who qualify as "enemy combatants." There is some debate as to the proper scope of this term, and the Government has never provided any court with the full criteria that it uses in classifying individuals as such. It has made clear, however, that, for purposes of this case, the "enemy combatant" that it is seeking to detain is an individual who, it alleges, was " 'part of or supporting forces hostile to the United States or coalition partners'" in Afghanistan and who "'engaged in an armed conflict against the United States'" there. We therefore answer only the narrow question before us: whether the detention of citizens falling within that definition is authorized.

The Government maintains that no explicit congressional authorization is required, because the Executive possesses plenary authority to detain pursuant to Article II of the Constitution. We do not reach the question whether Article II provides such authority, however, because we agree with the Government's alternative position, that Congress has in fact authorized Hamdi's detention, through the AUMF.

Our analysis on that point, set forth below, substantially overlaps with our analysis of Hamdi's principal argument for the illegality of his detention. He posits that his detention is forbidden by 18 U.S.C. § 4001(a). Section 4001(a) states that "[n]o citizen shall be imprisoned or otherwise detained by the United States except pursuant to an Act of Congress." Congress passed § 4001(a) in 1971 as part of a bill to repeal the Emergency Detention Act of 1950, which provided procedures for executive detention, during times of emergency, of individuals deemed likely to engage in espionage or sabotage. Congress was particularly concerned about the possibility that the Act could be used to reprise the Japanese internment camps of World War II. The Government . . . maintains that § 4001(a) is satisfied, because Hamdi is being detained "pursuant to an Act of Congress"—the AUMF. . . . [F]or the reasons that follow, we conclude that the AUMF is explicit congressional authorization for the detention of individuals in the narrow category we describe (assuming, without deciding, that such authorization is required), and that the AUMF satisfied § 4001(a)'s requirement that a detention be "pursuant to an Act of Congress" (assuming, without deciding, that § 4001(a) applies to military detentions).

The AUMF authorizes the President to use "all necessary and appropriate force" against "nations, organizations, or persons" associated with the September 11, 2001, terrorist attacks. There can be no doubt that individuals who fought against the United States in Afghanistan as part of the Taliban, an organization known to have supported the al Qaeda terrorist network responsible for those attacks, are individuals Congress sought to target in passing the AUMF. We conclude that detention of individuals falling into the limited category we are considering, for the duration of the particular conflict in which they were captured, is so fundamental and accepted an incident to war as to be an exercise of the "necessary and appropriate force" Congress has authorized the President to use.

The capture and detention of lawful combatants and the capture, detention, and trial of unlawful combatants, by "universal agreement and practice," are "important incident[s] of war." *Ex parte Quirin*. The purpose of detention is to prevent captured individuals from returning to the field of battle and taking up arms once again. . . .

There is no bar to this nation's holding one of its own citizens as an enemy combatant. In *Quirin*, one of the detainees, Haupt, alleged that he was a naturalized United States citizen. . . . While Haupt was tried for violations of the law of war, nothing in *Quirin* suggests that his citizenship would have precluded his mere detention for the duration of the relevant hostilities. . . . Nor can we see any reason for drawing such a line here. . . .

In light of these principles, it is of no moment that the AUMF does not use specific language of detention. Because detention to prevent a combatant's return to the battlefield is a fundamental incident of waging war, in permitting the use of "necessary and appropriate force," Congress has clearly and unmistakably authorized detention in the narrow circumstances considered here.

Hamdi objects, nevertheless, that Congress has not authorized the *indefinite* detention to which he is now subject. The Government responds that "the detention of enemy combatants during World War II was just as 'indefinite' while that war was being fought." We take Hamdi's objection to be not to the lack of certainty regarding the date on which the conflict will end, but to the substantial prospect of perpetual detention. We recognize that the national security underpinnings of the "war on terror," although crucially important, are broad and malleable. As the Government concedes, "given its unconventional nature, the current conflict is unlikely to end with a formal cease-fire agreement." The prospect Hamdi raises is therefore not far-fetched. If the Government does not consider this unconventional war won for two generations, and if it maintains during that time that Hamdi might, if released, rejoin forces fighting against the United States, then the position it has taken throughout the litigation of this case suggests that Hamdi's detention could last for the rest of his life.

It is a clearly established principle of the law of war that detention may last no longer than active hostilities. See Article 118 of the Geneva Convention (III) Relative to the Treatment of Prisoners of

War, August 12, 1949 ("Prisoners of war shall be released and repatriated without delay after the cessation of active hostilities"). . . .

Hamdi contends that the AUMF does not authorize indefinite or perpetual detention. Certainly, we agree that indefinite detention for the purpose of interrogation is not authorized. Further, we understand Congress's grant of authority for the use of "necessary and appropriate force" to include the authority to detain for the duration of the relevant conflict, and our understanding is based on longstanding law-of-war principles. If the practical circumstances of a given conflict are entirely unlike those of the conflicts that informed the development of the law of war, that understanding may unravel. But that is not the situation we face as of this date. Active combat operations against Taliban fighters apparently are ongoing in Afghanistan. . . . The United States may detain, for the duration of these hostilities, individuals legitimately determined to be Taliban combatants who "engaged in an armed conflict against the United States." If the record establishes that United States troops are still involved in active combat in Afghanistan, those detentions are part of the exercise of "necessary and appropriate force," and therefore are authorized by the AUMF. . . .

III

Even in cases in which the detention of enemy combatants is legally authorized, there remains the question of what process is constitutionally due to a citizen who disputes his enemy-combatant status. Hamdi argues that he is owed a meaningful and timely hearing and that "extra-judicial detention [that] begins and ends with the submission of an affidavit based on third-hand hearsay" does not comport with the Fifth and Fourteenth Amendments. The Government counters that any more process than was provided below would be both unworkable and "constitutionally intolerable." Our resolution of this dispute requires a careful examination both of the writ of habeas corpus, which Hamdi now seeks to employ as a mechanism of judicial review, and of the Due Process Clause, which informs the procedural contours of that mechanism in this instance.

A

Though they reach radically different conclusions on the process that ought to attend the present proceeding, the parties begin on common ground. All agree that, absent suspension, the writ of habeas corpus remains available to every individual detained within the United States. US Const., Art. I, § 9, cl. 2 ("The Privilege of the Writ of Habeas Corpus shall not be suspended, unless when in Cases of Rebellion or Invasion the public Safety may require it"). Only in the rarest of circumstances has Congress seen fit to suspend the writ. At all other times, it has remained a critical check on the Executive, ensuring that it does not detain individuals except in accordance with law. All agree suspension of the writ has not occurred here. Thus, it is undisputed that Hamdi was properly before an Article III court to challenge his detention under 28 U.S.C. § 2241. Further, all agree that § 2241 and its companion provisions provide at least a skeletal outline of the procedures to be afforded a petitioner in federal habeas review. Most notably, § 2243 provides that "the person detained may, under oath, deny any of the facts set forth in the return or allege any other material facts," and § 2246 allows the taking of evidence in habeas proceedings by deposition, affidavit, or interrogatories.

The simple outline of § 2241 makes clear both that Congress envisioned that habeas petitioners would have some opportunity to present and rebut facts and that courts in cases like this retain some ability to vary the ways in which they do so as mandated by due process. The Government recognizes the basic procedural protections required by the habeas statute, but asks us to hold that, given both the flexibility of the habeas mechanism and the circumstances presented in this case, the presentation of the Mobbs Declaration to the habeas court completed the required factual development. It suggests two separate reasons for its position that no further process is due.

B

First, the Government urges the adoption of the Fourth Circuit's holding below—that because it is "undisputed" that Hamdi's seizure took place in a combat zone, the habeas determination can be made purely as a matter of law, with no further hearing or fact-finding necessary. This argument is easily rejected. As the dissenters from the denial of rehearing en banc noted, the circumstances surrounding Hamdi's seizure cannot in any way be characterized as "undisputed," as "those circumstances are neither conceded in fact, nor susceptible to concession in law, because Hamdi has not been permitted to speak for himself or even through counsel as to those circumstances." (Luttig, J., dissenting from denial of rehearing en banc). . . . Further, the "facts" that constitute the alleged concession are insufficient to support Hamdi's detention. Under the definition of enemy combatant that we accept today as falling within the scope of Congress's authorization, Hamdi would need to be "part of or supporting forces hostile to the United States or coalition partners" and "engaged in an armed conflict against the United States" to justify his detention in the United States for the duration of the relevant conflict (Brief for Respondents 3). The habeas petition states only that "[w]hen seized by the United States Government, Mr. Hamdi resided in Afghanistan." An assertion that one *resided* in a country in which combat operations are taking place is not a concession that one was "*captured* in a zone of active combat operations in a foreign theater of war," and certainly is not a concession that one was "part of or supporting forces hostile to the United States or coalition partners" and "engaged in an armed conflict against the United States." Accordingly, we reject any argument that Hamdi has made concessions that eliminate any right to further process.

C

The Government's second argument requires closer consideration. This is the argument that further factual exploration is unwarranted and inappropriate in light of the extraordinary constitutional interests at stake. Under the Government's most extreme rendition of this argument, "[r]espect for separation of powers and the limited institutional capabilities of courts in matters of military decision making in connection with an ongoing conflict" ought to eliminate entirely any individual process, restricting the courts to investigating only whether legal authorization exists for the broader detention scheme. At most, the Government argues, courts should review its determination that a citizen is an enemy combatant under a very deferential "some evidence" standard. . . . Under this review, a court would assume the accuracy of the Government's articulated basis for Hamdi's detention, as set forth in the Mobbs Declaration, and assess only whether that articulated basis was a legitimate one. . . .

In response, Hamdi emphasizes that this Court consistently has recognized that an individual challenging his detention may not be held at the will of the Executive without recourse to some proceeding before a neutral tribunal to determine whether the Executive's asserted justifications for that detention have basis in fact and warrant in law. He argues that the Fourth Circuit inappropriately "ceded power to the Executive during wartime to define the conduct for which a citizen may be detained, judge whether that citizen has engaged in the proscribed conduct, and imprison that citizen indefinitely," and that due process demands that he receive a hearing in which he may challenge the Mobbs Declaration and adduce his own counter evidence. The District Court, agreeing with Hamdi, apparently believed that the appropriate process would approach the process that accompanies a criminal trial. It therefore disapproved of the hearsay nature of the Mobbs Declaration and anticipated quite extensive discovery of various military affairs. Anything less, it concluded, would not be "meaningful judicial review."

Both of these positions highlight legitimate concerns. And both emphasize the tension that often exists between the autonomy that the Government asserts is necessary in order to pursue effectively a particular goal and the process that a citizen contends he is due before he is deprived of a constitutional right. The ordinary mechanism that we use for balancing such serious competing interests, and for determining the procedures that are necessary to ensure that a citizen is not "deprived of life, liberty, or property, without due process of law," US Const., Amdt. 5, is the test that we articulated in *Mathews v. Eldridge* (1976). *Mathews* dictates that the process due in any given instance is determined by weighing "the private interest that will be affected by the official action" against the Government's asserted interest, "including the function involved" and the burdens the Government would face in providing greater process. The *Mathews* calculus then contemplates a judicious balancing of these concerns, through an analysis of "the risk of an erroneous deprivation" of the private interest if the process were reduced and the "probable value, if any, of additional or substitute safeguards." We take each of these steps in turn.

1

It is beyond question that substantial interests lie on both sides of the scale in this case. Hamdi's "private interest . . . affected by the official action," is the most elemental of liberty interests—the interest in being free from physical detention by one's own government.

Nor is the weight on this side of the *Mathews* scale offset by the circumstances of war or the accusation of treasonous behavior, for "[i]t is clear that commitment for *any* purpose constitutes a significant deprivation of liberty that requires due process protection," *Jones v. United States* (1983), and at this stage in the *Mathews* calculus, we consider the interest of the *erroneously* detained individual. Indeed, as amicus briefs from media and relief organizations emphasize, the risk of erroneous deprivation of a citizen's liberty in the absence of sufficient process here is very real. See Brief for Ameri-Cares et al. as *Amici Curiae* 13–22 (noting ways in which "[t]he nature of humanitarian relief work and journalism present a significant risk of mistaken military detentions"). Moreover, as critical as the Government's interest may be in detaining those who actually pose an immediate threat to the national security of the United States during ongoing international conflict, history and common sense teach us that an unchecked system of detention carries the potential to become a means for oppression and abuse of others who do not present that sort of threat. See *Ex parte Milligan* (1866) ("[The Founders] knew—the history of the world told them—the nation they were founding, be its existence short or long, would be involved in war; how often or how long continued, human foresight could not tell; and that unlimited power, wherever lodged at such a time, was especially hazardous to freemen"). Because we live in a society in which "[m]ere public intolerance or animosity cannot constitutionally justify the deprivation of a person's physical liberty," *O'Connor v. Donaldson* (1975), our starting point for the *Mathews v. Eldridge* analysis is unaltered by the allegations surrounding the particular detainee or the organizations with which he is alleged to have associated. We reaffirm today the fundamental nature of a citizen's right to be free from involuntary confinement by his own government without due process of law, and we weigh the opposing governmental interests against the curtailment of liberty that such confinement entails.

2

On the other side of the scale are the weighty and sensitive governmental interests in ensuring that those who have in fact fought with the enemy during a war do not return to battle against the United States. As discussed above, the law of war and the realities of combat may render such detentions both necessary and appropriate, and our due process analysis need not blink at those realities. Without doubt, our Constitution recognizes that core strategic matters of warmaking belong in the hands of those who are best positioned and most politically accountable for making them. *Department of Navy v. Egan* (1988) (noting the reluctance of the courts "to intrude upon the authority of the Executive in military and national security affairs"); *Youngstown Sheet & Tube Co. v. Sawyer* (1952) (acknowledging "broad powers in military commanders engaged in day-to-day fighting in a theater of war").

The Government also argues at some length that its interests in reducing the process available to alleged enemy combatants are heightened by the practical difficulties that would accompany a system of trial-like process. In its view, military officers who are engaged in the serious work of waging battle would be unnecessarily and dangerously distracted by litigation half a world away, and discovery into military operations would both intrude on the sensitive secrets of national defense and result in a futile search for evidence buried under the rubble of war. To the extent that these burdens are triggered by heightened procedures, they are properly taken into account in our due process analysis.

3

Striking the proper constitutional balance here is of great importance to the nation during this period of ongoing combat. But it is equally vital that our calculus not give short shrift to the values that this country holds dear or to the privilege that is American citizenship. It is during our most challenging and uncertain moments that our nation's commitment to due process is most severely tested; and it is in those times that we must preserve our commitment at home to the principles for which we fight abroad.

With due recognition of these competing concerns, we believe that neither the process proposed by the Government nor the process apparently envisioned by the District Court below strikes the proper constitutional balance when a United States citizen is detained in the United States as an enemy combatant. That is, "the risk of erroneous deprivation" of a detainee's liberty interest is unacceptably high under the Government's proposed rule, while some of the "additional or substitute procedural safeguards" suggested by the District Court are unwarranted in light of their limited "probable value" and the burdens they may impose on the military in such cases (*Mathews*).

We therefore hold that a citizen-detainee seeking to challenge his classification as an enemy combatant must receive notice of the factual basis for his classification, and a fair opportunity to rebut the Government's factual assertions before a neutral decision maker. These essential constitutional promises may not be eroded.

At the same time, the exigencies of the circumstances may demand that, aside from these core elements, enemy combatant proceedings may be tailored to alleviate their uncommon potential to burden the Executive at a time of ongoing military conflict. Hearsay, for example, may need to be accepted as the most reliable available evidence from the Government in such a proceeding. Likewise, the Constitution would not be offended by a presumption in favor of the Government's evidence, so long as that presumption remained a rebuttable one and fair opportunity for rebuttal were provided. Thus, once the Government puts forth credible evidence that the habeas petitioner meets the enemy-combatant criteria, the onus could shift to the petitioner to rebut that evidence with more persuasive evidence that he falls outside the criteria. A burden-shifting scheme of this sort would meet the goal of ensuring that the errant tourist, embedded journalist, or local aid worker has a chance to prove military error while giving due regard to the Executive once it has put forth meaningful support for its conclusion that the detainee is in fact an enemy combatant. In the words of *Mathews*, process of this sort would sufficiently address the "risk of erroneous deprivation" of a detainee's liberty interest while eliminating certain procedures that have questionable additional value in light of the burden on the Government.

We think it unlikely that this basic process will have the dire impact on the central functions of warmaking that the Government forecasts. The parties agree that initial captures on the battlefield need not receive the process we have discussed here; that process is due only when the determination is made to *continue* to hold those who have been seized. The Government has made clear in its briefing that documentation regarding battlefield detainees already is kept in the ordinary course of military affairs. Any factfinding imposition created by requiring a knowledgeable affiant to summarize these records to an independent tribunal is a minimal one. Likewise, arguments that military officers ought not have to wage war under the threat of litigation lose much of their steam when factual disputes at enemy-combatant hearings are limited to the alleged combatant's acts. This focus meddles little, if at all, in the strategy or conduct of war, inquiring only into the appropriateness of continuing to detain an individual claimed to have taken up arms against the United States. While we accord the greatest respect and consideration to the judgments of military authorities in matters relating to the actual prosecution of a war, and recognize that the scope of that discretion necessarily is wide, it does not infringe on the core role of the military for the courts to exercise their own time-honored and constitutionally mandated roles of reviewing and resolving claims like those presented here.

In sum, while the full protections that accompany challenges to detentions in other settings may prove unworkable and inappropriate in the enemy-combatant setting, the threats to military operations posed by a basic system of independent review are not so weighty as to trump a citizen's core rights to challenge meaningfully the Government's case and to be heard by an impartial adjudicator.

D

In so holding, we necessarily reject the Government's assertion that separation of powers principles mandate a heavily circumscribed role for the courts in such circumstances. Indeed, the position that the courts must forgo any examination of the individual case and focus exclusively on the legality of the broader detention scheme cannot be mandated by any reasonable view of separation of powers, as this approach serves only to *condense* power into a single branch of government. We have long since made clear that a state of war is not a blank check for the President when it comes to the rights of the nation's citizens. Whatever power the United States Constitution envisions for the Executive in its exchanges with other nations or with enemy organizations in times of conflict, it most assuredly envisions a role for all three branches when individual liberties are at stake. Likewise, we have made clear that, unless Congress acts to suspend it, the Great Writ of habeas corpus allows the Judicial Branch to play a necessary role in maintaining this delicate balance of governance, serving as an important judicial check on the Executive's discretion in the realm of detentions. Thus, while we do not question that our due process assessment must pay keen attention to the particular burdens faced by the Executive in the context of military action, it would turn our system of checks and balances on its head to suggest that a citizen could not make his way to court with a challenge to the factual basis for his detention by his government, simply because the Executive opposes making available such a challenge. Absent suspension of the writ by Congress, a citizen detained as an enemy combatant is entitled to this process.

Because we conclude that due process demands some system for a citizen detainee to refute his classification, the proposed "some evidence" standard is inadequate. Any process in which the Executive's factual assertions go wholly unchallenged or are simply presumed correct without any opportunity for the alleged combatant to demonstrate otherwise falls constitutionally short. . . . Plainly, the "process" Hamdi has received is not that to which he is entitled under the Due Process Clause.

There remains the possibility that the standards we have articulated could be met by an appropriately authorized and properly constituted military tribunal. Indeed, it is notable that military regulations already provide for such process in related instances, dictating that tribunals be made available to determine the status of enemy detainees who assert prisoner-of-war status under the Geneva Convention. In the absence of such process, however, a court that receives a petition for a writ of habeas corpus from an alleged enemy combatant must itself ensure that the minimum requirements of due process are achieved. Both courts below recognized as much, focusing their energies on the question of whether Hamdi was due an opportunity to rebut the Government's case against him. The Government, too, proceeded on this assumption, presenting its affidavit and then seeking that it be evaluated under a deferential standard of review based on burdens that it alleged would accompany any greater process. As we have discussed, a habeas court in a case such as this may accept affidavit evidence like that contained in the Mobbs Declaration, so long as it also permits the alleged combatant to present his own factual case to rebut the Government's return. We anticipate that a District Court would proceed with the caution that we have indicated is necessary in this setting, engaging in a factfinding process that is both prudent and incremental. We have no reason to doubt that courts faced with these sensitive matters will pay proper heed both to the matters of national security that might arise in an individual case and to the constitutional limitations safeguarding essential liberties that remain vibrant even in times of security concerns.

IV

... The judgment of the United States Court of Appeals for the Fourth Circuit is vacated, and the case is remanded for further proceedings.

It is so ordered.

Justice Souter, with whom Justice Ginsburg joins, concurring in part, dissenting in part, and concurring in the judgment.

According to Yaser Hamdi's petition for writ of habeas corpus, brought on his behalf by his father, the Government of the United States is detaining him, an American citizen on American soil, with the explanation that he was seized on the field of battle in Afghanistan, having been on the enemy side. It is undisputed that the Government has not charged him with espionage, treason, or any other crime under domestic law. It is likewise undisputed that for one year and nine months, on the basis of an Executive designation of Hamdi as an "enemy combatant," the Government denied him the right to send or receive any communication beyond the prison where he was held and, in particular, denied him access to counsel to represent him. The Government asserts a right to hold Hamdi under these conditions indefinitely, that is, until the Government determines that the United States is no longer threatened by the terrorism exemplified in the attacks of September 11, 2001.

In these proceedings on Hamdi's petition, he seeks to challenge the facts claimed by the Government as the basis for holding him as an enemy combatant. And in this Court he presses the distinct argument that the Government's claim, even if true, would not implicate any authority for holding him that would satisfy 18 U.S.C. § 4001(a) (Non-Detention Act), which bars imprisonment or detention of a citizen "except pursuant to an Act of Congress."

The Government responds that Hamdi's incommunicado imprisonment as an enemy combatant seized on the field of battle falls within the President's power as Commander in Chief under the laws and usages of war, and is in any event authorized by two statutes. Accordingly, the Government contends that Hamdi has no basis for any challenge by petition for habeas except to his own status as an enemy combatant; and even that challenge may go no further than to enquire whether "some evidence" supports Hamdi's designation; if there is "some evidence," Hamdi should remain locked up at the discretion of the Executive. At the argument of this case, in fact, the Government went further and suggested that as long as a prisoner could challenge his enemy combatant designation when responding to interrogation during incommunicado detention he was accorded sufficient process to support his designation as an enemy combatant. Since on either view judicial enquiry so limited would be virtually worthless as a way to contest detention, the Government's concession of jurisdiction to hear Hamdi's habeas claim is more theoretical than practical, leaving the assertion of Executive authority close to unconditional.

The plurality rejects any such limit on the exercise of habeas jurisdiction and so far I agree with its opinion. The plurality does, however, accept the Government's position that if Hamdi's designation as an enemy combatant is correct, his detention (at least as to some period) is authorized by an Act of Congress as required by § 4001(a), that is, by the Authorization for Use of Military Force, (hereinafter Force Resolution). Here, I disagree and respectfully dissent. The Government has failed to demonstrate that the Force Resolution authorizes the detention complained of here even on the facts the Government claims. If the Government raises nothing further than the record now shows, the Non-Detention Act entitles Hamdi to be released. . . .

II

The threshold issue is how broadly or narrowly to read the Non-Detention Act, the tone of which is severe: "No citizen shall be imprisoned or otherwise detained by the United States except pursuant to an Act of Congress." . . . For a number of reasons, the prohibition within § 4001(a) has to be read broadly to accord the statute a long reach and to impose a burden of justification on the Government.

First, the circumstances in which the Act was adopted point the way to this interpretation. The provision superseded a cold-war statute, the Emergency Detention Act of 1950, which had authorized the Attorney General, in time of emergency, to detain anyone reasonably thought likely to engage in espionage or sabotage. That statute was repealed in 1971 out of fear that it could authorize a repetition of the World War II internment of citizens of Japanese ancestry; Congress meant to preclude another episode like the one described in *Korematsu v. United States* (1944). While Congress might simply have struck the 1950 statute, in considering the repealer the point was made that the existing statute provided some express procedural protection, without which the Executive would seem to be subject to no statutory limits protecting individual liberty. . . .

The fact that Congress intended to guard against a repetition of the World War II internments when it repealed the 1950 statute and gave us § 4001(a) provides a powerful reason to think that § 4001(a) was meant to require clear congressional authorization before any citizen can be placed in a cell. It is not merely that the legislative history shows that § 4001(a) was thought necessary in anticipation of times just like the present, in which the safety of the country is threatened. To appreciate what is most significant, one must only recall that the internments of the 1940's were accomplished by Executive action. Although an Act of Congress ratified and confirmed an Executive order authorizing the military to exclude individuals from defined areas and to accommodate those it might remove, the statute said nothing whatever about the detention of those who might be removed; internment camps were creatures of the Executive, and confinement in them rested on assertion of Executive authority. When, therefore, Congress repealed the 1950 Act and adopted § 4001(a) for the purpose of avoiding another *Korematsu*, it intended to preclude reliance on vague congressional authority . . . .

Finally, even if history had spared us the cautionary example of the internments in World War II, even if there had been no *Korematsu* . . . there would be a compelling reason to read § 4001(a) to demand manifest authority to detain before detention is authorized. The defining character of American constitutional government is its constant tension between security and liberty, serving both by partial helpings of each. In a government of separated powers, deciding finally on what is a reasonable degree of guaranteed liberty whether in peace or war (or some condition in between) is not well entrusted to the Executive Branch of Government, whose particular responsibility is to maintain security. For reasons of inescapable human nature, the branch of the Government asked to counter a serious threat is not the branch on which to rest the nation's entire reliance in striking the balance between the will to win and the cost in liberty on the way to victory; the responsibility for security will naturally amplify the claim that security legitimately raises. A reasonable balance is more likely to be reached on the judgment of a different branch, just as Madison said in remarking that "the constant aim is to divide and arrange the several offices in such a manner as that each may be a check on the other—that the private interest of every individual may be a sentinel over the public rights" (The Federalist No. 51). Hence the need for an assessment by Congress before citizens are subject to lockup, and likewise the need for a clearly expressed congressional resolution of the competing claims.

III

Under this principle of reading § 4001(a) robustly to require a clear statement of authorization to detain, none of the Government's arguments suffices to justify Hamdi's detention. . . .

B

. . . [T]here is the Government's claim, accepted by the Court, that the terms of the Force Resolution are adequate to authorize detention of an enemy combatant under the circumstances described, a claim the Government fails to support sufficiently to satisfy § 4001(a) as read to require a clear statement of authority to detain. Since the Force Resolution was adopted one week after the attacks of September 11, 2001, it naturally speaks with some generality, but its focus is clear, and that is on the use of military power. It is fairly read to authorize the use of armies and weapons, whether against other armies or individual terrorists. But . . . it never so much as uses the word detention, and there is no reason to think Congress might have perceived any need to augment Executive power to deal with dangerous citizens within the United States, given the well-stocked statutory arsenal of defined criminal offenses covering the gamut of actions that a citizen sympathetic to terrorists might commit.

C

Even so, there is one argument for treating the Force Resolution as sufficiently clear to authorize detention of a citizen consistently with § 4001(a). Assuming the argument to be sound, however, the Government is in no position to claim its advantage.

Because the Force Resolution authorizes the use of military force in acts of war by the United States, the argument goes, it is reasonably clear that the military and its Commander in Chief are authorized to deal with enemy belligerents according to the treaties and customs known collectively as the laws of war. Accordingly, the United States may detain captured enemies, and *Ex parte Quirin*, may perhaps be claimed for the proposition that the American citizenship of such a captive does not as such limit the Government's power to deal with him under the usages of war. Thus, the Government here repeatedly argues that Hamdi's detention amounts to nothing more than customary detention of a captive taken on the field of battle: if the usages of war are fairly authorized by the Force Resolution, Hamdi's detention is authorized for purposes of § 4001(a).

There is no need, however, to address the merits of such an argument in all possible circumstances. For now it is enough to recognize that the Government's stated legal position in its campaign against the Taliban (among whom Hamdi was allegedly captured) is apparently at odds with its claim here to be acting in accordance with customary law of war and hence to be within the terms of the Force Resolution in its detention of Hamdi. In a statement of its legal position cited in its brief, the Government says that "the Geneva Convention applies to the Taliban detainees." Hamdi presumably is such a detainee, since according to the Government's own account, he was taken bearing arms on the Taliban side of a field of battle in Afghanistan. He would therefore seem to qualify for treatment as a prisoner of war under the Third Geneva Convention, to which the United States is a party.

By holding him incommunicado, however, the Government obviously has not been treating him as a prisoner of war, and in fact the Government claims that no Taliban detainee is entitled to prisoner of war status. This treatment appears to be a violation of the Geneva Convention provision that even in cases of doubt, captives are entitled to be treated as prisoners of war "until such time as their status has been determined by a competent tribunal." . . .

Whether, or to what degree, the Government is in fact violating the Geneva Convention and is thus acting outside the customary usages of war are not matters I can resolve at this point. What I can say, though, is that the Government has not made out its claim that in detaining Hamdi in the manner described, it is acting in accord with the laws of war authorized to be applied against citizens by the Force Resolution. I conclude accordingly that the Government has failed to support the position that the Force Resolution authorizes the described detention of Hamdi for purposes of § 4001(a). . . .

D

. . . [I]n a moment of genuine emergency, when the Government must act with no time for deliberation, the Executive may be able to detain a citizen if there is reason to fear he is an imminent threat to the safety of the nation and its people (though I doubt there is any want of statutory authority). This case, however, does not present that question, because an emergency power of necessity must at least be limited by the emergency; Hamdi has been locked up for over two years.

Whether insisting on the careful scrutiny of emergency claims or on a vigorous reading of § 4001(a), we are heirs to a tradition given voice eight hundred years ago by Magna Carta, which, on the barons' insistence, confined executive power by "the law of the land."

IV

Because I find Hamdi's detention forbidden by § 4001(a) and unauthorized by the Force Resolution, I would not reach any questions of what process he may be due in litigating disputed issues in a proceeding under the habeas statute or prior to the habeas enquiry itself. For me, it suffices that the Government has failed to justify holding him in the absence of a further Act of Congress, criminal charges, a showing that the detention conforms to the laws of war, or a demonstration that § 4001(a) is unconstitutional. I would therefore vacate the judgment of the Court of Appeals and remand for proceedings consistent with this view.

Since this disposition does not command a majority of the Court, however, the need to give practical effect to the conclusions of eight members of the Court rejecting the Government's position calls for me to join with the plurality in ordering remand on terms closest to those I would impose. Although I think litigation of Hamdi's status as an enemy combatant is unnecessary, the terms of the plurality's remand will allow Hamdi to offer evidence that he is not an enemy combatant, and he should at the least have the benefit of that opportunity.

It should go without saying that in joining with the plurality to produce a judgment, I do not adopt the plurality's resolution of constitutional issues that I would not reach. . . .

Subject to these qualifications, I join with the plurality in a judgment of the Court vacating the Fourth Circuit's judgment and remanding the case.

Justice Scalia, with whom Justice Stevens joins, dissenting.

Petitioner, a presumed American citizen, has been imprisoned without charge or hearing in the Norfolk and Charleston Naval Brigs for more than two years, on the allegation that he is an enemy combatant who bore arms against his country for the Taliban. His father claims to the contrary that he is an inexperienced aid worker caught in the wrong place at the wrong time. This case brings into conflict the competing demands of national security and our citizens' constitutional right to personal liberty. Although I share the Court's evident unease as it seeks to reconcile the two, I do not agree with its resolution.

Where the Government accuses a citizen of waging war against it, our constitutional tradition has been to prosecute him in federal court for treason or some other crime. Where the exigencies of war prevent that, the Constitution's Suspension Clause, Art. I, § 9, cl. 2, allows Congress to relax the usual protections temporarily. Absent suspension, however, the Executive's assertion of military exigency has not been thought sufficient to permit detention without charge. No one contends that the congressional Authorization for Use of Military Force, on which the Government relies to justify its actions here, is an implementation of the Suspension Clause. Accordingly, I would reverse the decision below.

I

The very core of liberty secured by our Anglo-Saxon system of separated powers has been freedom from indefinite imprisonment at the will of the Executive. . . .

The gist of the Due Process Clause, as understood at the founding and since, was to force the Government to follow those common-law procedures traditionally deemed necessary before depriving a person of life, liberty, or property. When a citizen was deprived of liberty because of alleged criminal conduct, those procedures typically required committal by a magistrate followed by indictment and trial. . . .

These due process rights have historically been vindicated by the writ of habeas corpus. . . .

The writ of habeas corpus was preserved in the Constitution—the only common-law writ to be explicitly mentioned. See Art. I, § 9, cl. 2. Hamilton lauded "the establishment of the writ of *habeas corpus* " in his Federalist defense as a means to protect against "the practice of arbitrary imprisonments . . . in all ages, [one of] the favourite and most formidable instruments of tyranny." . . .

II

. . . Our Federal Constitution contains a provision explicitly permitting suspension, but limiting the situations in which it may be invoked: "The privilege of the Writ of Habeas Corpus shall not be suspended, unless when in Cases of Rebellion or Invasion the public Safety may require it." Art. I, § 9, cl. 2. Although this provision does not state that suspension must be effected by, or authorized by, a legislative act, it has been so understood, consistent with English practice and the Clause's placement in Article I.

The Suspension Clause was by design a safety valve, the Constitution's only "express provision for exercise of extraordinary authority because of a crisis." *Youngstown Sheet & Tube Co. v. Sawyer* (1952) (Jackson, J., concurring). Very early in the nation's history, President Jefferson unsuccessfully sought a suspension of habeas corpus to deal with Aaron Burr's conspiracy to overthrow the Government. During the Civil War, Congress passed its first Act authorizing Executive suspension of the writ of habeas corpus, to the relief of those many who thought President Lincoln's unauthorized proclamations of suspension unconstitutional. Later Presidential proclamations of suspension relied upon the congressional authorization. . . .

V

. . . Hamdi is entitled to a habeas decree requiring his release unless (1) criminal proceedings are promptly brought, or (2) Congress has suspended the writ of habeas corpus. A suspension of the writ could, of course, lay down conditions for continued detention, similar to those that today's opinion prescribes under the Due Process Clause. But there is a world of difference between the people's representatives' determining the need for that suspension (and prescribing the conditions for it), and this Court's doing so.

The plurality finds justification for Hamdi's imprisonment in the Authorization for Use of Military Force, which provides:

That the President is authorized to use all necessary and appropriate force against those nations, organizations, or persons he determines planned, authorized, committed, or aided the terrorist attacks that occurred on September 11, 2001, or harbored such organizations or persons, in order to prevent any future acts of international terrorism against the United States by such nations, organizations or persons. § 2(a)

This is not remotely a congressional suspension of the writ, and no one claims that it is. Contrary to the plurality's view, I do not think this statute even authorizes detention of a citizen with the clarity necessary to satisfy the interpretive canon that statutes should be construed so as to avoid grave constitutional concerns, . . . or with the clarity necessary to overcome the statutory prescription that "[n]o citizen shall be imprisoned or otherwise detained by the United States except pursuant to an Act of Congress." 18 U.S.C. § 4001(a). But even if it did, I would not permit it to overcome Hamdi's entitlement to habeas corpus relief. The Suspension Clause of the Constitution, which carefully circumscribes the conditions under which the writ can be withheld, would be a sham if it could be evaded by congressional prescription of requirements *other than the common-law requirement of committal for criminal prosecution* that render the writ, though available, unavailing. If the Suspension Clause does not guarantee the citizen that he will either be tried or released, unless the conditions for suspending the writ exist and the grave action of suspending the writ has been taken; if it merely guarantees the citizen that he will not be detained unless Congress by ordinary legislation says he can be detained; it guarantees him very little indeed. . . .

. . . It is not the habeas court's function to make illegal detention legal by supplying a process that the Government could have provided, but chose not to. If Hamdi is being imprisoned in violation of the Constitution (because without due process of law), then his habeas petition should be granted; the Executive may then hand him over to the criminal authorities, whose detention for the purpose of prosecution will be lawful, or else must release him.

There is a certain harmony of approach in the plurality's making up for Congress's failure to invoke the Suspension Clause and its making up for the Executive's failure to apply what it says are needed procedures—an approach that reflects what might be called a Mr. Fix-it Mentality. The plurality seems to view it as its mission to Make Everything Come Out Right, rather than merely to decree the consequences, as far as individual rights are concerned, of the other two branches' actions and omissions. Has the Legislature failed to suspend the writ in the current dire emergency? Well, we will remedy that failure by prescribing the reasonable conditions that a suspension should have included. And has the Executive failed to live up to those reasonable conditions? Well, we will ourselves make that failure good, so that this dangerous fellow (if he is dangerous) need not be set free. The problem with this approach is not only that it steps out of the courts' modest and limited role in a democratic society; but that by repeatedly doing what it thinks the political branches ought to do it encourages their lassitude and saps the vitality of government by the people.

VI

Several limitations give my views in this matter a relatively narrow compass. They apply only to citizens, accused of being enemy combatants, who are detained within the territorial jurisdiction of a federal court. This is not likely to be a numerous group; currently we know of only two, Hamdi and Jose Padilla. Where the citizen is captured outside and held outside the United States, the constitutional requirements may be different. Moreover, even within the United States, the accused citizen–enemy combatant may lawfully be detained once prosecution is in progress or in contemplation. The Government has been notably successful in securing conviction, and hence long-term custody or execution, of those who have waged war against the state.

I frankly do not know whether these tools are sufficient to meet the Government's security needs, including the need to obtain intelligence through interrogation. It is far beyond my competence, or the Court's competence, to determine that. But it is not beyond Congress's. If the situation demands it, the Executive can ask Congress to authorize suspension of the writ—which can be made subject to whatever conditions Congress deems appropriate, including even the procedural novelties invented by the plurality today. To be sure, suspension is limited by the Constitution to cases of rebellion or invasion. But whether the attacks of September 11, 2001, constitute an "invasion," and whether those attacks still justify suspension several years later, are questions for Congress rather than this Court. If civil rights are to be curtailed during wartime, it must be done openly and democratically, as the Constitution requires, rather than by silent erosion through an opinion of this Court.

The Founders well understood the difficult tradeoff between safety and freedom. "Safety from external danger," Hamilton declared,

> is the most powerful director of national conduct. Even the ardent love of liberty will, after a time, give way to its dictates. The violent destruction of life and property incident to war; the continual effort and alarm attendant on a state of continual danger, will compel nations the most attached to liberty, to resort for repose and security to institutions which have a tendency to destroy their civil and political rights. To be more safe, they, at length, become willing to run the risk of being less free. *The Federalist*, No. 8.

The Founders warned us about the risk, and equipped us with a Constitution designed to deal with it.

Many think it not only inevitable but entirely proper that liberty give way to security in times of national crisis—that, at the extremes of military exigency, *inter arma silent leges*. Whatever the general merits of the view that war silences law or modulates its voice, that view has no place in the interpretation and application of a Constitution designed precisely to confront war and, in a manner that accords with democratic principles, to accommodate it. Because the Court has proceeded to meet the current emergency in a manner the Constitution does not envision, I respectfully dissent.

Justice Thomas dissenting.

The Executive Branch, acting pursuant to the powers vested in the President by the Constitution and with explicit congressional approval, has determined that Yaser Hamdi is an enemy combatant and should be detained. This detention falls squarely within the Federal Government's war powers, and we lack the expertise and capacity to second-guess that decision. As such, petitioners' habeas challenge should fail, and there is no reason to remand the case. The plurality reaches a contrary conclusion by failing adequately to consider basic principles of the constitutional structure as it relates to national security and foreign affairs and by using the balancing scheme of *Mathews v. Eldridge*. I do not think that the Federal Government's war powers can be balanced away by this Court. Arguably, Congress could provide for additional procedural protections, but until it does, we have no right to insist upon them. But even if I were to agree with the general approach the plurality takes, I could not accept the particulars. The plurality utterly fails to account for the Government's compelling interests and for our own institutional inability to weigh competing concerns correctly. I respectfully dissent.

I

"It is 'obvious and unarguable' that no governmental interest is more compelling than the security of the Nation." *Haig v. Agee* (1981). The national security, after all, is the primary responsibility and purpose of the Federal Government. . . .

The Founders intended that the President have primary responsibility—along with the necessary power—to protect the national security and to conduct the nation's foreign relations. They did so principally because the structural advantages of a unitary Executive are essential in these domains. . . .

These structural advantages are most important in the national-security and foreign-affairs contexts. "Of all the cares or concerns of government, the direction of war most peculiarly demands those qualities which distinguish the exercise of power by a single hand." *The Federalist*, No. 74 (A. Hamilton). . . . To this end, the Constitution vests in the President "[t]he executive Power," Art. II, § 1, provides that he "shall be Commander in Chief of the" armed forces, § 2, and places in him the power to recognize foreign governments, § 3.

This Court has long recognized these features and has accordingly held that the President has *constitutional* authority to protect the national security and that this authority carries with it broad discretion. . . .

Congress, to be sure, has a substantial and essential role in both foreign affairs and national security. But it is crucial to recognize that *judicial* interference in these domains destroys the purpose of vesting primary responsibility in a unitary Executive. . . .

III

I agree with the plurality that the Federal Government has power to detain those that the Executive Branch determines to be enemy combatants. But I do not think that the plurality has adequately explained the breadth of the President's authority to detain enemy combatants, an authority that includes making virtually conclusive factual findings. In my view, the structural considerations discussed above, as recognized in our precedent, demonstrate that we lack the capacity and responsibility to second-guess this determination. . . .

IV

. . . Ultimately, the plurality's dismissive treatment of the Government's asserted interests arises from its apparent belief that enemy-combatant determinations are not part of "the actual prosecution of a war," or one of the "central functions of warmaking." This seems wrong: Taking *and holding* enemy combatants is a quintessential aspect of the prosecution of war. See, e.g., . . . *Quirin*. Moreover, this highlights serious difficulties in applying the plurality's balancing approach here. First, in the war context, we know neither the strength of the Government's interests nor the costs of imposing additional process.

Second, it is at least difficult to explain why the result should be different for other military operations that the plurality would ostensibly recognize as "central functions of warmaking." . . . Because a decision to bomb a particular target might extinguish *life* interests, the plurality's analysis seems to require notice to potential targets. To take one more example, in November 2002, a Central Intelligence Agency (CIA) Predator drone fired a Hellfire missile at a vehicle in Yemen carrying an al Qaeda leader, a citizen of the United States, and four others. It is not clear whether the CIA knew that an American was in the vehicle. But the plurality's due process would seem to require notice and opportunity to respond here as well. . . . I offer these examples not because I think the plurality would demand additional process in these situations but because it clearly would not. The result here should be the same.

I realize that many military operations are, in some sense, necessary. But many, if not most, are merely expedient, and I see no principled distinction between the military operation the plurality condemns today (the holding of an enemy combatant based on the process given Hamdi) from a variety of other military operations. In truth, I doubt that there is any sensible, bright-line distinction. It could be argued that bombings and missile strikes are an inherent part of war, and as long as our forces do not violate the laws of war, it is of no constitutional moment that civilians might be killed. But this does not serve to distinguish this case because it is also consistent with the laws of war to detain enemy combatants exactly as the Government has detained Hamdi. . . .

Undeniably, Hamdi has been deprived of a serious interest, one actually protected by the Due Process Clause. Against this, however, is the Government's overriding interest in protecting the nation. If a deprivation of liberty can be justified by the need to protect a town, the protection of the nation, a fortiori, justifies it. . . .

For these reasons, I would affirm the judgment of the Court of Appeals.

CONTRIBUTORS

RICHARD COHEN, syndicated columnist for the *Washington Post*.

ALAN M. DERSHOWITZ, Felix Frankfurter Professor of Law, Harvard University.

VIET D. DINH, Professor of Law, Georgetown University Law Center; Former Assistant Attorney General, Office of Legal Policy, United States Department of Justice.

DAVID A. HARRIS, Balk Professor of Law and Values, University of Toledo College of Law.

NAT HENTOFF, author, *Village Voice* columnist, and frequent contributor to such publications as the *Wall Street Journal*, the *New York Times*, the *New Republic*, *Commonweal*, *Atlantic*, and the *New Yorker*.

PHILIP B. HEYMANN, James Barr Ames Professor of Law, Harvard University.

ARYEH NEIER, author, columnist, president of the Open Society Institute and the Soros Foundation, and former executive director of Human Rights Watch.

CHRISTIAN PARENTI, author and a fellow at the City University of New York's Center for Place, Culture, and Politics.

JOHN T. PARRY, Associate Professor of Law, University of Pittsburgh.

EYAL PRESS, journalist whose work has appeared in such publications as the *New York Times Magazine*, the *Nation*, and the *Atlantic Monthly*.

WILLIAM REHNQUIST, chief justice, United States Supreme Court.

STEPHEN J. SCHULHOFER, the Robert B. McKay Professor of Law at New York University.

JAY STANLEY, communications director of the Technology and Liberty Program of the American Civil Liberties Union.

BARRY STEINHARDT, attorney and director of the American Civil Liberties Union's Technology and Liberty Program.

STUART TAYLOR JR., senior writer and columnist for the *National Journal* and a contributing editor at *Newsweek*.

WELSH S. WHITE, Professor of Law, University of Pittsburgh.

FRANK H. WU, Professor of Law, Howard University, adjunct professor at Columbia University.

JOHN C. YOO, Professor of Law, University of California, at Berkeley; Former Deputy Assistant Attorney General, US Department of Justice.

INDEX